The Principles of Project Management

The Principles of Project Management

**Preface by
John R. Adams**

Library of Congress Cataloging-in-Publication Data

Principles of project management: collected handbooks from the
   Project Management Institute/ with a new introduction by John R.
   Adams
       p.   cm.
   Includes bibliographical references and index.
   ISBN: 1–880410–30–3 (pbk.)
     1. Industrial project management—Handbooks, manuals, etc.
I. Project Management Institute
HD69.P75P677   1996
658.4'04––dc21   96-51592
                                            CIP

Book Team
Editor-in-Chief
James S. Pennypacker

Managing Editor	*Editor, Book Division*
Dewey L. Messer	Jeannette M. Cabanis
Graphic Designer	*Associate Editor*
Michelle Owen	Sandy Jenkins
Acquisitions Editor	*Production Coordinator*
Bobby R. Hensley	Mark S. Parker

Editorial Production Associate
Lisa Woodring

PMI books are available at quantity discounts. For more
information, please write to the Business Manager, PMI
Publications Division, 40 Colonial Square, Sylva, NC 28779. Or
contact your local bookstore.

The paper used in this book complies with the Permanent Paper
Standard issued by the National Information Standards
Organization (Z39.48—1984).

10   9   8   7   6   5   4

Table of Contents

The Principles of Project Management

Figures and Tables

An Organization Development Approach to Project Management

Team Building for Project Managers

Conflict Management for Project Managers

Preface

In 1979, PMI was just beginning to develop its professionalism programs. Matt Perry was assembling a team of well-known project managers to develop the first version of what was to become known as the *Project Management Body of Knowledge* (now known as the *PMBOK Guide*), a written outline of what we believed a manager needed to know and understand to function as a project manager. The first certification exam was a gleam in the eye of Dr. M. Dean Martin, who would shortly be commissioned by the PMI Board of Directors to develop a proposal and design PMI's certification program. The first degree program in the field would not begin offering classes for eight more years. David Cleland and Russ Archibald were writing in the field, but the literature of project management was very limited, particularly literature that drew from accepted academic fields and was written specifically to be of help to neophyte project managers. It was clear that the literature of project management was limited both in quantity and in academic quality, and that the literature would have to be expanded dramatically if there was to be any hope of developing the project management field into a recognized and accepted profession.

As PMI's Director of Educational Services, much of these efforts to develop the profession fell under my purview. While the resources PMI could devote to these efforts was very limited, there were several academics who were committed to contributing to the project management profession. A program was needed that would allow these academics to contribute their specialized talents and at the same time provide a literature that would support the *PMBOK Guide* as it was developed.

What developed was a series of "handbooks" drawn from relevant academic literature, but designed to incorporate only that portion of a specific academic topic that was particularly relevant to the project manager and the project management profession. Project management oriented professors, with the aid of research assistants, were asked to develop specialized, 30–60 page handbooks, small and compact enough to be kept readily available for reference on a project manager's desk, that summarized the topic in a readable and graphic manner. The research assistant was specified to help acquaint young future management professionals with project management as a possible career. The professor was provided with a $300 grant to help develop the manuscript and fund the research assistant, and with recognition for authoring the handbook.

The results of several year's work are reprinted in this document. The topics were apparently well-chosen. The handbooks have served as primary *PMBOK Guide* references for over 12 years, and are still being used for that purpose. Several of the research assistant co-authors have in fact gone on to build their own careers in our project management profession. Two of the professors, Dr. M. Dean Martin and Dr. Linn Stuckenbruck, have died during this period, but their work lives on to help current project managers understand the challenges of this unique profession.

Speaking for all the authors, we hope you find these works both interesting and useful to you, and that they help you develop and advance in your career.

Sincerely,

Dr. John R. Adams

Organizing for Project Management

Dwayne P. Cable
and
John R. Adams

Introduction

Purpose

The Industrial Revolution, which started in the United States around 1790, established a continuing element of change that we Americans have grown accustomed to and, to a great extent, even demand in our organizations as a means of dealing with societal and business problems. Because of this continuing change in technologies, markets, laws, customer and management attitudes, to name a few areas, today's managers realize that methods of controlling and directing organizations must be dynamic in nature and have the capability of adjusting to the unexpected. Wallace, in his or her article "The Winchester-Western Division Concept of Product Planning," labeled management's attempts at structuring organizations to accommodate this rate of change as the "Organizational Revolution".[1] This monograph's primary purpose is to track and iterate the ways in which management has responded organizationally to solve problems and bring about needed changes.

Overview

Problems arise in every organization. Such problems as what products to develop, should capacity be expanded, should a computer be purchased, or the effect of changes in the law on the market position of a firm are just a few of an endless number of continuing problems about which management must concern itself if the firm is to survive. These problems and their alternative solutions establish some elements of change around which the organization must adapt (develop product C, construct a new production facility, install a computer, etc.). Projects are generally established to carry out these changes and someone is always responsible for each project's successful completion.

This monograph briefly defines the project and the management concept through which project objectives are fulfilled. Following that brief review is a detailed explanation of the typical organizational structures used to attain project fulfillment. The following forms of organization are reviewed:
- The functional organization
- The project expeditor organization
- The project coordinator organization
- The weak matrix organization
- The strong matrix organization
- The projectized organization.

When discussing the form or structure of an organization, the level of authority the project manager enjoys depends primarily on which of these structures is chosen. Figure 1 presents a continuum upon which the level of authority and the various organizational structures may be related.

The project manager within the functional, expeditor, coordinator, and weak matrix forms of organization has little or no formal authority and typically no separate project team exists. The person responsible for the project must thus rely heavily on interpersonal skills to satisfactorily complete the project. The strong matrix and fully projectized structures have a much higher level of formal authority assigned to the project manager, with an established project team. Each structure has its advantages and disadvantages, which must be carefully weighed when deciding what organizational style would be best for a given project and the environment (internal and external to the firm) within which it must function.

Every project is unique in terms of the problems that arise, the priorities and resources assigned it, the environment in which it operates, and the project manager's attitude and style used to guide and control project activities. Hence, the organizational structure for the project must be designed to fit within that project's operating constraints. The organizational structure initially implemented may not be the same structure used throughout the life cycle of the project due to changes in priorities, available resources, project personnel, laws, and other contingencies. Regardless of the project management structure chosen, management must realize that a dynamic state of equilibrium between limited personnel and financial resources and the objectives of the project will be necessary if project management is to be successful in their particular parent organization.

Projects and Project Management

Projects

Nearly every activity within an organization could be labeled a project possessing unique characteristics and varying levels of importance to the parent organization. Every activity has a starting and ending point, and one person is normally the ultimate responsible agent. However, the activities usually designated as projects typically occur only once in an organization, and are usually needed to accomplish one or more of four basic objectives:
- Create change
- Implement strategic plans
- Fulfill contractual agreements
- Solve specified problems.

A project may be needed to create change in an organization, such as expanding the production facilities, building a new corporate headquarters, or

Figure 1. Organization/Authority Continuum

Project Manager's Authority

None	Low		Medium		High
Functional Organization	Project Expeditor Organization	Project Coordinator Organization	Weak Matrix Organization	Strong Matrix Organization	Projectized Organization

modifying present facilities to meet federal, state, or local environmental requirements. A project or a series of projects may be established to carry out various aspects of a firm's long-term strategic planning, such as to conduct a feasibility study for a new product or to undertake research to develop new processes—both requiring several years of work. Many firms, especially architectural, engineering, accounting, advertising and construction firms, generate their revenues through large contractual arrangements. When a construction firm builds a new production facility or an accounting firm conducts an annual audit for a client, one of the most effective ways of managing the effort is to establish the contract as a project and assign responsibility for its accomplishment to a project manager. Most every organization must expect, and hence plan for, contingencies because of continuously changing market, social, and legal requirements in its environment. When alternative solutions to organizational problems must be generated and evaluated, ad hoc or permanent "committees" are typically formed to fulfill this function. These alternatives are reported back to top management for their decision making purposes. These "committees," when formalized, are clearly seen as projects. All projects solve some type of problem, but projects may also be established simply to determine and define feasible alternative solutions to problems: determining various corporate tax strategies, ascertaining the feasibility of new technologies, or evaluating different market possibilities are but three examples of such projects.

Because of differing objectives, priorities, time, and cost constraints, every project is unique. However, Stuckenbruck identifies seven primary characteristics that are common to all projects:

1. *Objective*: All projects are established to fulfill some need or requirement specified by management. Each has a specific goal to reach.[2]

2. *Schedule*: Generally, projects have a certain target; a point in time within which they must be accomplished.[3]

3. *Complexity*: This point refers to whether the technology exists to achieve the project objectives. If not, one must either find alternatives to

reaching the objectives or else extend the schedule to develop the necessary technology.[4]

4. *Size and nature of the task*: Project goals can only be achieved within the established time, cost, and schedule constraints by developing an adequate, step-by-step plan of action; once prepared, this plan of action constitutes a project strategy.[5]

5. *Resources*: Every project will have use of certain resources (labor and management personnel, equipment, materials, facilities, finances, etc.) in order to carry out task requirements. Since all resources are limited, the objective would be to persuade the owners of those resources to commit the necessary amounts to the project. This, of course, assumes the owners are both capable and willing to commit those resources.[6]

6. *Organizational structure*: An individual must be given the responsibility for the project. This "project manager" must fulfill the project objectives within the constraints specified by the management of the parent organization. It is very important to ascertain if the project strategy developed can function effectively through the ordinary decision-making and information channels of the present organization. This 'meshing' of project requirements into the existing organization is a very critical aspect to ensuring effective accomplishment of project objectives. The level of authority the project manager will possess and the amount of resources that are to be assigned to the project should aide in determining the organizational structure to be used.[7]

7. *Information and control system*: The information and control systems of an organization are generally structured to handle problems through the typical functional lines of authority. Cost information, for example, generated in the more prevalent functional organization, will be accumulated in such "generic" accounts as purchasing, materials, work-in-progress etc., for the entire organization, investment center, or profit center. The project manager is more interested in those portions of the purchasing, materials, and work-in-progress accounts that are directly involved with the project. Most computer systems and their programs report cost data in the "generic" fashion, thus being of little use to the project manager. Because of these problems, different accumulating processes and new financial reports must be developed. This is a process in which both the project manager and the project team should fully participate.[8]

Primarily, projects are established to fulfill top management goals and objectives. These goals and objectives may include carrying out long-range strategic plan, determining alternatives to certain specific major problems, creating changes in the organizations, or generating specified revenues. Every project has its unique characteristics that must be delicately meshed into the parent organization's structure in order to effectively achieve project objectives within time, cost, and schedule constraints.

Project Management

In the past, a company typically decided to undertake a project effort, assigned the project and the "necessary" resources to a carefully selected individual and contended that they were using some aspect of project management. The organizational implications of this new form of management was of little importance. Although the basic concepts of project management are simple, applying these basics to existing organizations is not. The most traumatic aspect of the process is the extensive reorganization or realignment of the existing organization that is necessary.[9] Efforts were needed to increase the importance of project management and define its concept. Many of these first efforts defined project management in terms of the project manager's role and emphasized the activities of integration. Richard P. Olsen, in his or her article "Can Project Management Be Defined?," provided a long-overdue convergence of ideology, methodology, and general practice of that period by defining project management as "... the application of a collection of tools and techniques ... to direct the use of diverse resources toward the accomplishment of a unique, complex, one-time task within time, cost, and quality constraints. Each task requires a particular mix of these tools and techniques structured to fit the task environment and life cycle (from conception to completion) of the task."[10]

Considerable uncertainty in decision-making exists because of the unique and complex characteristics typical of projects. As this uncertainty increases, management typically responds by either reducing the amount of information it demands for project decisions or by increasing information handling capacity through the application of more costly procedures.[11] Lower performance, poorer decisions, and higher than acceptable levels of uncertainty, however, make reducing the quantities of information required an unacceptable alternative for project completion. Project management provides the other alternative—an avenue by which specialized information is brought closer to those needing to make decisions.

Just as every project has its uniqueness and complexities, so too does the management process which guides and controls those activities. Every project affects the parent organization to some extent. Production facilities, equipment, and labor used in the parent organization's revenue generation process may be needed temporarily to accomplish certain project tasks. Employing project management technologies minimizes the disruption of routine business activities in many cases by placing under a single command all of the skills, technologies, and resources needed to realize the project. The skills required depend on each specific project and the resources available at that time. The greater the amount of adjustments a parent organization must make to fulfill project objectives, the greater chance exists for project failure.[12] Changes within an organization, especially shifts in authority, cause high levels of conflict, which may entice those affected to sabotage or impede project efforts.

The form of project management will be unique for every project venture and will change throughout the project life cycle. Project managers need to understand these changes, how they will be developed, when they will occur, and how to ease their disruptive effects on the parent organization as well as on the project. The first key, however, is to understand the organizational alternatives available to the project manager.

Organizational Alternatives

There are many alternative organizational approaches for the management of projects. Unfortunately, much of the published work simplistically refers to the "project" or the "matrix" forms of organization, leaving the impression that these are clearly defined organizational styles that serve to identify project efforts.[13] Approaches to organization structure are as unique as the projects and the managers that accomplish them.

Differentiation and Integration

Every business organization in existence experiences problems in various areas of their operations. Difficulties arise in properly accumulating costs for tax and reporting purposes, in the inventory and production control areas, in the sales and marketing areas, and in the contracting and procurement areas, just to name a few. Management can most effectively deal with these problems by creating specific areas of the organization, such as accounting, production, and marketing, where those individuals possessing the required expertise could be grouped and assigned to solve those problems. This separation process, known as "differentiation," was defined by Lawrence and Lorsch as "… the state of segmentation of the organizational system into subsystems. Each of which tend to develop particular attributes in relation to the requirements posed by the relevant external environment."[14] Depending on the size of the organization, differentiation may occur both horizontally and vertically. Some organizations have many levels of management (high vertical differentiation) with numerous departmental separations (high horizontal differentiation).[15] The level of differentiation hinges on the variety and types of problems the organization must continuously deal with.

Once the organization differentiates itself sufficiently to satisfactorily deal with all major problems arising from its environmental requirements, all the parts must be combined into a coordinated effort toward the attainment of organizational goals. Lawrence and Lorsch call this coordinating effort "integration" and define it as "… the process of achieving unity of effort among the various subsystems in the accomplishment of the organization's task."[16] Both differentiation and integration are measured on a continuum, and the

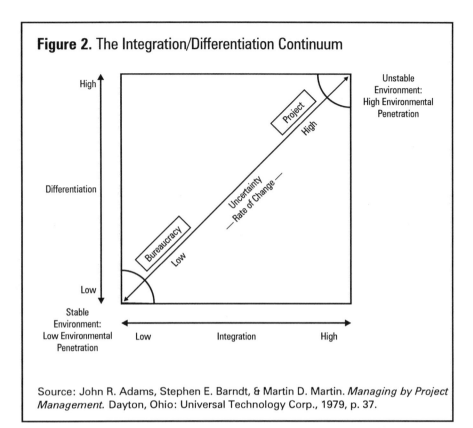

Figure 2. The Integration/Differentiation Continuum

Source: John R. Adams, Stephen E. Barndt, & Martin D. Martin. *Managing by Project Management.* Dayton, Ohio: Universal Technology Corp., 1979, p. 37.

level of differentiation and integration needed by a specific organization is contingent on the organization's task and the environment in which it operates. Adams, Barndt, and Martin provide in Figure 2 an Integration/Differentiation Continuum that merges the uncertainty issue which exists in every organization with the differentiation and integration concepts.

One could conceivably classify every organization somewhere in this continuum. As previously stated, each organization must match the demands of its environment and, if properly positioned in this continuum, that organization may successfully and efficiently do so. A bureaucratic form of organization would be appropriate where the relevant technology is relatively well developed, the relevant conditions in the environment are slow to change, and the problems faced by the organization are similar to those it has dealt with in the past. In a bureaucratic structure, differentiation and integration are low and the organization faces little uncertainty. Project organizations occupy the other end of the continuum because, by definition, they were specifically developed to cope with rapid and dynamic rates of change and highly uncertain environments."[17] For project-oriented organizations like IBM and most construction firms, high-technology and a dynamic environment dictate a high level of uncertainty. Hence, to be successful, high levels of both integration and differentiation are necessary.[18]

Adams, Barndt, and Martin state there are three unique characteristics of work efforts that are typical of a project—a high differentiation and high integration form of organization:[19]

1. Advanced technology
2. Professional personnel
3. High levels of uncertainty.

Advanced technology: Depending on the final product, the entire project may use many types of new technology, all of which have their own level of uncertainty. Each technology has its own uncertainties in the environment, thus requiring sufficient levels of differentiation to deal with those problems. Likewise, a significant integration effort would be required to obtain the optimal utilization of those technologies.[20]

Professional personnel: "A major characteristic of a project organization is that it typically employs a very high percentage of professionals ... (requiring) a base of specialized intellectual and practical knowledge acquired through education and experience."[21] When diverse technologies must be used in projects, technical professionals are obviously required to apply their technical specialties to the project goals. The traditional incentives used in non-professional jobs usually have little effect on the professional. "Professionals claim special status within organizations based on autonomy, authority of expertise, high ethical standards, collegial evaluation of performance, and service to societal rather than personal interests."[22] This should provide a hint to the unique management problems that will exist in the project organization. Management must put their emphasis on horizontal communications and control systems and the "reasons" behind work efforts to provide effective guidance of professionals. For this reason, professional management specialists are also required as part of the project team.

Level of uncertainty: As mentioned earlier, advanced technology possesses an aura of uncertainty in itself, but technology is not the only source of uncertainty within the project organization. Cost and schedule estimates are just that—educated guesses that cannot provide exact costs and time tables. Costs fluctuate and schedules provide only ranges of time within which tasks need to be completed. Both cost and schedule variances may impact the entire project. "The larger the effort in terms of costs, and the longer the anticipated duration of the task to be accomplished, the greater the level of uncertainty."[23] Some projects coordinate efforts with organizations external to the parent organization, such as governmental agencies, contractors, subcontractors, and suppliers. If estimates are received from these outside organizations, a higher level of uncertainty will exist in both the time and cost figures because the statistical methods and confidence levels utilized in preparing those figures as well as the quality with which the figures are developed cannot be totally controlled by the project or its parent organization.

In other words, large work efforts involving both high costs and numerous estimates, and expecting to involve a number of independent organizations over a long period of time, tend to require highly differentiated and integrated forms of organizations capable of dealing with high levels of uncertainty.[24] They tend to require the project type of organization.[25]

Forms of Organizational Structures

Uniqueness represents the basic premise of project management and, as such, the form of organizational structure chosen will be as original as the project characteristics and organizational environment in which it will operate. One method employed in selecting organizational structures is to identify the extent of authority top management is willing to delegate to the project manager: the one responsible for integrating all project tasks within time, cost, and schedule constraints. As shown in Figure 1 and repeated here for the reader's convenience, the literature supports six major approaches to project organizational structure: functional, project expeditor, project coordinator, strong and weak matrix, and the projectized organization. Each organizational structure is typified by the level of formal authority accorded the project manager. The level of authority is therefore an indicator of the organizational structure appropriate to effectively fulfill project objectives. The project manager, within the functional, project expeditor, and project coordinator forms of organizational structures, possesses little formal authority to assure appropriate project coordination and little decision-making takes place. A moderate level of formal authority is provided in a weak matrix structure. On the other end of the continuum, in the strong matrix and fully projectized organizational structures, the project manager typically maintains exceptional control over project activities and has a specific project team assigned.

Each organizational structure previously mentioned is adequately detailed with a discussion of their advantages and disadvantages in the material that follows. Understanding the characteristics of each project, the level of uncertainty that exists in each project environment, and the strengths and weaknesses involved in the following organizational structures is the first step in developing an appropriate project organization for a high probability of success.

The Functional Organizational Form

The most prevalent organizational structure in existence today is the basic hierarchical, functionally oriented structure based on such management theories as task specialization line and staff divisions of responsibility, approximately equal delegations of authority and responsibility, and limited spans of control.[26] A separation (differentiation) of problem areas is usually accom-

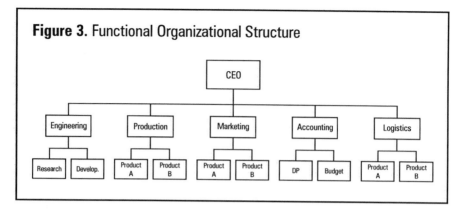

Figure 3. Functional Organizational Structure

plished, and these are dealt with by people grouped by specialty (production, marketing, engineering, accounting, etc.) and managed as functional units. The principle behind the "Doctrine of Specialization" is that it is easier to manage specialists if they are grouped together and supervised by an individual possessing somewhat similar skills and experiences.[27] Figure 3 represents a typical functional organizational structure. The functional arrangement centralizes similar resources, provides mutual support by physical propinquity, and clearly defines career paths for its participants. Every individual in the organization, in theory, reports to only one superior.

Difficulties with the functional organizational structure start in a multiple project environment because of conflicts that arise over the relative priorities of different projects in competition for limited resources.[28] In addition, project members place more emphasis on their functional specialty, usually to the detriment of the overall project, and are not motivated to do otherwise since their career paths lie in the functional, specialized organization. The functional organization represents one end of the authority continuum presented in Figure 1. Technically, the project manager has no formal authority and thus must rely totally on the informal power structure and interpersonal skills to realize project objectives. Even with these problems there are still many organizations that accomplish projects within functional constraints.[29] It should be noted that the term "functional" is used in this discussion to represent several methods of hierarchical organization design methods, which include differentiating substructures of the organization by specific product or product groups, by types of customers, by different levels or styles of technology, or by geographical location.

Project Organizational Structure

To avoid many of the conflicts and other problems experienced within the hierarchical, functional organization, a separate, "vertical" organization is frequently established. Technology for this style of structure varies with the technical backgrounds of the writers. Those most well established in the field of project management and concerned with the technical accuracy of its terminology refer to this "vertical" organization as the "projectized" organizational structure. A review of the available literature surfaced two other terms, the product and the program organization, which are used in various industries to refer to this same type of organizational structure. Figure 4 represents a projectized organization in its purest form. The purely projectized organization occupies the other end of the authority continuum presented in Figure 1. In this structure, the project manager has total authority over the project and retains the flexibility to acquire resources needed for the project from either within or outside the parent organization, subject only to the time, cost, and performance constraints identified as project targets. Personnel are specifically assigned to the project and report directly to the project manager (not to their former, functional superiors), thus placing at least short-term career progression of each team member within the project manager's responsibility. One of the objectives here is to overcome the functional loyalty that exists in the functional organizational form by developing a project loyalty. As demonstrated in Figure 4, the parent organization remains functionally organized while a temporary and smaller organization structure is established to fulfill the project objectives. Personnel are assigned from the parent functional organization (production, engineering, accounting, etc.) to provide their services specifically for the project. It takes a special individual to stop working (temporarily) for their functional supervisors, go to work on a project reporting to the project manager, and then later return to their previous job and functional supervisors. The project team, then, includes those individuals that supervise the functional units within the project. This structure establishes a unity of command for the project and promotes more effective informal communications channels between the project manager and his or her team, and among the project team members.

Establishing this new "suborganization" creates specialized problems. First, there may be duplications of facilities and an inefficient use of resources. Because all resources needed to accomplish the project are specifically assigned to the project, some resources may be committed for time periods when they are not really necessary or when they could have been more effectively used (from the parent organization's viewpoint) elsewhere. An interesting assumption taken here is that the necessary resources are available for assignment. Next, by definition of a project, all project team members work themselves "out of a job" and must be reassigned: either fired, assigned to another project, or returned to their prior functional unit. "Often … those individuals lose their "home" in the functional structure while they are off working for the project."[30] Top management should recognize this fact and show that career progression for these individuals will not be negatively affected.

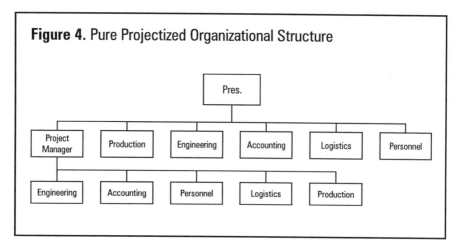

Figure 4. Pure Projectized Organizational Structure

In reality, neither extreme end of the authority continuum, the totally functional nor the purely projectized organizations, are often used in project undertakings. The project manager typically possesses some but not total functional authority for the coordination/integration of project activities. In deciding what organizational form would be best for both the project and its parent organization, however, the project manager's control over resources, particularly manpower, remains the most critical decision factor.

The Project Expeditor

One practical organization where a project manager approach is used, but with little formal authority, is in the "project expeditor" form of organizational structure. The project expeditor (PE) acts basically as a staff assistant to the executive (VP of Marketing, Engineering, etc.) who ultimately has responsibility for the project. The workers for the project remain in their functional organization and provide assistance on an as-needed basis. The project expeditor can make few if any decisions of his or her own, but can make recommendations to the executive responsible for the effort. The expeditor's primary responsibility lies in assuring the timely arrival of parts/materials and completion of tasks. Figure 5 represents an example of the project expeditor form of organization.

The project expeditor's primary responsibility lies in the area of communications. He or she must forward decisions made by his or her superior to those people actually working on the project communicate back any problems, and offer suggestions to resolve those problems. Since the expeditor cannot personally make or enforce decisions, special "people" skills and unique technical abilities are necessary to support his or her efforts to fulfill project objectives. The people skills are not primarily needed to motivate workers but to persuade those in positions of authority to keep project efforts moving.

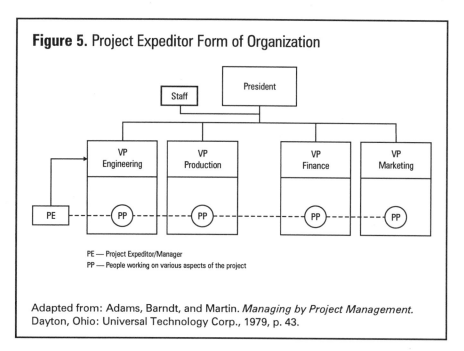

Figure 5. Project Expeditor Form of Organization

PE — Project Expeditor/Manager
PP — People working on various aspects of the project

Adapted from: Adams, Barndt, and Martin. *Managing by Project Management.* Dayton, Ohio: Universal Technology Corp., 1979, p. 43.

Hence, true loyalty to the project usually does not exist except on the part of the project manager.

This form of organizational structure is most used in the traditional functional organization where the project's importance and costs are relatively low. Small projects ($10k–$200k) might typically be considered in this class and use some form of the expeditor structure.

The Project Coordinator

Obviously, if a project is to be accomplished in a timely and efficient manner, those people in control need to be loyal to the project as opposed to their functional organization. Project loyalty from functional managers, however, can be tremendously difficult to establish. As the project takes on more significance to the parent organization, the project expeditor is moved out of his or her facilitator position into a staff function reporting to a much higher level manager in the hierarchical echelon. This type of organization leads to an increased level of authority and responsibility and a new name: "project coordinator." Again, the size of projects in terms of dollars remains small in relation to the entire organization but the authority and loyalty issues are improved. Figure 6 represents an example of the project coordinator form of organizational structure.

The project coordinator has the authority to assign work to individuals in the functional organizations. The functional manager still has authority to

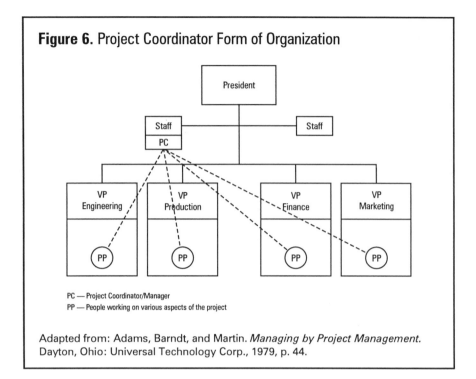

Figure 6. Project Coordinator Form of Organization

President

Staff — PC

Staff

VP Engineering

VP Production

VP Finance

VP Marketing

PP

PP

PP

PP

PC — Project Coordinator/Manager
PP — People working on various aspects of the project

Adapted from: Adams, Barndt, and Martin. *Managing by Project Management.* Dayton, Ohio: Universal Technology Corp., 1979, p. 44.

perform merit reviews but cannot enforce professional or organizational standards in the accomplishment of project activities. In essence, the functional manager is forced to share authority and resources with the project coordinator. Also, the individuals performing the work aspects of the project are, in reality, having to satisfy both the project manager and their functional supervisors. Both characteristics indicate a high conflict situation which management must learn to minimize. Kerzner indicates three shortcomings of the project coordinator form (Kerzner calls this the "Line-Staff" form) of organization:

- Upper-level management was not ready to cope with the problems arising from shared authority.
- Upper-level managers were reluctant to relinquish any of their power and authority to project managers.
- Line-staff project managers who reported to a division head did not have any authority or control over those portions of a project in other divisions, i.e., the project manager in the engineering division could not direct activities in the manufacturing division.[31]

These shortcomings and others previously mentioned must be considered in relation to the size (dollar costs and quantities of resources involved) of the project and the priority assigned it by the parent organization. A pro-

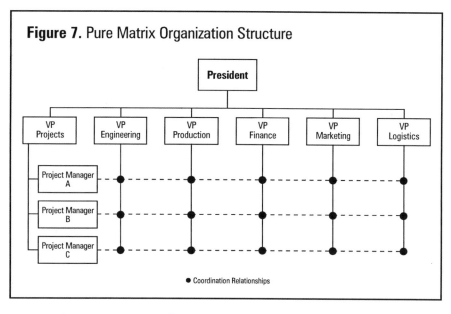

Figure 7. Pure Matrix Organization Structure

President

VP Projects | VP Engineering | VP Production | VP Finance | VP Marketing | VP Logistics

Project Manager A

Project Manager B

Project Manager C

● Coordination Relationships

ject coordinator structure will typify small to medium-sized projects with lower levels of importance to the parent organization.

Matrix Organization

In an effort to maximize the strengths and minimize the weaknesses of both the project and functional organizational structures, modifications to these approaches developed a new organization style called the "matrix organization." The matrix organization maintains the functional (vertical) lines of authority while establishing a relatively permanent horizontal structure that assumes a continuous inflow of projects and that is designed to interact with all functional units supporting the projects. Figure 7 depicts a pure matrix organizational structure.

The term "matrix" has its origin in the United States aerospace industry and the term represents the grid-like relationships shown in Figure 7. Davis and Lawrence define a matrix organization as "… any organization that employs a 'multiple command system' that includes not only a multiple command structure but also related support mechanisms and an associated organizational culture and behavior pattern."[32] The matrix organizational structure was established to fill a very definite real-world need for managing several very large, complex projects simultaneously without sufficient resources to totally projectize each project. With the exception of the fully projectized structure, previous organizational structures were incapable of handling the extensive projects frequently found being managed through various forms of the matrix.

Table 1. Advantages of a Matrix Organization Form.

1. Highly visible project objectives.
2. Improved project manager control over resources.
3. Rapid responses to contingencies.
4. More support obtained from functional organizations.
5. Maximum efficient utilization can be made of scarce resources.
6. Coordination efforts across functional lines improved.
7. Better balance between time, cost, quality, and performance.
8. More effective horizontal and vertical dissemination of information.
9. Project termination effort is not the traumatic event that it can be in a projectized organization.
10. A strong, technical base is easier to develop and have available to all projects equally.
11. Each person retains their "home" after project realization.
12. Morale problems are less frequent.
13. Conflicts are minimal and more easily resolved.
14. The matrix structure provides excellent training for prospective project managers.

Adapted from both:
  Harold Kerzner. *Project Management: A Systems Approach to Planning, Scheduling, and Controlling.* New York: Van Nostrand Reinhold Company, 1979, p. 55.
  Linn C. Stuckenbruck. *The Implementation of Project Management: The Professionals Handbook.* Reading, Mass.: Addison-Wesley Publishing Company, 1981. pp. 76–78.

One result of establishing a matrix structure is that those working on the project frequently have two bosses. Such a person is caught in the middle between two supervisors, each having their own demands and expectations. The functional reporting line is vertical to his or her functional supervisor, while for work assignment and control, the reporting line is horizontal to the project manager. This promotes a high-conflict situation for all concerned: the individual worker, the project manager, and the functional manager. To control the level of conflict, the roles, responsibilities, and authorities of everyone must be clearly defined and documented. Unfortunately, this is rarely if ever accomplished.

This open violation of the unity of command principle can be very frustrating for the employee working on several projects simultaneously. The thought of two supervisors may be hard for many managers to adjust to. In addition, because of multiple projects, there are four or five people that one must report to for different activities. This must be a frustrating situation at best. Most organizational theorists feel that the lack of a clear-cut, single line

Organizing for Project Management

Table 2. Disadvantages of a Matrix Organization Form.

1. Not cost effective from a company-wide viewpoint because of excess administrative personnel.
2. Project personnel must report to more than one boss.
3. The matrix structure is more complex to monitor and control.
4. Tougher problems with resource allocations and project priorities.
5. Functional managers may have differing priorities than the project manager and may follow those priorities at the detriment of the project.
6. Extensive efforts needed to establish policies and procedures.
7. There exists a greater chance of duplications of effort because each project organization operates independently.
8. Higher potential for conflict exists in a matrix due to differing priorities, power struggles, and competition for scarce resources.

Adapted from both:
   Harold Kerzner. *Project Management: A Systems Approach to Planning, Scheduling, and Controlling.* New York: Van Nostrand Reinhold Company, 1979, p. 56.
   Linn C. Stuckenbruck. *The Implementation of Project Management: The Professionals Handbook.* Project Management Institute, Addison-Wesley Publishing Company, Reading, Mass., 1981, pp. 78–80.

of responsibility and authority will result in a clear case of managerial ineffectiveness. This result has yet to be documented and substantiated in the case of the matrix.[33]

The matrix organizational structure is an attempt to create a synergistic atmosphere within which the company may fulfill project objectives while maintaining their hierarchical activities. The "turf issue" (This is my project … This is my department … etc.) must be recognized in a matrix structure and plans and procedures developed to minimize its negative affects. Senior functional and project managers in decision-making capacities must look beyond personal aspirations and consider the effects of their decisions on other organizations and projects within the parent organization.

Though this organizational form is complex, the advantages of the matrix can go far beyond project management in general. Table 1 provides a summary of many advantages ascribed to the matrix organization, while Table 2 presents its disadvantages.[34]

Davis and Lawrence separate problem areas of the matrix organizational structure into nine "pathologies": power struggles, anarchy, groupitis, collapse during economic crunch, excessive overhead, decision strangulation, sinking, layering, and navel gazing.[35] Brief definitions of these "pathologies"

Table 3. Matrix Pathologies.

1. Power struggles: Because of the ambiguity and shared power inherent in a matrix structure, power struggles are both inevitable and extremely difficult to prevent.
2. Anarchy: Though a highly unlikely event, a company may experience traumatic effects in a matrix when an extended period of stress is placed upon it and may eventually completely destroy the firm.
3. Groupitis: Confusing matrix behavior with group decision-making. Complete business decisions need not be accomplished in group meetings.
4. Collapse during economic crunch: Typically, the matrix structure is used during prosperous times and sidelined during hard times.
5. Excessive overhead: The matrix structure gives the appearance, initially, of doubling administrative costs but as the matrix matures these costs decrease and productivity gains appear.
6. Decision strangulation: With increased administrative personnel, the decision-making process may become sluggish.
7. Sinking: The observation that top management believes the working matrix structure sinks to lower levels of management.
8. Layering: Refers to the situation where matrices appear within other matrices.
9. Navel gazing: Becoming too absorbed with internal operations to the detriment of the world outside the organization.

Adapted from: Stanley M. Davis and Paul R. Lawrence. *Matrix*. Reading, Mass.: Addison-Wesley Publishing Company, 1977, pp. 129–144.

are presented in Table 3. These problems are not unique to the matrix structure but seem somewhat more prevalent in it.[36]

Strong vs. Weak Matrix

Discussions of strong and weak matrix organizations have appeared frequently in the published literature. The terms "strong" and "weak" should not be interpreted as suggesting good or bad connations. Rather, they refer to the relative importance and power of the integrative function in the matrix. In essence, the issue lies with the balance of power between the functional and project managers. According to Stuckenbruck, in his or her article "The Matrix Organization," this balance of power may be shifted in either direction by changing any one or any combination of the following three factors:

1. "The administrative relationship—The levels at which the project and involved functional managers report, and the backing they receive from top management.

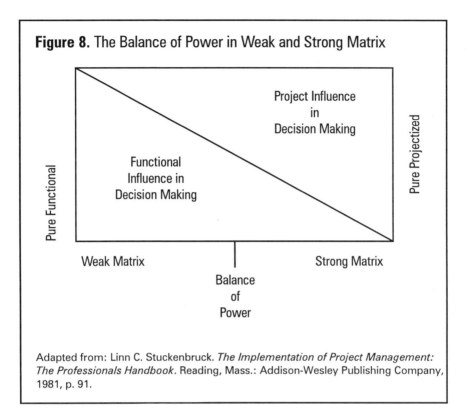

Figure 8. The Balance of Power in Weak and Strong Matrix

Project Influence in Decision Making

Functional Influence in Decision Making

Pure Functional

Pure Projectized

Weak Matrix

Strong Matrix

Balance of Power

Adapted from: Linn C. Stuckenbruck. *The Implementation of Project Management: The Professionals Handbook*. Reading, Mass.: Addison-Wesley Publishing Company, 1981, p. 91.

2. "The physical relationship—The physical distances between the various people involved in the project.

3. "The time spent on the project—The amount of time spent on the project by the respective managers."[37]

A strong matrix has the balance of power shifted in the project manager's direction, while the power distribution in a weak matrix favors the functional manager. The higher up the hierarchical echelon the project manager reports, the more physically separated the project team members are from their functional organizations, and the more full-time members on the project, the stronger the matrix structure. Galbraith agrees, as shown in Figure 8. He describes the managerial alternatives as a continuum ranging from the purely functional to a purely projectized structure, with the strong and weak matrix being defined as the amount of decision making influence possessed by the project and functional managers, respectively.[38]

Figure 9 combines the authority continuum presented in Figure 1 with the organizational continuum discussed by Youker[39] to develop an improved understanding of the type of organization most appropriate for different types of projects. The organizational continuum is based on the percent of personnel

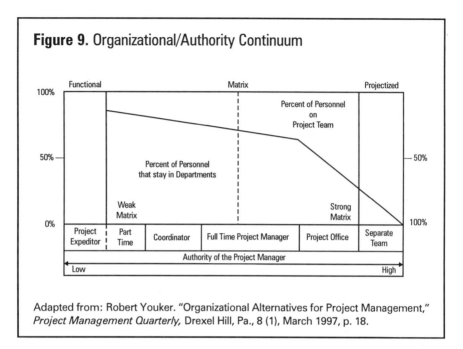

Figure 9. Organizational/Authority Continuum

Adapted from: Robert Youker. "Organizational Alternatives for Project Management," *Project Management Quarterly,* Drexel Hill, Pa., 8 (1), March 1997, p. 18.

who are full-time members of the project team. In the functional organization there are no individuals assigned to the project team. Consequently, no project manager exists and there is no project authority delegated. The weak matrix starts when an individual is given part-time responsibility to coordinate project efforts across functional department lines. As the part-time coordinator devotes more time to the project, project authority increases and the matrix becomes stronger. Eventually, as the project becomes more important, a full-time project manager is assigned, perhaps with a few specialized assistants. The establishment of a project office signifies the start of the strong matrix. In the projectized organization, essentially 100 percent of the personnel needed on the project are assigned to the project, and the project manager has essentially total responsibility for the project.

The Practical Organization for Projects

The functional, matrix and projectized organizations were discussed for clarity in their "pure" theoretical forms. In fact, few large organizations involved in multiple projects use any single form of organization. Rather, they employ a variety of organizational forms, selecting the one that seems most appropriate for the particular project in question. Thus, it is possible, even probable, that all forms of project organizations will be used to varying degrees on different projects and on the same project at different levels. Actual organizational charts for large companies involved with numerous projects can become quite complex. Figure 10 represents a simplified organization familiar to the authors, which undertakes several projects in various levels of the firm, with each project manager commanding varying levels of authority and resources. Each project requires coordination efforts with many organizations within and outside the parent company.

In Figure 10, projects A–E are shown in a full strong matrix organization, with the project managers reporting to the Project Management Department—the "manager of project managers." This individual also supervises a Project Control unit whose purpose is to provide the data collection and analysis efforts normally associated with project management network planning and control systems. Project F, however, is a particularly large and important effort. Its project manager reports directly to the Vice President for Engineering and Construction, while drawing on the services of the Project Management Department's Project Control unit. Project F is at least partially projectized, and there is little question within the entire parent organization of the importance or priority possessed by Project F and the Project F manager. It should be noted that all of these projects, A through F, must coordinate and work with a variety of departments supervised by several vice presidents, as well as government agencies and public groups outside of the parent organization. Meanwhile in the Accounting Department, a project expeditor works on some smaller project coordinating the activities of various departments working under the Vice President for Administrative Services. Not shown in this figure are the wide range of projects and project organization styles undertaken, mainly in the area of facilities maintenance and modification, under the Vice President for Operations.

The practical organization thus uses all the forms of project organization discussed earlier. The size and importance of the particular project determines the type of organization selected and the authority and responsibility delegated to the particular project manager. It is this mix of varying organizational structures that makes the practical application of project management techniques such a complex undertaking in most large organizations. As stated previously, organizational structures are as unique as the projects, their managers, the parent organization, and the environment within which they all operate. Table 4 presents 12 key factors that should provide assistance in deciding which organizational structure is most appropriate.

By matching the characteristics of the proposed project with the criteria indicated in Table 4, a basic understanding of the most appropriate organizational structures can be achieved. For example, if uncertainty, complexity, time criticality, and importance are relatively high, the technology is complex, the size of the project is large or moderately large, and the duration is expected to be moderate to long, then that project may be an excellent candidate for either a strong matrix or fully projectized organizational structure.

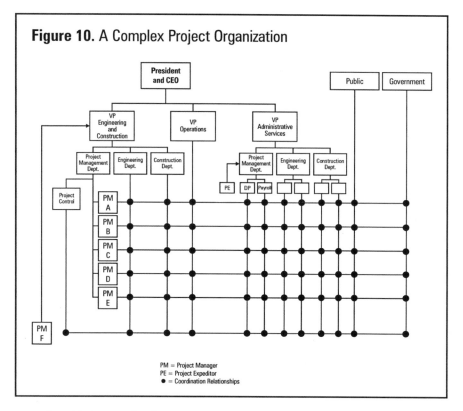

Figure 10. A Complex Project Organization

PM = Project Manager
PE = Project Expeditor
● = Coordination Relationships

In addition to the decision criteria presented in Table 4, three other factors should be considered before a final choice is made. First, one must determine if there exists ways to improve coordination and commitment in the functional structure without moving to a matrix or projectized structure. If so, much disruption and conflict may be avoided. Next, one must determine what variations of the matrix that might exist for the particular situation and determine the advantages and disadvantages of each variation. Finally, one must determine the relationship that exists between organizational design, the abilities of the project manager, and the planning and reporting system of the organization,[40] as presented in Figure 11. For the project organization to be successful, the project manager must possess broad skills, both people and technical, to manage the organization toward project completion. The planning and reporting system may be quite simple in a project organization but complex in the traditional functional organization.

Youker provides some "survival" techniques that may be useful, regardless of the project organization structure chosen:[41]

1. Have a charter from top management clearly defining responsibilities and authority for both the project managers and the functional departments.

Table 4. Key Factors of Organizational Structures

Project Characteristic	Functional	Matrix		Projectized
		Weak	Strong	
Uncertainty	Low	Moderate	High	High
Technology	Standard	Standard	Complex	New
Complexity	Low	Low	Medium	High
Duration	Short	Medium	Medium	Long
Size	Small	Small	Medium	Large
Importance	Low	Moderate	Moderate	High
Customer	Diverse	Diverse	3 or 4	One
Interdependency (within)	Low	Medium	Medium	High
Interdependency (between)	High	Medium	Medium	Low
Time Criticality	Low	Moderate	Moderate	High
Resource Criticality	Depends	Depends	Depends	Depends
Differentiation	Low	Low	High	Medium

Adapted from: Robert Youker. "Organizational Alternatives For Project Management," *Project Management Quarterly*, Drexel Hill, Pa. 8 (1), March 1977, p. 21.

2. Learn how to anticipate and constructively channel conflict.

3. Develop methods to promote teamwork.

4. Documented approval of objectives, plans and budgets provide the project manager with the needed leverage to assure departmental commitments; use them.

5. Obtain documented department head approval as well as the lower-level task leaders'.

6. The project manager should avoid conflict with the functional department head and carry the problem through the matrix manager.

7. Utilize the management-by-objectives approach and do not supervise the functional departments too closely.

8. Reduce uncertainty through careful and continuous planning.

Summary

The functional structure will work for many organizations and their unique projects if adequate communications can be achieved with minimum disruption of the organization. The matrix structure requires changes in the organization and a coordinated effort of the entire firm. Care must be exercised

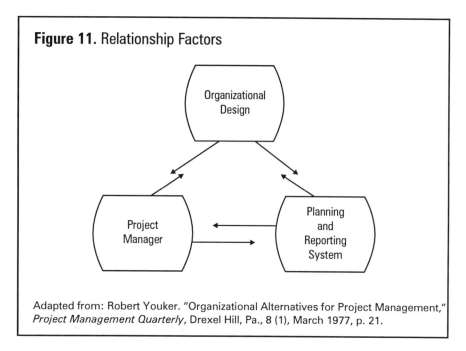

Figure 11. Relationship Factors

Organizational Design

Project Manager

Planning and Reporting System

Adapted from: Robert Youker. "Organizational Alternatives for Project Management," *Project Management Quarterly*, Drexel Hill, Pa., 8 (1), March 1977, p. 21.

in choosing and training the expeditor, coordinator, or manager. To be effective and successful, the project supervisor should have both good interpersonal skills and the appropriate technical knowledge.

The projectized structure may be the simplest approach from the viewpoint of the project manager, but it may be detrimental to both the functional organization and top-level management. In reality, especially for large organizations, combinations of all the project organization methods are typically developed. The complexity of the coordination effort increases with this "hybrid" structure, however, and one must be aware of the relative strengths and weaknesses of each structure, carefully selecting that most appropriate for each project as it is undertaken.

By accepting one of the project management structures, all associated personnel must recognize that the organization is taking an enormous step from which there may be no return. More management positions may need to be created under the constraint of limited personnel and financial resources. Regardless of the project management structure chosen, management must realize that a dynamic state of equilibrium will be necessary if project management is to be successful in their particular parent organization.

Endnotes

1. W.L. Wallace, "The Winchester-Western Division Concept of Product Planning," New Haven, Conn.: Olin Mathieson Corporation, January 1963, pp. 2–3.

2. Linn C. Stuckenbruck, ed., *The Implementation of Project Management: The Professionals Handbook,* Reading, Mass.: Addison-Wesley, 1981, pp. 53–57. Article written by James N. Salapatas.

3. Ibid.

4. Ibid.

5. Ibid.

6. Ibid.

7. Ibid., p. 56.

8. Ibid.

9. Ibid., p. 5l.

Richard P. Olsen, "Can Project Management Be Defined?," *Project Management Quarterly*, 2 (1), 1971, pp. 12–14.

11. Jay R. Galbraith, *Organizational Design,* Reading, Mass.: Addison-Wesley, 1977.

12. David I. Cleland, "Defining a Project Management System," *Project Management Quarterly*, 8 (4), 1977, p. 39.

13. John R. Adams, Stephen E. Barndt, and Martin D. Martin, *Managing by Project Management,* Dayton, Ohio: Universal Technology Corp., 1979, p. 33.

14. Paul R. Lawrence and Jay W. Lorsch, *Studies in Organizational Design*, Homewood, Ill.: Richard D. Irwin, 1970, p. 89.

15. Adams, et al., p. 34.

16. Lawrence, et al., p. 92.

17. Adams, et al., p. 37.

18. Ibid.

19. Ibid., pp. 38–40.

20. Ibid.

21. Ibid.

22. Author C. Bulter, "Project Management: A Study in Organizational Conflict," *Academy of Management Journal 16* (1), March 1973, pp. 84–101.

23. Adams, et al., p. 41.

24. Ibid.

25. Ibid.

26. Robert Youker, "Organizational Alternatives for Project Management," *Project Management Quarterly*, 8 (1), March 1977, p. 18.

27. Ibid.

28. Ibid., p. 19.

29. Ibid.

30. Ibid.

31. Harold Kerzner, *Project Management: A Systems Approach to Planning, Scheduling, and Controlling*, New York : Van Nostrand Reinhold, 1979, p. 49.

32. Stanley M. Davis and Paul R. Lawrence, *Matrix,* Reading, Mass.: Addison-Wesley, 1977, p. 3.

33. Galbraith, et al., p. 167.

34. Many of the ideas were drawn from Kenner, et al., pp. 55–56; Stuckenbruck, et al., pp. 76–80.

35. Davis, et al., pp. 129–144.

36. Ibid.

37. Stuckenbruck, et al., p. 89.

38. Jay R. Galbraith, "Matrix Organizational Designs," *Business Horizons*, February 1971, pp. 29–40.

39. Youker, et al., p. 22.

40. Ibid., p. 21.

41. Ibid.

References

Adams, John R., Stephen Barndt, and Martin D. Martin. *Managing By Project Management*. Dayton, Ohio: Universal Technology Corp., 1979.

Bulter, Author C. "Project Management: A Study in Organizational Conflict." *Academy of Management Journal*, 16 (1), March 1973, pp. 84–10l.

Cleland, David I. "Defining a Project Management System." *Project Management Quarterly*, 8 (4), 1977, p. 39.

Davis, Stanley M., and Paul R. Lawrence. *Matrix*. Reading, Mass.: Addison-Wesley, 1977, p. 3.

Galbraith, Jay R. "Matrix Organization Designs." *Business Horizons,* February 1971, pp. 29–40.

Galbraith, Jay R. *Organizational Design*. Reading, Mass.: Addison-Wesley, 1977.

Kerzner, Harold, *Project Management: A Systems Approach to Planning, Scheduling and Controlling*. New York: Van Nostrand Reinhold, 1979.

Lawrence, Paul R., and Jay W. Lorsch. *Studies in Organizational Design*. Homewood, Ill.: Richard D. Irwin, 1970, p. 89.

Olsen, Richard F. "Can Project Management Be Defined?" *Project Management Quarterly*, 2 (1), 1971, pp. 12–14.

Stuckenbruck, Linn C. *The Implementation of Project Management: The Professionals Handbook*. Reading, Mass.: Addison-Wesley, 1981.

Wallace, W.L., "The Winchester-Western Division Concept of Product Planning." New Haven: Olin Mathieson Corporation, January 1963, pp. 2–3.

Youker, Robert. "Organizational Alternatives for Project Management." *Project Management Quarterly, 8* (1), March 1977.

The Project Manager's Work Environment: Coping With Time and Stress

Paul C. Dinsmore,
Martin Dean Martin,
and
Gary T. Huettel

Introduction

Success for the project manager is to a large degree dependent on the environment which structures job tasks and impacts the individual. For the individual to perform effectively, knowledge of key environmental variables is critical. Two such variables that can either enhance or degrade performance are time and stress. Time is one of the project manager's most limited resources. Once time has been expended there is no recovery. The minutes, hours and days pass, and associated with this passage are opportunities and problems. Proper time management allows the project manager to seize and benefit from opportunities and to solve or at least alleviate problems. The converse is also true.

Time seems to be a flexible resource, but as continuous daily decisions are made as to how it is expended, the limited and constrained nature of time becomes apparent. This comprehension caused by the passage of time and the difficulty associated with assigning priorities for task execution has a tendency to place the project manager in a continuous stress condition. Thus, stress builds and can lead to poor performance and poor health for the project manager. The purpose of this monograph is to explore the time and stress concepts, their relationship, and to identify ideas and techniques that will better enable the project manager to more effectively allocate and use time while concurrently coping with the effects of stress. Time management is examined first, then stress management.

Time Management

Time management deals with how the project manager uses the time available during a working hour, day, week, or other time interval. The environment for the project manager is illustrated in Figure 1. The project manager is constantly bombarded by various stimuli that originate either from within (internal) or without (external) the firm. External factors include ecological, political, social, economic and technological variables. These variables cover such items as the competition, governmental rulings, changes in technology, and a host of others. Internal variables include plans, policies, rules, direction provided by top management and peers, and other organizational constraints. The internal and external variables interact to create stimuli that impact the project manager's resultant decisions. These forces place a premium on the effective use of available time and create job-related stress for the project manager. The decisions that emanate from this environment subsequently impact the project team in terms of the quality of its productivity, morale, and growth. The second and dual impact is on the project task in terms of performance, cost and schedule outcomes. Thus, management by the

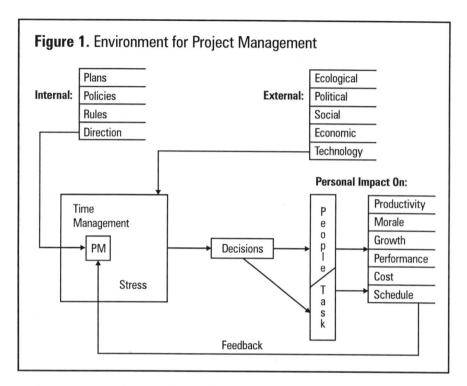

Figure 1. Environment for Project Management

Internal: Plans, Policies, Rules, Direction

External: Ecological, Political, Social, Economic, Technology

Personal Impact On: Productivity, Morale, Growth, Performance, Cost, Schedule

Time Management, PM, Stress, Decisions, People, Task, Feedback

project manager of personal time becomes a critical consideration. Feedback closes the loop and helps determine the proper corrective action. However, this corrective action must include not only changes in the decision-making process, but also changes in the way the project manager uses available time. The nature of time and how project managers use the available time are factors that need to be examined.

Evolution of the Time Challenge

The invention of time-measuring devices created the concept of linear time, or what might be called in modern times "living by the clock." Sebastian de Grazia[1] says that linear time is contrary to natural time, which is instinctual and governed by the oscillations of nature, marked only by the biological and social milestones of life. Living on linear time is a learned discipline and is contrary to Man's natural way of dealing with the periods marked by the turning of the globe.

With the advent of the Industrial Age, the need for more production at less cost sparked awareness for increasing "productivity," which involves the factor time; i.e., X number of units produced in Y periods of time, or a project to be completed within a certain time frame. Although projects can be traced to ancient times, featuring undertakings such as the Egyptian Pyramids and the Great Wall of China, project work as known today is fundamentally an outcropping of the Industrial Age and shares the industrialists' concern for getting a job done within a given time frame. Perhaps the only truly significant break-through in project-time analytics came in the emerging Space Age of the early 1660s with the successful application of PERT/CPM networks. Project people were then able to dissect the linear or chronological time requirements and cross-relate the activities on a network which defined inter-relationships. It then became possible to determine with a greater degree of accuracy "what should be done, and when."

Today with sophisticated network planning and scheduling systems, project managers find themselves caught between the idea of linear time—a learned chronological concept—and natural time, which resonates with a deeper unclocked human perception of life. This inner conflict, reflecting the inability of most people to fully program themselves on linear time, is one hypothesis for explaining why team members are often incapable of making happen on a timely basis that which the insensitive "unnatural" linear system would dictate.

The Time Problem Itself

The project manager, who spent early childhood years on natural time—happily oblivious to the ticking of the clock—finds himself or herself in adulthood enmeshed in a project environment, where success or failure may be measured by accomplishing tasks within given time constraints. He or she is now exposed to sophisticated techniques, such as computer-linked network systems, which are used to determine concrete time requirements for the project. He or she faces a rational planning and scheduling system that analyzes project time needs and subsequently plots out the project's time-task requirements with impassionate objectivity. Project management systems, then, are geared to handle linear time requirements.

But what about the project manager? Is the project manager fully tuned to the project's time needs? More importantly, how does he or she manage his or her own time? If the project has a system for dealing with its linear time needs, does the project manager have a system for dealing with perhaps the most important of project resources, the project manager's own managerial time? Are those principles of planning and scheduling—accepted as basic tenants for the project—applied with the same fervor by the project manager when organizing his or her own workday?

The project manager may feel at times that the challenge is insurmountable. Given the constraints of time, quality, cost and the political environment, he or she faces a daily basketful of ambiguities and "impossible" tasks, which he or she is supposed to field in stride as he or she plans his or her next strategic project moves. A 36-hour day would seemingly better fit the project manager's driving schedule, rather than the sparse 24 hours, which must also accommodate personal and family life.

The particular time crunch felt by the project manager may have its logical explanations. After all, he or she is by circumstance and design the hub of project activities. Directly or indirectly, everything revolves about him. He or she sticks his or her fingers and nose into a wide range of subjects varying from minor to major importance. As time's chronometer spins away, the day's hours seem to shrink, crises mount, and people and telephones clamor for a few moments of the project manager's time. The naked reality is that "there aren't enough hours in the day"—and the harried project manager must somehow conciliate his or her responsibilities with that limited fleeting resource called time.

Not all project managers, of course, fit into the overburdened model just described. Some have natural or developed abilities for making the right managerial moves—including mapping out strategic planning, motivating, team-building, delegating, systems development—the job gets done, and necessary time is available to tend to the important project issues. However, because the project manager's pressure-packed situation is special, his or her time resources can take on a particularly elusive character.

There are numerous reasons that make the project manager's situation unique. He or she not only has to ride herd on his or her subordinate project team, responsible for activities like design, project engineering, supply, construction, planning and scheduling, logistical and support systems, but must ultimately coordinate client relations, governmental and regulatory agencies, emergency situations, special consultants, financing agencies, joint venture partners and anyone else who may impact project results.

The project manager's time management habits have far-reaching effects. The pace for the project staff is set by the project manager's style. Deadline-setting, goal-meeting and productivity are also directly influenced. Project posture on meeting management, paper-handling and interruptions are likewise triggered by the project manager's time management moves. Although many of these problems are common to managers at large, the project manager's troubles are in some ways peculiar. For instance:[2]

- A prime project function is to be a fast-tracking integrator, which implies intense interaction with people.
- High pressure due to schedule and cost requirements causes a tendency toward working longer hours to "catch up."
- Projects are often performed in multiple shifts, requiring a broader management time-spread.
- As the project hub, the project manager maintains extensive contact at all levels, including superior (client, joint venture boards, parent company management), lateral and dotted line (functional and matrix managers, ma-

jor contractors and suppliers, parent company specialized staff), and subordinate (line and project staff).

All the classic time management barriers of excess paperwork, overloaded meeting schedules, extensive one-on-one interviews, and constant interruptions by the secretary, passersby and telephone must be hurdled by the project manager. Once clear of those obstacles, the project manager can shift more efforts from reacting (responding to actions initiated by others) to proacting (taking initiative on subjects that will ultimately result in project benefit). A weeding-out system is needed to sort out nonproductive time-consumers from those few important subjects that are truly worthy of attention. For the project manager this is particularly difficult due to the great number of activities to be administered.

A special knack, bordering on genius, seems to enable some project managers to direct projects to timely and successful completion in spite of an ambient of apparent managerial chaos. For those blessed with this rare ability, a brisk change in pace of daily habits might prove highly prejudicial. Such project managers are probably destined to complete their careers "winging it" from one project to the next, gathering laurels of success for their exceptional natural talent. Most project managers, however,—not blessed with this genius-like prowess—find that systematically eliminating some major time bottlenecks and rearranging daily priorities can spark an increase in project output. The "average" project manager endowed with reasonable professional talents can boost productivity considerably by heeding some simple hints drawn from the literature on executive time management. The "well-above-average" project manager can also raise his or her effectiveness level by applying those tips found compatible with his or her management style, making the workday even more productive. Research results infer an awareness by project management professionals for a need to improve time management practice—starting with the project manager.[3]

The Survey

A time management survey was made at the Joint Project Management Institute/Internet Symposium held in Boston, Massachusetts, in October 1981. At the symposium over 800 project management professionals from around the world attended three days of debates and discussions on project management. Four hundred questionnaires were randomly distributed during the event. Seventy-eight completed forms were returned.

About a third of the respondents indicated that they were working in manufacturing-related industry at the time of the survey. The remaining respondents were evenly distributed between architects and engineers (A&Es), contractors, independent consultants, and miscellaneous other categories.

Figure 2. Personal Time Philosophy

Composite Time Philosophy	Percentage of Total Philosophy
a) "I determine how I use my time."	46.4
b) "Others determine how I use my time."	25.9
c) "The system determines how I use my time."	27.7
	100.0%

Of the 78 questionnaires, 31 were answered by professionals carrying titles of project director or project manager. The remaining categories included president or member of the board, vice-president or manager of operations, regional or area manager, chief engineer or construction manager, department or section head in a project structure, functional department or section head, consultant or professor. Those categories were distributed quite evenly. Thirty-eight respondents indicated that they had logged between 10 and 20 years in project management. Seventeen of those surveyed had more than 30 years of experience. The remainder had less than 10 years in the project management field.

Time Usage
The group surveyed showed an average workday of slightly more than nine hours. The major time user was shown to be meetings, taking up somewhat less than two hours daily (108 minutes based on a nine-hour day). Routine paperwork, telephone conversations, closed-door concentration and one-on-one listening, all varied within the boundaries of 65–81 minutes and represented major time consumers for the respondents. The remaining time, composing about one-quarter of the respondents' workday, was distributed between seven items of lesser impact as shown in Figure 3.

Causes
The respondents were asked to distribute points between items (a), (b), and (c) given in Figure 2, thus arbitrating the composition of their own personal time philosophy. The resulting distribution of total time philosophy is shown in the chart.

The results indicate that more than half of the respondents' composite time philosophy is made up of views which accept that time is outside their personal control [items (b) and (c), summing 53.6 percent]. On the other hand, the remaining component of 46.4 percent reflects a strong, "I chart my

Figure 3. Time Distribution of Respondents' Average Work Day

Activity	Percent Time Spent on Activity	Minutes Spent on Activity
• Routine paperwork	15	81
• Telephone Conversations	12	65
• Meetings	20	108
• Closed-door concentration for planning analysis and control	12	65
• One-one listening, interviewing or coaching	14	75
• Coffee, chats, rest stops	4	22
• Business lunches extending over normal lunch period	2	11
• Time-consuming conversations and interruptions	6	32
• Time you really can't account for	5	27
• Travel (time spent en route during working hours)	3	16
• Reading professional literature	4	22
• Other	3	16
TOTAL	100%	540

own path" factor in the respondents' philosophies. When asked to identify the items that represented the most serious causes of time management problems, the returns indicated the following items in order of gravity—with 1 representing the most serious cause; 7, the least serious cause:

1. Difficulty in saying no
2. Lack of self-discipline
3. Lack of time management awareness in the organization
4. Less-than-fully-competent employees
5. Excessive bureaucracy in the organization
6. Poor utilization of secretary or assistant
7. Tendency to centralize, not delegate.

Search for Solutions

The respondents were given five solutions for the problem of dealing with an increased workload and asked to prioritize from one to five the solutions which they considered best. The results are as follows:

1. Delegate more (involve others)
2. Do less work (eliminate some work items)
3. Let things slide (delay)
4. Work longer (more hours)
5. Work harder (faster).

Scheduling Daily Activities

When asked to indicate which phrase best reflects thoughts on scheduling daily activities, the respondents replied as follows:

- "I schedule all activities daily and allot specific periods of time for each." (14 percent)
- "I list to-do items but don't allocate specific time periods." (51 percent)
- "I carry my agenda in my head." (3 percent)
- "I note some items on the agenda but most of the day is not formally scheduled." (32 percent)

Thus, the majority of the professionals polled (51 percent) indicated that they did not formally schedule daily activities, although they did prepare "to-do" lists. Only 14 percent responded that their work was fully programmed time-wise. Almost one-third showed partial scheduling practices, and only 3 percent avoided any attempt at scheduling.

Project Priorities

A hypothetical sequencing problem was presented in the survey as follows: "As project manager for a $100 million industrial plant that is four months behind schedule, assuming you had made the following to-do list in a given day, give the sequence in which you would perform the following items (number from 1 to 12)." Here is the sequence that resulted by summing the responses:

1. Analyze progress report to determine appropriate corrective measures.
2. Think about how to get back on schedule.
3. Review milestone dates.
4. Approve drawings for release to contractor.
5. Listen to contractor's complaints on interference.
6. Sign checks for paying suppliers.
7. Review project management organization to see how it can better meet the needs.
8. Read and sign correspondence.
9. Lobby with the client.
10. Draft reply to nasty letter from client.
11. Interview junior engineers.
12. Read revision 4 to the construction management manual.

The sequence that resulted from the survey shows priority emphasis on action items necessary to put the project back on schedule. Items of lesser immediate impact were shown at the end of the list.

Delegation

The two most important reasons for delegating, in accordance with survey results were:

- "Increases managerial effectiveness."
- "Provides stimulus to subordinates."

Other items that were considered important, but to a lesser degree, were:

- "Allows time to think."
- "Opens new horizons (for you, the boss)."
- "Avoids one-man-band tendency."

Justifications given by the respondents for not delegating to a greater degree were:

- "Subjects are too confidential to involve others."
- "My subordinates aren't sufficiently qualified."
- "I can do it better."
- "I already delegate enough."

Meetings

The survey showed that the participants attended over six meetings per week. In those meetings an average of 25 percent of the time was spent on off-the-track banter, generalized complaining, lobbying for pet causes, and other nonproductive items. When asked, "What do you think contributed toward eventual nonproductiveness of the last meeting you attended?," the three most prevalent responses were:

- "The meeting wasn't properly planned (no written objective or detailed agenda)"
- "Inept leadership"
- "Undisciplined participants."

Time Bottlenecks

The respondents' grading of "time bottlenecks," per magnitude of the time problem presented, resulted in the following sequence:

- In-coming phone calls
- Meetings I go to
- Routine paperwork
- Interruptions by colleagues
- Interruptions by subordinates
- Interruptions by third parties
- Interruptions by boss

- Outgoing phone calls
- Schedule appointments
- Interruptions by secretary
- Meetings I call.

The respondents' perception of "time bottlenecks" varies only slightly with that shown under "time usage," as shown in Table A; common emphasis is given to the major time problems of meetings, telephone use, paperwork and one-on-one dealings with various parties.

Solutions

Solutions to time problems, or for improving the use of managerial time, were given by the respondents per the following prioritized list:
- Question whether certain things should be done at all.
- Start disciplining interruptions.
- Start using an agenda regularly.
- Delegate more.
- Eliminate part of paperwork.
- Start closing door to office.

The sequence selected suggests an awareness that "there's not enough time to do it all," yet the reluctance to "close the door to office," indicates a tendency towards "hands on" management. If priorities are indeed as reflected above, the poll mirrors the managers' expectations that time can be rationalized without creating excessive communication barriers. These solutions and others will be examined after the essentials of time management are explored.

Time Management Cornerstones

Executive time management has been the topic of much professional literature; dozens of books are available to tell the business person how to manage a day (or more correctly perhaps, how to manage *himself* or *herself* during the day). Some books extend the concepts to life management, laying out guidelines for a more personal approach to handling time. Others present specific "how-to" procedures and map out the route to timely success for a special audience, such as executives, hospital administrators, or the working mother. Although focused at differing audiences, the books carry many common themes that are held by the authors to be universally applicable. Selected major themes from the literature are summarized in the following section.

How is Time Used?

Peter Drucker suggests in the training film "Management Time"[4] that managers should actually make a time log, registering for a week just how the day's time is used. He recommends that a secretary or assistant jot down the boss's time usage—or that the manager makes notes throughout the day. From a review of such a time log at the week's end, the manager typically finds a misuse of time in one or more of the following ways: (1) snap judgments made on highly important subjects; (2) telephone conversations that go on and on; (3) periods of incessant interruptions in which virtually nothing of significance is accomplished; (4) dwelling on unimportant subjects, which could well be delegated or ignored; (5) periods of paper slavery in which much unnecessary paper is handled.

Drucker holds in the firm that when confronted with the *facts*, i.e., a log of how time was *really* spent during the week, the manager is forced to take stock and improve time habits. The time log might be called an "awareness bell" designed for the manager to look habits in the mirror and take subsequent corrective action. The log then is simply a prop—though highly effective, according to Drucker—to motivate the manager to tackle the "time bottlenecks" and formulate a truly proactive managerial stance. The following major time bottlenecks are found to dominate many managers' days:[5]

- Paperwork—requiring signature or reading
- Meetings—scheduled or otherwise
- One-on-one listening, problem-solving, and coaching
- Telephone calls—incoming and outgoing.

Gaining time involves aiming a steely eye at each item in an effort to sweep away wasted motions and time-killers. Some pointers for keeping precious minutes from the major time consumers are covered in the next section.

The Managerial Microcosm

The results of the survey discussed earlier reveal several methods that the project manager may use to better use available time. The basic idea of management involved certain functions that the project manager should apply for overall management of the project; they include planning, organization, control, direction, staffing, communication, and coordination. These functions can also be applied to the microcosm where the project manager works each day in terms of time management for personal activities. Thus, methods or techniques which can be placed in these functional categories will be discussed briefly in terms of planning, organization, control and coordination, and direction and communication. Staffing will not be involved.

Planning

This function deals with the establishment by the project manager of those objectives that must be accomplished during a given time period, such as a month, week, or day. Some useful techniques that will assist the project manager in planning for how time should be used are the next concern.

Figure 4. Chart of Time Allocation per Pareto's Principle

Group	Percent of Subjects Competing for Project Manager's Attention	Percent of Time Which Should be Allocated to the Group of Items
A	10	70
B	20	20
C	70	10

Pareto's Principle

Pareto's Principle has applications in numerous fields, including sales, materials management, maintenance.[6] Simply stated, Pareto's Principle says that the significant items in a given group normally represent a relatively small portion of the total items in the group.

Pareto's Principle establishes criteria for discrimination when confronted with a large number of items. Arranged in groups of A, B and C (group A representing the most important subjects), Pareto's Principle applied to the manager's time yields a distribution as shown in Figure 4.

The 70-20-10 percentage reflects a generally accepted rule of thumb for Pareto distributions. Pareto's Principle applied to time management basically says that unequal treatment should be given to the various subjects confronting the project manager. According to the standard Pareto distribution, up to 70 percent of the project manager's time should be applied to "A" subjects, such as:

• Selection of key staff members
• Developing project plans
• Establishing overall project relationships
• Review of project budget requirements
• Decisions regarding project control systems
• Establishing reporting criteria
• Developing and motivating staff.

"B" and "C" subjects, representing lesser priorities, should be put into proper perspective with corresponding allocation of only 20 percent and 10 percent of management time (See Figure 5).

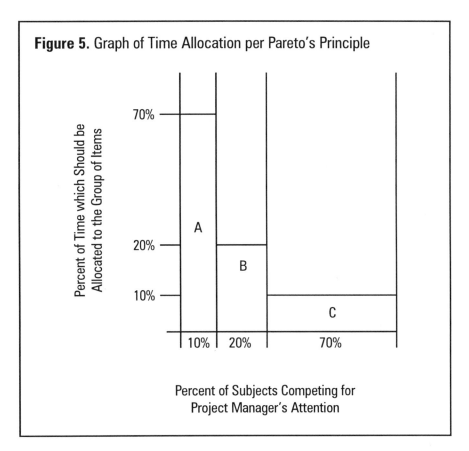

Figure 5. Graph of Time Allocation per Pareto's Principle

Percent of Time which Should be Allocated to the Group of Items

70%

20%

A

10%

B

C

10%   20%   70%

Percent of Subjects Competing for
Project Manager's Attention

Scheduling Time vs. Work

After a day of little or no forward progress, many project managers have asked themselves, "What did I really accomplish today?" And the answer is often not encouraging! One explanation is that the project manager is led astray by the whims and urgencies of others, thus draining time from more relevant subjects. Peter Drucker[7] takes the position that managers do not accomplish what they should because their approach is wrong; i.e., they try to cram an ever-expanding mass (all the work that comes at them from sundry directions) into a limited, unstretchable compartment (their working time). Drucker contends that work should be trimmed and prioritized to meet the immutable limitations of time, rather than using the opposing approach. Trying to make time expand is somewhat like trying to pour more water into a glass than it will hold; it's no wonder that no matter how hard some project managers drive, they still find themselves up to their earlobes in work, and complain that 24 hours a day are not enough!

Figure 6. Sample Daily Activity List

DATE: _____

TO DO ITEMS:

1. Talk to project engineer about delay in concrete work.
2. Telephone client about specification change.
3. Check delivery date for portable pump.
4. Etc.

Drucker says plan time first, then plan work. In other words, lay out the day in terms of specific blocks of time, then fit priority items (relevant important subjects) into those time periods. For the lesser important subjects, figure out another way to get them done (delegate, reorganize, eliminate, etc.).

Daily Activity List

One tool that is useful for time management is the daily activity list. Typically, this should be developed in the early morning or the evening before. The project manager should list those tasks or activities that need attention so as to keep the project on track. A sample list is illustrated in Figure 6. Generally, an individual will overplan, thus, not all items will be completed. The most critical item should receive priority treatment. Items may be worked concurrently and some may be carried over or even deleted during the day.

Weekly Schedule

Another useful time management planning device is the schedule of planned activities by day and hour. This tool is illustrated in Figure 7, and is self-explanatory. It is a very useful tool and can be used in conjunction with the daily activity list. Once again activities may be worked concurrently and some may have to be rescheduled based on the events that occur during a given day.

Goal Setting

Much time is lost because project goals are either nonexistent or they are vague and ambiguous. Broad goals for establishing project boundaries are typically set forth in the project charter. The project team is then responsible for setting project goals within this overall context. Basically, goals establish targets that then serve to direct project behavior and activities. Clear and con-

Figure 7. Schedule of Planned Activities

	Monday	Tuesday	Wednesday	Thursday	Friday
8:00 – 9:00					
9:00 – 10:00					
10:00 – 11:00					
11:00 – 12:00					
12:00 – 1:00					
1:00 – 2:00					
2:00 – 3:00					
3:00 – 4:00					
4:00 – 5:00					
5:00 – 6:00					
Evening					

cise goals serve to structure behavior so that people perform in the most effective and efficient manner. Thus, they become standards which the individual can use to establish personal goals and the necessary activities to achieve the goals. Criteria for establishing goals are listed in Figure 8. These criteria are self-explanatory and will not be discussed in detail.[8] The weekly plan outlined in Figure 6 can be consolidated with the concept of weekly objectives. This integration is illustrated in Figure 9.

Plan for Appointments

Appointments should be scheduled for specific time periods during the workday. They should begin promptly and end on the same note. Sufficient time between appointments should be scheduled to provide for handling of unexpected time demands. This type of interruption will normally be caused by unscheduled telephone calls and drop-in appointments. For best time use, callers should be asked to leave their names and telephone numbers for subsequent follow-up, rather than have the immediate meeting interrupted. Unscheduled appointments should consume no more than 15–20 percent of appointment time.[9] The decision as to how much of the workday should be allotted to appointments should be based on experience and the state of project affairs.

```
┌─────────────────────────────────────────────────────────────┐
│  Figure 8. Goal Setting Criteria                             │
│                                                              │
│      1. State end result                                     │
│      2. Challenging                                          │
│      3. Measurable                                           │
│      4. Attainable                                           │
│      5. Compared Against Alternatives                        │
│      6. Understandable                                       │
│      7. Contemporary                                         │
│      8. Attainable                                           │
│      9. Congruent                                            │
│                                                              │
└─────────────────────────────────────────────────────────────┘
```

Uncertainty Reduction

The project manager consistently makes decisions in the face of varying degrees of uncertainty. Often uncertainty causes the project manager to delay decisions, which leads to stress and ineffective time use. Rather than be a victim of uncertainty, the project manager should plan and structure control systems so that two-way communication is maximized.[10] Another consideration relates to the use of management information systems, reports, personal discussions, meetings, and other feedback systems to obtain high-quality, recent information to reduce uncertainty in terms of decision-making.

Organization

This function deals with the grouping and ordering of activities so that they are completed in the most efficient and effective manner. Several techniques can assist the project manager in this area.

Time Matrix

Project managers, from a classical viewpoint, should focus on activities that will assure completion of a quality project, on time and within budget; i.e., subjects which are really important as far as the project's objectives are concerned. Since the project manager is high on "the most-sought-after-persons" list, it is natural that he or she has a sizeable "wheat and chaff" problem—a need for a filter system to ensure adequate time is spent on "wheaty" subjects. A big system-clogger in project management is the abundance of mini-urgencies, which pockmark the manager's day and often push aside other subjects of greater project relevance.

Important subjects, in terms of project management, are those which are relevant in terms of meeting project goals. Urgencies, on the other hand, are characterized by a pressing need to have a given activity completed in a short time span, yet having no necessary relationship with importance. An abun-

Figure 9. Consolidated Objectives and Time Schedule (Weekly)

Date: _____ / _____ / _____

Plan for Week of _____					
Weekly Objectives:	Associated Activities:	Priority			Day/Time For Activity:
		1	2	3	

dance of urgent items over an extended period carries the indelible stamp of sloppy planning and/or poor management. The question arises, however, if really important matters are not characterized by urgency and vice versa. In other words, isn't an urgent subject automatically important, and an important one therefore urgent? The importance/urgency matrix shown in the book *Manage Your Time, Manage Your Work Manage Yourself* by Merrill C. Douglass and Donna N. Douglass is helpful for putting this relationship into perspective.[11] See Figure 10.

The matrix shows four distinct relationships between urgency and importance. Quadrant 1 indicates a situation of "crisis" characterized by a subject that is both important and urgent (a major casting flaw in a critical path equipment item; or, the client wants to make a major design change). Quadrant 2 represents the planning and control mode—the subjects are important, but somehow are not red-flagged with urgency (basic planning, training sessions, development of subordinates). Quadrant 3 encompasses subjects that are relatively unimportant but carry the urgent label. Many telephone calls, one-on-one conversations, and "urgent" pieces of correspondence fall into this box. Quadrant 4 represents genuine time-wasters (items that are unimportant

Figure 10. Importance/Urgency Matrix

	Important	Not Important
Urgent	1	3
Not Urgent	2	4

and not urgent). Examples of these subjects are over-emphasis on procedures, excessive efficiency consciousness in detriment to effectiveness, and chats about yesterday's football game.

A typical time distribution shows crisis Quadrant 1 demanding (and getting) its fair share of attention, while Quadrant 2 has its rightful share syphoned off by the trivia and time-wasters of Quadrants 3 and 4. The result is insufficient planning and control, which subsequently produces more crises and urgent trivia. The logical solution for breaking out of this circle is concentration on important matters (Quadrants 1 and 2), which will tend to attenuate the effects of time-gobbling Quadrants 3 and 4.

Setting Priorities by Groupings

Ask yourself, "If you really need to see all that paper?" Just because it lands on your desk doesn't mean you should spend time with it. With your secretary's aid, make a list of all documents that cross your desk and classify the subjects in groups of priorities A, B and C. Then, by delegating, eliminating and condensing, drastically reduce the time spent on C items and, to a lesser degree, on those of group B, thus allowing time for A priorities.

Control and Coordination

Control and coordination activities deal with the tracking of progress in an effort to save time later by identifying and dealing as early as possible with problems. Problems, like a mustard plant, generally grow from small seeds. Deviations from plan need to be detected and corrective action initiated. Several techniques and ideas apply here.

Discipline and Structure Meetings

You need to go back to the basics! Does everybody know what the subject is—what is the objective of the meeting? It's amazing how many people don't know what the meeting is all about (sometimes not even the leader has a clear idea). See that project group leaders know the fundamentals for running a meeting. Establish meeting objectives clearly in a memo, meeting notice, or other written form. Prior to the meeting make an itemized agenda and afterwards register the results with meeting notes. Avoid "instantaneous problem solving." Direct discussion initially toward alternate solutions in order to explore the full potential of the group. Create an "open" atmosphere (all ideas are valid). Once this stage of exploration is completed, have the group narrow in on the solution. The result may be a better solution obtained by consensus, and paradoxically, time is saved as the procedure minimizes entrenched argumentation and standoff positions. A detailed checklist for conducting an effective committee meeting is outlined below:

General Comments

1. Committees may be formal or informal in terms of structure. Some purposes for committees include to generate a specific product, to brainstorm ideas, to provide a social relief valve, to keep individuals busy, and to delay a decision on an issue.

2. The charter for a committee should clearly give the leader (chairperson) the authority to lead the group and to make decisions.

3. The selection of committee members is critical. They must be qualified and have authority to represent their specific functional area.

4. The leader must possess authority to replace those who consistently block committee activities.

5. Committee members must want to serve on the specific committee.

6. Committee members must attend meetings and not be permitted to send substitutes.

7. Committee meetings should be closed and free from interruptions. Members need to concentrate on the task at hand.

Actions to Complete Prior to Meetings

1. An agenda should be prepared and sent to members before each meeting. Members may be requested to submit agenda items. Each member should bring their agenda copy to the meeting. Have extra copies on hand in case some individuals forget.

2. If written or published materials are to be discussed during the meeting they should be distributed in advance with each member studying and reviewing them prior to the meeting.

3. If possible, a meeting schedule for the duration of the assignment should be developed. Members need to reserve these dates. Meetings should begin and end promptly. They should be held in a set location and with a fixed time. The committee should meet only when it is necessary. Don't have a meeting just to have one.

Meeting Issues

1. *First Meeting*:

- Provide a clear statement of the committee's objectives(s) to each member. Discuss to ensure that each person understands what is to be achieved.
- Organize committee—appoint secretary or other persons as required. Assign tasks if necessary, such as subcommittee chairpersons.

- Be prepared to lay out and thoroughly discuss the task at hand. Use PERT, CPM, milestone charts, networking, etc., to describe task and schedule. Assign specific tasks.
- Consider whether subcommittees will be required. Their work will be completed between meetings with reports to facilitate committee meeting. The optimal committee size is 8–10 members. Subcommittees maybe justified for committees larger than this. Large committees place a premium on planning, organization, communication, coordination and control.
- The method for decision-making should be selected and discussed, i.e., vote, consensus, etc.

2. *All Meetings*:

- Committee members must be prepared to participate in meetings.
- The agenda needs to be followed—limit digression—leader is a facilitator and must bring the discussion on track when digressions occur.
- Atmosphere for meetings needs to be such that people feel free to comment in an open and candid manner.
- Territorial issues must be evaluated in the context of the common benefit.
- Keep track of agreements or decisions and summarize them at the end of each meeting.
- Prior to adjournment, clearly establish what must be accomplished prior to the next meeting and by whom.

3. *Post-Meeting Issues*:

- Each member *must follow-up* and complete assigned tasks.
- Coordination and communication should be accomplished as problems arise.
- Each member should inform his or her functional personnel of status and issues.
- If necessary, summarize committee deliberations in writing.

4. *Other Factors*:

- It is not unusual for conflict to occur based on ego, turf considerations, conflict between personal and group goals, communication problems, etc.
- Conflict cannot be eliminated; it needs to be managed. Conflict resolution modes include forcing, smoothing, withdrawal, superordinate goal, compromise, and problem solving.
- Be willing to cope with "group think," "hidden agendas," and other dysfunctional behavior.

Telephone Code of Conduct

Steer clear of being a slave to the telephone. Group outgoing calls to get them out of the way. Avoid incoming call interruptions when working on important matters (call back at a specified time). If you have to make daily long-distance calls, try scheduling a specific hour of the day. Avoid grabbing the phone on impulse—organize thoughts and discuss all subjects in an orderly sequence.

The pointers given suggest optimizing the managerial workday by rationalizing time used in paperwork, meetings, one-on-one contacts and telephone conversations. The suggestions capture in summary form many of the classical time management "solutions" that appear to be applicable in the project management world. Management experts contend that by applying the timely principles exemplified in the suggestions given more time will be available for working on important project matters.

Such a "formula" approach may be regarded as simplistic, however. Due to the wide diversity in project manager's styles, personalities, backgrounds, prior successes and failures, aspirations, etc., a time management posture cannot be "ready made" to fit all. Rather, a customized approach is needed, with the project manager acting as his or her own stylist, selecting those pointers that are consistent with his or her projected managerial profile.

Use of Time-Saving Devices

The project manager has a vast array of time-saving devices available for use in this electronic age. One of the most accessible is the dictaphone. In many cases the project manager has limited access to clerical assistance. The dictaphone, however, is available for dictation on a practically unlimited basis. Memos, letters, and written communication can be dictated and then typed later, when clerical assistance is available. Also of use are portable tape recorders; personal computers; video-tape players; calculators; telephone answering machines; other special telephone features such as call forwarding, repeat dialing, etc.; copiers, including facsimile reproduction machines, memory typewriters, word processors; and a host of other labor-and time-saving devices.[12]

Paper Control

Often it seems that the project manager is inundated with paper of all types, including letters, memos, plans, blueprints, contracts, and drawings. Incoming paperwork needs to be prioritized on receipt and dealt with accordingly. Items should be handled as few times as possible. Where clerical assistance is available, personnel can be instructed to act as a filter and thereby help minimize the incoming flow. One system for dealing with paperwork classifies items as toss—wastebasket; refer—referral out-box; act—action box or reading file; and file—file as appropriate.[13]

Filing Systems

Much time is often spent looking for documents for reference and other purposes. Time can be saved by proper filing of documents so that they can be easily located when needed. However, judgment needs to be applied. Not every document needs to be retained. A filing program needs to be structured and orderly.[14] Each file needs to be labeled with meaningful and generic labels. Active and inactive files need to be segregated. Files must be arranged in some order that will provide easy accessibility. Periodically, the files need to be purged of outdated, inactive, and extraneous materials.

Avoid Organization Traps

Organizational pressures to conform to systems quite often lead to situations where the project manager reacts to situations without really considering choices, alternatives or responsibilities. Such traps consume time that could be more meaningfully used for other purposes.[15] Such traps include procrastination, activity, telephone, drop-in visitor, meetings and a host of other time wasters that rob us of flexibility, create stress, and in general permit the organization to control and direct time usage, rather than the other way around. The key is for the project manager to recognize these traps and to gain control of time use. The effective outcome is that the individual gains control of the organization and is better able to budget time use.

Self-Analysis for Control

An analysis of how the project manager spends the available time during a workday is a good starting point for change. It is an introspective process and requires honest answers. A series of questions as illustrated in Figure 11 are posed. The project manager then tries to honestly answer each question.

1. How much time do I spend on the telephone?
2. Do I devote more time to individual calls than is necessary?
3. Can I say "no" to requests for my services? Etc.

The questions can relate to meetings, handling correspondence, planning, and reading habits. They should be fairly exhaustive and tailored to the individual's job profile. The resultant answers are analyzed to identify areas that need to be changed and improved.

Direction and Communication

The project manager is a supervisor and must spend considerable time in dealing with subordinates. Time savings can also accrue in this area of endeavor. Some examples follow.

Limit Interaction Time

Does every visitor wandering into an office need to be received? And remain for as long as they wish? Obviously not. Many visitors will be as well off talking to the manager's subordinates. The project manager has the prerogative to set the time limits on interviews. A secretary can help articulate an interview agenda. (This does not eliminate periods of "open door policy" essential for project pulse-taking).

Time Management Self Analysis:

1. How much time do I spend on the telephone?
2. Do I devote more time to individual calls than is necessary?
3. Can I say "no" to requests for my services, Etc.?

Delegation

Many project managers have experienced situations where a subordinate has not performed according to plan and discussions. The tendency in reaction to this situation is to micromanage, i.e., not to delegate. However, this reaction is a mistake. Subordinates must learn to manage their own time. Accordingly, the project manager needs to recognize the value of delegation and delegate where possible. Some reasons favoring delegation are listed in Figure 12. To delegate, however, is not to forget. The project manager should periodically check the performance to ensure these plans are being effectively executed by subordinates. If this is not the case, then immediate corrective action should be taken.

1. Increases managerial effectiveness.
2. Provides project manager time to think.
3. Provides opportunity for subordinates to grow.
4. Avoids one-man show syndrome.
5. Stimulates creative thinking.
6. Reduces crisis atmosphere.

Two-Way Communication

The project manager should ensure that an atmosphere exists where subordinates can and will report problems without fear of undue and unwarranted punishment. This two-way flow of information is critical. It helps to minimize surprises. The basic condition to foster this flow of information is trust.

Conclusion

Project managers occupy extremely demanding positions. The project manager's time is sought by everyone involved in the project; therefore, it must be managed effectively to achieve project success. The project manager can better time-management practices by improving daily time habits based on

---

Figure 12. Reasons to Delegate

1. Increases managerial effectiveness.
2. Provides PM time to think
3. Provides opportunity for subordinates to grow.
4. Avoids one-man show syndrome.
5. Stimulates creative thinking.
6. Reduces crisis atmosphere.

---

commonsense criteria. There are no magic formulas for improving management productivity, but the principles for bettering time usage are elementary; project managers who are capable of dominating complicated and esoteric project concepts can easily put time management rules into effect. The hints given in this monograph are offered as a guideline for the project manager or other project personnel to test and adjust existing time habits that may not be meeting project needs.

The survey results given in this monograph show the respondent's awareness of the importance for effectively managing time. Ideas for improving time habits can be grouped into the following points:

- Learn how time is really being used (time log).
- Rationalize time bottlenecks such as paperwork, meetings, one-on-one contacts and coaching, per detailed tips given.
- Use time on a prioritized, scheduled basis, giving emphasis to important items over those which appear urgent.

John Quincy Adams[16] said in *The Hour Glass*, "Time was—Time shall be—Drain the glass—But where in time is now?"

The project manager's dilemma is captured in Adams' concept of fleeting "nowness." For project requirements to be met, the project manager's time perception must be keen and time management habits solid. Attention to the project manager's own time can spark a productivity payoff, leading the way to quality projects completed within budget and on schedule.

Stress Management

All occupations have a certain amount of stress associated with them, but the project manager, with an endless list of demands, deadlines, and problems, is exposed to more stress than most. If the project manager is unable to cope with stress, he or she will be subject to anxiety, headaches, ulcers, or any one of a number of stress-related ailments. However, if the project manager is aware of the environmental stress as it is encountered and is able to manage it, he or she can manipulate it into a driving force that will make him or her more productive as well as remove much of the worry from life.

Nature of Stress

Most people believe stress is part of having a job, but few realize how damaging stress can be. The collective costs of stress on American industry is incredible, it is estimated stress causes between seventy-five billion and one hundred billion dollars to be lost each year in absenteeism, reduced productivity, and health-related expenses.[17] Heart attacks alone, many of which are related to job stress, cost more than twenty-six billion dollars annually in disability payments and medical bills.[18] These statistics show stress is more pervasive and costly than anybody would imagine.

Stress makes its presence known at the workplace by leading to increased worker turnover, resignations, and absenteeism. The list of human ailments directly or indirectly related to stress is almost infinite: heart attacks, high blood pressure, peptic ulcers, depression, insomnia, psychosomatic diseases, anxiety, colds, diarrhea, constipation, nasal congestion, asthma, chest pains, back and neck pains, skin disorders, kidney damage, cholesterol deposits, arteriosclerosis, colitis, impotency, and many others. Approximately 70 percent of the physical problems that bring people to doctors are related to stress and lifestyle.[19] With all the pain and suffering stress can lead to, it is important for the project manager to be able to manage this potential killer.

Background on Stress

The most prevalent definition of stress comes from Dr. Hans Selye, who has been researching stress since 1936. His definition is "stress is the nonspecific (psychological) response of the body to any demand made upon it."[20] A more general definition states that "stress is a response to pressures, responsibilities, and real or imaginary threats from the environment."[21] Stress is a response, not the elements that cause it. The factors that produce stress are called *stressors*.

Stress is not a clear-cut, specific response to a situation. A specific response is a particular outcome resulting from the corresponding stimulus, such as perspiring when you are hot or feeling pain when you are cut. Because stress does not lead to only one predictable response, it is not a specific response. Stress responses differ from person to person, what is stressful to one person may be invigorating to another. The fact that one may get a headache after receiving an unfavorable evaluation from the boss or have an upset stomach when thinking about overdue work shows that the stress response is variable. In some instances stress may not produce any symptoms! Unfortunately, although stress may evidence its presence in many ways, it inwardly builds up over periods of time and leads to many internal disorders.

Any activity or situation a person is involved in produces stimuli that cause stress. The human body is designed to experience some stress each day. Even if a person were completely removed from all stress, this isolation from stress would act as a stressor. While it is natural for people to experience some stress each day, experiencing too much will result in grave consequences.

Although there is only one kind of stress, it manifests itself in two completely different ways. Both the joy one receives from falling in love and the heartburn one obtains during hectic days are produced by stress. The beneficial symptoms of stress, the vigor and exhilaration produced by certain situations, are called *eustress*. Conversely, the detrimental effects of stress, such as anxiety and worrying, are called *distress*. Eustress does not promote distress or internal disorders, but distress leads to more deaths in the United States and all the other industrialized countries than any other cause.[22] Stress is unavoidable; the project manager should try to minimize distress and maximize eustress.

Everybody knows that stress and strain are usually coupled, but few know the difference between them. While stress is the response to a situation, *strain* is the psychological or physiological changes that take place within the individual as a result. In short, *stress is the cause and strain is the symptom*.

Stress Defined

When the body encounters a stressor, it goes through a three-stage reaction process. Dr. Hans Selye called this reaction pattern the General Adaptation Syndrome (G.A.S.).[23] The first stage, the alarm reaction, begins as soon as the body perceives a stressor. In this stage the person feels a "fight or flight" sensation. He or she wants to either avoid the stressor or fight it. The body biochemically fights the stress by releasing hormones from the endocrine glands.[24] These hormones either try to return the body to its previous steady state or invigorate the body to battle the stressor. During the alarm reaction, the body's heartbeat, blood pressure, blood flow, demand for oxygen, and blood sugar level rise, muscles become tense, pupils become dilated, and digestion slows down.[25]

Following the alarm stage is the resistance stage. During the resistance stage the body adapts to the stressor and tries to resist it. If the body is able to overcome the stressor, it then mends the damage that occurred during the alarm stage. The physical manifestations of stress disappear and the body is then more resistant to the stressor. However, although the body is more resistant to stress, it is less resistant to other invading pathogens.

When the body can no longer adapt to the stress, it enters the final stage of the G.A.S.—the exhaustion reaction. The length of time a person's body can maintain the resistance stage before becoming exhausted is highly variable and contingent upon numerous factors, including the individual and the gravity of the stressor. During exhaustion, the symptoms of the alarm reaction reappear but the body is powerless to do anything about it. Thus, the body is at the mercy of stress and succumbs to headaches, ulcers, high blood pressure, and heart attacks.

There are many physiological and psychological factors that produce stress. Some general physiological causes are insufficient amount of sleep, improper diet, and being fatigued. A few psychological stress factors are a person's feelings, emotions, and the way he or she views his or her environment. Even though both types of stressors affect people, psychological causes of stress are more common and severe.

All people have different personalities, and some personality types are more subject to stress than others. The hard-driving project manager with "type A" personality is more likely to have problems with stress than a more passive coworker. While all project managers are exposed to stress, those with aggressive, goal-achieving personalities should be even more concerned with stress than their more easygoing contemporaries.

Sources of Stress

The sources of stress that a project manager encounters at the office are too numerous to count. Most of the work-related stressors, such as job insecurity or excessive demands on time, are daily occurrences in which the project manager has limited control. Once the project manager realizes the personal affect of these uncontrollable factors, an improved condition will exist to manage the stress and reduce the personal disturbance. A significant step in stress reduction will be accomplished.

Figure 13 summarizes some of the sources of job-related stress. Since each individual perceives stressors differently, readers may feel some of the conditions listed do not produce stress. However, the list contains recognized factors that do stress some executives. These stressors are not listed in any order of importance.

Individual Stress Management

The first step in managing stress is to become familiar with the nature of the stress responses and their effects on the body. All people need to get to know their own normal work styles so they can tell when and how they are affected by stress. Once the project manager knows how his or her stress response works and what triggers it, he or she is in a position to identify these stressors. A project manager can use several methods to help identify sources of stress.

Stress Diary
One way is by keeping a diary at work of the stress symptoms encountered and their apparent causes. Eventually, patterns of source-symptoms relationships will emerge and the sources will be revealed.

Mechanical Devices

Another more complicated strategy of identifying stressors involves either a blood pressure or pulse rate measuring device. After engaging in an activity at work, the project manager can measure pulse with a pulsimeter, and then record the activity and its consequential pulse rate. Accumulating this information on many activities will allow the executive to determine which activities increase or decrease blood flow rate. By seeing which events increased the blood flow, the project manager has identified sources of stress. Once the executive is aware of the elevated blood pressure due to an activity, he or she should relax and think of ways to reduce the stress that has been encountered. Because the project manager has an idea of which activities are stressful and which are not, stress can consciously be reduced at work. By performing non-stressful activities between stressful ones, or by formulating a schedule that balances stressful and nonstressful activities, the project manager can prevent stress from building up throughout the course of the day.

Identification of Stress Situations

Recognizing which situations are sources of stress allows an executive to mentally prepare himself or herself to reduce their impact. Being aware of stressors enables the project manager to foresee some stressful situations before they occur, and this provides he or she with an opportunity to work his or her way around them. By delegating potential stressors to someone who does not find them stressful, or by manipulating the circumstances leading to them, the project manager can bypass or mollify some stressful activities.

With the knowledge of stress and its sources, the project manager is able to reduce the number of or even remove some stressful activities from the schedule. He or she can control the amount of stressors he or she is exposed to by regulating participation in stressful events. The project manager also has the ability to influence the stressors other organization members are subject to by determining which activities they should engage in or refrain from. By limiting the stressors others are subject to, the total level of stress within the organization can be reduced.

Work Schedule

It is helpful for the project manager to be familiar with the times of the day he or she is most productive. Arranging the schedule to fit stressful activities into times when the project manager is refreshed will limit the amount of stress they deliver. The better rested the project manager is the more likely he or she will be able to overcome stress. Conversely, stress has a much greater impact on people when they are run-down and tired.

An important aspect of managing stress is controlling the stress responses. Once a person knows how his or her body reacts to stress, it is possible for him or her to regulate his or her responses. Many people have de-

Figure 13. Sources of Stress

Sources of Job Stress

- Job insecurity
- Lack of praise for good performance
- Problems with co-workers, clients
- Lack of clean job description
- Career ambitions that have fallen through
- Feeling your talents are not fully used
- Having little decision making power to influence outcomes that reflect on the person
- Having the responsibility to complete a project, but not the authority needed
- Lacking control of a situation
- Lack of communication on the job
- Demands on time
- Too fast or too slow a pace
- Unfinished business
- Getting involved in too many abligations and duties
- Being involved in activities that do not contribute to your goals
- Individual's priorities differing from the leader's
- Trying to fit several activities into the time it should take for one
- Too many demands
- The fear of what might happen
- Following orders
- Having your accomplishments ignored or rejected
- Changes in jobs

veloped bad habits in responding to stress, such as headaches and heartburn, which could be avoided. To alleviate some undesirable affects of stress, the project manager should be aware of his or her stress response. When a stress reaction is experienced, relax and try to control the response. A person is in a much better position to cope with stress' if he or she can relax throughout the stress reaction. By remaining calm and collected during a stress response, the project manager has avoided otherwise unpleasant stress effects. Controlling stress responses allows a person to defend himself or herself from the detriment of stress. When the project manager has achieved the ability to control stress responses so as to remain calm and unnerved throughout the day, a significant step in stress management has been accomplished.

Attitude Adaptation

Attitude plays a role in the amount of stress one experiences. If a person is motivated by "have to" or "should", his or her attitude will promote stress.[26] However, if a person has a positive attitude toward a project, the undertaking will be more pleasurable and less stressful. Changing unfavorable attitudes toward a project to favorable ones will reduce the stress caused by the project. Everybody knows it is easier to work on an enjoyable task than a disliked one, so it is sensible to change attitudes of drudgery to attitudes of enthusiasm.

Personal Organization

Avoiding the accumulation of incomplete tasks helps in stress management. Closing all the loose ends eliminates further stress produced by unfinished business. Maintaining a comfortable pace of life is critical to coping with stress. If a person's pace of life is too hectic, one does not have a chance of getting away from stress. Having too many things going on all the time is a relentless source of stress. The project manager should have a pace of life that is suitable for him or her to prevent excessive stress. It is important for a person to have a private life as well as a work life. Life is not all work, and those who believe it is will become stress victims. An enjoyable private life provides an escape from the stress of work and allows a person to be happier and healthier. Taking on more commitments than you can handle is a common source of stress. To avoid participating in more activities than he or she is comfortable with, the project manager must know his or her limits. Once he or she is involved with as many commitments as he or she can manage, the project manager should not undertake any more. Although it is hard to say no to people, it may be necessary to prevent becoming overcommitted. It is better to refrain from some commitments than to be stressed by too many.

Leisure Activity

Away from the office, two activities which reduce stress are exercise and meditation. For each of these pastimes to help, a person must enjoy it. If a person exercises to reduce stress, but hates physical exertion, exercising becomes a stressor in itself. A disliked pastime will not help reduce stress. Meditation is certainly not for everyone, but for those who enjoy it is a good way to escape from stress. Participating in enjoyable activities is a pleasant way of reducing stress. Activities which do not reduce stress are smoking, drinking, and taking drugs. These ineffective responses to stress only produce temporary effects and do not deal with the actual causes of stress. Relying too heavily on temporary escapes from stress can lead to more stress than not indulging at all.

Managerial Integration

There is a way stress can be used to the project manager's advantage. Some of the techniques used in reducing stress also can lead to improved performance. By taking precautions against future stress, such as competing an assignment before the pressures of the deadline are felt, a project manager can work on projects before they become stressful. Getting assignments under control before time demands set in allows the project manager to be more productive, effective, and less stressed. It is beneficial to let the fear of time stress cause a project manager to schedule each week's activities in advance. Pitting outcomes of work against the fear of stress will make the project manager work extra hard to avoid the stress, which also leads to improved productivity.

For each project, the project manager should establish goals and ethical guidelines. When working on the project, the executive should abide by the ethics established in his or her guidelines. The list of goals shows the project manager which objectives to concentrate on. A plan should accompany the goals to specify the activities needed for their achievement. Besides describing the activities, the plan should state how they are to be implemented. A plan enables the project manager to follow a concrete course of action, thus reducing the stress of uncertainties from the project.

Organizational Stress Management

Not only is stress management important to the individual, but to the organization as well. Because individuals perform the tasks that lead to organizational goals, stress management that improves employee productivity will also benefit the organization. To get the maximum contribution from each employee, the organization should provide an atmosphere that promotes eustress and minimizes distress. Organizational stress is the stress that a person receives when dealing with any organizational or project demand. It originates within the organization and affects the employees.

Organizational stress can produce strain on employees and lead to reduced productivity, so it is important that it is properly managed. Effectively managed organizational stress can lead to improved worker performance and satisfaction, which is beneficial to both the individual and the organization.

Stress within the organization has many direct and indirect consequences. Problems caused directly by organizational stress are absenteeism, tardiness, and worker turnover. Indirect affects include low morale, reduced motivation, and dissatisfaction among employees.

Because some stress is needed for superior performance, organizations should maintain a tolerable stress level. The organization should manage a stress level that promotes performance but is not detrimental to employees. Using absenteeism, tardiness, and worker turnover rates, an organization can approximate its stress level. For a more comprehensive analysis of its stress level, employee interviews, questionnaires, and direct observation can be used.

Organizations can make great strides in managing stress by promoting a friendly, cooperative atmosphere for employees. If workers are happy with the company, their office environment, and enjoy working with their coworkers, they will be more satisfied and content with their jobs. Employee satisfaction will lead to increased performance and less strain on organization members.

Companies can promote a positive atmosphere by respecting employees and treating them fairly. Employees should receive feedback about their activities from bosses to let them know where they stand. Managers should let subordinates know how they want things done and encourage them to always do their best. The company should have a fair promotion policy based on criteria in which the employee is made aware. If employees feel respected and know what is expected of them, organizational stress will be minimized.

Organizations can prevent or reduce stress through their personnel departments. When offering jobs to people, the personnel department should inform the candidate of all the details about the job so the person does not get any wrong expectations. If an employee takes a new position and it turns out to be different from original expectations, stress will remain as long as the position is held. The personnel department can avoid employee misunderstandings through proper explanation of job requirements and ramifications in the first place.

The personnel department should place individuals into positions for which they are suited. Employees should be assigned to jobs they are capable of handling, or they will face frustration and impending failure. Individuals who work best under stressful conditions are better off in managerial positions and easily stressed people are comfortable with less-demanding jobs. People also should be assigned to superiors or groups they can get along with. Employees will perform better if they like their immediate coworkers. A disliked boss can be a tremendous source of stress for employees. Proper placement of individuals reduces organizational stress and spares employees from a great deal of future stress.

A company can incorporate stress management in to its medical plan. As part of its medical program, an organization keeps health records of employees. When an individual complains of stress-related ailments, a company doctor can review the person's record and look for stress indicators such as high blood pressure or a heart condition. If a person has a history of stress ailments, job stress should be reviewed carefully. Rather than risk a heart attack, the company should either change the demands of the person's job or transfer the person to a less stressful position. If the employee is actually transferred, the organization must not let the position change appear as a demotion or the employee's self-esteem and status may suffer. Good medical records allow a company to document the physical effects of its organizational stress and become aware of high stress levels and over-stressed employees.

Organizations can reduce stress on employees by providing pleasant working conditions. People naturally feel less stress and more productive in enjoyable surroundings. The company should maintain a comfortable temperature, proper lighting in its offices and have some sort of smoking policy for its employees. Offices should be aesthetic, with desks arranged to minimize interruptions. Working in a pleasant environment allows employees to forget about discomfort and helps them to concentrate on their work.

Conclusions

Organizations have many ways of monitoring stress levels and influencing the stress situation. The goal of the organization stress policy is to manage stress in such a way that it promotes performance without being harmful to employees. Because all companies are different, each organization must have its own stress management policy, which it can adapt to the work environment.

Summary

Project managers and related project personnel are highly trained and valuable individuals. They represent critical resources for their companies. Productivity and project success can be promoted and enhanced if these individuals realize that personal time is an equally critical resource that must be conserved and managed. In turn, efficient and effective time management can reduce personal and organizational stress.

The rhythms of life surround us daily. They include cosmic rhythms, such as the orbiting Earth, winds and weather and magnetism; seasonal rhythms, such as winter, summer, fall and spring; and a host of other rhythms.[27] As such, they create and impact the project manager's environment and sense of time. Superimposed on this scenario are the constraints which are derived from how time is measured and scheduled. Variations between natural and measured time create stress. This stress can be reduced by effective time and stress management. These environmental factors have been discussed separately for the sake of clarity; however, the fact remains—they are innately related. The project manager who recognizes this fact and takes positive action to cope with stress and time is enhancing both the probability of project and personal success.

Endnotes

1. S. De Grazia, *Of Time Work & Leisure*, The Twentieth Century Fund, Inc., USA, 1962.

2. Paul C. Dinsmore and D.I. Cleland, "Project Management, A Day at a Time," unpublished manuscript prepared for *Worldwide Projects Magazine*, July, 1982.

3. Special thanks to Dr. David I. Cleland of the University of Pittsburgh who oversaw the compilation of the survey data by the staff personnel, and offered helpful comments.

4. P.F. Drucker, "Management Time," filmed by B.N.A., USA.

5. Paul C. Dinsmore, "Put a Time Resource Leveler on Your Day," *Project Management Quarterly, 8* (4), December 1981, pp. 43–46.

6. M.E., Douglass and N.D. Douglass, *Manage Your Time, Manage Your Work, Manage Yourself*, New York: Amacom, 1980.

7. P.F. Drucker, *The Effective Executive*, London: Williams Heinemann Ltd., 1967.

8. Robert Albanese, *Managing Toward Accountability for Performance*, 3rd ed., Homewood, Ill.: Richard D. Irwin, Inc., 1981, pp. 34–40.

9. Stephanie Winston, *The Organized Executive*, New York: W.W. Norton & Company, 1983, pp. 226–230.

10. Martin Dean Martin and Kathleen Miller, "Planning and Control as Reciprocal Communication," *Proceedings of the 1980 Project Management Seminar/Symposium*, Drexel Hill, Pa.: The Project Management Institute, pp. II–H. 1 through II–H. 7.

11. Op. cit. Douglass and Douglass.

12. Op. cit. Winston, pp. 309–310.

13. Ibid., pp. 58–59.

14. Ibid., pp. 105–106.

15. Samuel A. Culbert, *The Organization Map*, New York: Basic Books, Inc., 1974.

16. J.Q. Adams, "The Hour Glass," quoted in *The Pocket Book of Quotations*, edited by Henry Davidoff, New York: Pocket Books, 1952.

17. James C. Quick and Jonathan D. Quick, *Organizational Stress and Preventive Management*, New York: McGraw-Hill Book Co., 1984.

18. Tom Cox, *Stress*, Baltimore, Md.: University Park Press, 1978.

19. John J. Parrino, *From Panic to Power—The Positive Use of Stress*, New York: John Wiley & Sons, Inc., 1979.

20. Mortimer H. Appley and Richard Turmbull, *Psychological Stress*, New York: Appleton-Century-Crofts, 1967.

21. David R. Frew, *Management of Stress*, Chicago: Nelson Hall, Inc., 1977.

22. Hans Selye, *Stress Without Distress*, Philadelphia, Penn.: Lippincott, 1974.

23. James W. Greenwood. III, and James W. Greenwood, Jr., *Managing Executive Stress: A Systems Approach*, New York: John Wiley & Sons, Inc., 1979.

24. Martin Shaffer, *Life After Stress*, New York: Plenum Press (Division Plenum Publishing Company), 1982.

25. Joseph L. Kearns, *Stress in Industry*, London: Priory Press Limited, 1973.

26. Michael C. Giammatteo and Dolores M. Giammatteo, *Executive Well-Being—Stress and Administrators*, Reston, Va.: National Association of Secondary School Principals, 1980.

27. Edward S. Ayensu and Philip Whitfield, *The Rhythms of Life*, New York: Crown Publishers, 1981.

References

Adams, J.Q. "The Hour Glass." *The Pocket Book of Quotations*, Henry Davidoff (ed.). New York: Pocket Books, 1952.

Albanese, Robert. *Managing Toward Accountability for Performance* (3rd ed.). Homewood, Ill.: Richard D. Irwin, Inc., 1981.

Appley, Mortimer H., and Richard Turmbull. *Psychological Stress*. New York: Appleton-Century-Crofts, 1967.

Ayensu, Edward S., and Philip Whitfield. *The Rhythms of Life*. New York: Crown Publishers, 1981.

Cleland, David I. "Time Management Survey." Compilation of time management survey data obtained from the Project Management Institute's Seminar/Symposium, Boston, Massachusetts, October 1981.

Cox, Tom. *Stress*. Baltimore, Md.: University Park Press, 1978.

Culbert, Samuel A. *The Organization Map*. New York: Basic Books. Inc., 1974.

De Grazia, S. *Of Time Work and Leisure*. The Twentieth Century Fund, Inc., USA, 1962.

Dinsmore, Paul C. "Put a Time Resource Leveler on Your Day." *Project Management Journal, 8* (4), December 1981.

Dinsmore, Paul C., and David I. Cleland. "Project Management, A Day at a Time." Unpublished manuscript prepared for *Worldwide Projects Magazine*, July 1982.

Douglass, M.E., and N.D. Douglass. *Manage Your Time, Manage Your Work, Manage Yourself*, New York: Amacom, 1980.

Drucker, P.C. "Management Time." Filmed by B.N.A., USA.

Frew, David R. *Management of Stress*. Chicago: Nelson-Hall, Inc., 1977.

Giammatteo, Michael C., and Dolores M. Giammatteo. *Executive Well-Being—Stress and Administrators*. Reston, Va.: National Association of Secondary School Principals, 1980.

Greenwood, III, James W., and James W. Greenwood, Jr. *Managing Executive Stress: A Systems Approach*. New York: Plenum Press (Division Plenum Publishing Company), 1982.

Kearns, Joseph L. *Stress in Industry*. London: Priory Press Limited, 1973.

Martin, Martin Dean, and Kathleen Miller. "Planning and Control as Reciprocal Communication." *Proceedings of the 1980 Project Management Seminar/Symposium*, Drexel Hill, Pa.: The Project Management Institute, pp. II-H-1 through II-H-7.

Parrino, John J. *From Panic to Power—The Positive Use of Stress*. New York: John Wiley & Sons, 1979.

Quick, James C., and D. Jonathan Quick. *Organizational Stress and Preventive Management*. New York: McGraw-Hill Book Company, 1984.

Selye, Hans. *Stress Without Distress*. Philadelphia: Lippincott, 1974.

Shaffer, Martin. *Life After Stress*. New York: Plenum Press (Division Plenum Publishing Company), 1982.

Winston, Stephanie. *The Organized Executive*. New York: W.W. Norton & Company, 1983.

Roles and Responsibilities of the Project Manager

John R. Adams
and
Brian W. Campbell

PART I

Introduction

To determine what a project manager does, it must first be determined what a project involves. According to Stewart, a project is concerned with four aspects of a work effort: scope, unfamiliarity, complexity, and stake.[1] The scope involves a single, predetermined result, which can be measured in terms of time, cost, and performance constraints. Unfamiliarity, in this case, deals with activities that typically occur only once and which contain many significant elements that are new to the people and/or the organization. In terms of a project, complexity would be any activity that is not routine and might involve advanced technology, a new mix of professional skills, or an unusual variety of organizational interfaces. Finally, the stake is determined by how much a failure would jeopardize the organization's financial position or its potential for achieving its goals. If an undertaking involves special concerns in one or more of these four areas, then the establishment of a project organization is likely to be warranted.[2]

If one were to think about some of the major projects of past to present times, they might think of such tasks as creating the Egyptian pyramids, the Eiffel Tower, the Panama Canal, or the World Trade Center. In tracing the origin of these or other specific projects or tasks, most would think of construction projects and the construction industry. As time passed, there also arose a need for project undertakings in the military, especially in the area of developing new weapon systems. Today, major projects have developed involving such additional fields as social welfare, natural sciences, and organizational behavior.

This monograph is broken down into two parts: the functions of a project manager and the education and experience necessary to be an effective project manager. Under the functions of a project manager, the areas covered include management functions and the project manager, interface management, the project manager as an integrator, the relationship of the project manager to other members of the organization, the relationship of the project manager to the customer, conflict management, basic functions of the project manager, and roles of the project manager. The second part of the monograph deals with education and experience, and is introduced later.

Management Functions and the Project Manager

Project management originated in the construction, engineering, and technical fields, but is now applied in a wide variety of areas. Most project managers are trained in the technology of their projects, but lack an understanding of the managerial functions necessary to do their jobs well. Thus, in defining the tasks of a project manager, a general understanding of the appropriate technical area must be assumed, while the definition of tasks concentrates on managerial requirements. As the need for projects has become more important and more common, a need has also arisen for someone to manage these projects. Any manager performs four basic functions or activities: planning, organizing, leading, and controlling. The project manager is responsible for performing these activities throughout the duration of the project. Upon recognition of the need for a project to fulfill certain requirements, the management personnel should begin the planning and design phase of the project to determine the life cycle of the project.[3] To be effective and enthusiastic about any project, the project manager should start out actively participating with other management personnel in planning and designing the project.[4] This involves determining in advance what a group should accomplish over a given period of time and how the goals are to be attained. Planning is the first step a project manager should take in beginning a project, and the plan must be made specific in terms of the time, cost, and resource commitments required to complete the work.

Before and during the project, the project manager must determine how the resources (human and physical) will be organized so the project is completed within the specified constraints of time, money, and performance requirements. By organizing the project, the project manager brings together under one structure the required individuals from the various supporting functional areas. These individuals may be with the project only a short period of time, but the contributions of each are critical to the project's success. It is up to the project manager to bring these people together in such a way that they can complete the project and solve the problems that will inevitably arise. By assembling these human resources under one organizational structure, if only for a brief period of time, the project manager temporarily combines the assets he or she requires to meet the needs set forth in the planning phase of the project. Organizing a project can only be successfully accomplished by the careful mixing of human, financial, and physical resources, at the proper time, and under a single direction of authority.

Perhaps one of the most important functions of a manager, but oftentimes the least mentioned, is the leadership function. This is also true for the manager of a project. Leading a group of people (project team) with differing expertise is a job that requires skill, knowledge, and an innate ability to communicate with people from various backgrounds. In order to lead personnel over whom he or she does not always have directive authority, the project manager must be well rounded in all of the functional and technical areas of the project. He or she must be a good negotiator, have good communication skills, and be easy to work with. Leadership is an important function for the project manager; for without the ability to lead people with different interests and ideas, the project manager probably would not see the completion of his or her project.

Finally, and also a very important management function, is the control function. Control can be defined as following plans set forth at the beginning of a project or assignment and evaluating the process in relation to time schedules, cost allocations, and given performance requirements.[5]

The control process comes into play when the initial plans are not adequate and must be revised to cope with new situations. Control can serve as a monitoring and corrective-action function to aid the manager in measuring the effectiveness and efficiency of his or her project.[6] Although control is mainly the responsibility of the project manager, he or she must count on each of the members of the project team to help him or her maintain control and to assist him or her in evaluating the project and solving problems that occur. Through the use of control, the project manager and his or her project team are able to complete the planned project in the most effective and efficient means possible and have an up-to-date idea of how well the project is progressing.

These managerial functions are not unique to the project manager, but the project manager would have a difficult time completing a project from beginning to end without using each of these functions extensively. Many project managers are promoted from the technical fields with no training or education in managerial functions. As a result, they tend to overemphasize the need to be involved in their particular area of expertise—the work that got them promoted. This is inevitably the technical aspect of the project. Technical material is unique to each project. What is needed of the project manager is a concentration in the management area, allowing others to perform the technical work. The project manager must be *knowledgeable* of the technical basis of the project. The primary function, however, is to manage it. He or she must confine his or her technical involvement to evaluating the technical work of others. His or her main effort must be in integrating, planning, and communicating for the single project goal. It is important that the project manager know how to implement these functions into the management of a project so that he or she can obtain the best results possible for the project and a good working relationship with those working with him or her on the project.

Interface Management

Interface management deals with identifying, documenting, scheduling, communicating, and monitoring interfaces related to the product and the project.[7] Management interfaces make up a major portion of this material. The project manager is a boundary spanner in that this person must coordinate across the various groups contributing to the project. The project/functional interface is a major aspect of this effort, and it has been pointed out that this important interface (project/functional) should be complementary for the project to run smoothly. Project management also involves three types of interfaces, which the project manager should be aware of and continually monitor for problems: personal interface, organizational interface, and system interface.[8]

Personal Interface

This interface can occur anytime two people are working on the same project and there is a potential for personal problems or conflict to exist.[9] If the two people work under the same line manager, the project manager usually has limited authority (unless he or she is their superior) and must call on the line manager to settle disputes. If the people are not in the same line or discipline, then the project manager assumes the role of mediator, with the ability to get line management to resolve the problem if necessary. Problems in the personal interface are even more difficult to solve when they involve two or more managers.[10] The project manager must be capable of dealing with all conflicts that involve people in or related to the project.

Organizational Interface

The organizational interface is probably the most difficult to deal with because not only does it involve people it also involves organizational goals and conflicting managerial styles.[11] Conflict can occur on the interface because of varying unit goals and because of misunderstandings of the technical language used within each organizational unit. These interfaces are primarily management interfaces dealing with actions, decisions, or approvals affecting the project; however, they can also involve units outside the immediate organization or project.[12]

System Interface

The system interface deals with the product, facility, construction, resources, or other types of non-people interfaces within the system itself or developed by the project. These system interfaces can be actual physical interfaces between interconnecting parts of the system or performance interfaces between various functional or product subsystems.[13] Some of the interfaces may include schedule problems where information passed on from one task to another is incorrect or delayed, a situation which can throw the project schedule off. Many of the technical problems generated as the project progresses are of this type. System interfaces are critical to the project's success and must be dealt with by the project manager, but not to the exclusion of the personal and organizational interfaces. Once again, many project managers understandably, because of their technical backgrounds, tend to over-involve themselves in technical system interfaces to the detriment of personal and organizational concerns.

The Project Manager as an Integrator

The Integration Process

Systems integration is the process by which the project manager attempts to coordinate the efforts of workers toward the accomplishment of group (project) goals.[14] Although any manager must be preoccupied with these goals, the project manager must be more concerned with the integration of the project team into a single functional unit. The project manager must be critically involved with this because of the many different functional personnel working toward a project goal. Integration of these individuals into one operational unit is important to the success of any project.

The project manager is the integrator in the matrix organization. Two of the most important tasks in this structure are problem solving and decision making between subsystems.[15] The project manager is the only person in the key position to solve the interface problems that occur. Three major problem/decision areas include: removal of administrative roadblocks or the setting of priorities; technical problems which necessitate decisions, changes in the scope, or tradeoffs among costs, schedules, and performance; and customer and client problems.[16] These are some of the problem areas the project manager must face in his or her primary job as an integrator.

Critical Actions in the Integration Process

The project manager should constantly be aware of the integration process. There are several steps or actions that must be taken and monitored to assure the integration process is going as planned and that conflicts are properly managed. The project manager is probably the only person who can start and approve these actions and continue the interaction process. Some of the important actions are:
- Plan for integration.
- Develop integrated work breakdown structure, schedule, and budget.
- Continually review and update project plan.
- Assure control and adherence to project plan.
- Assure design for integrated system.
- Resolve conflict situations.
- Remove roadblocks.
- Set priorities.
- Make administrative and technical decisions across interfaces.
- Resolve customer or client problems.
- Assure the project transfer takes place.
- Maintain communication links across interfaces.[17]

Power Relationships of the Project Manager With Different Members of the Organization

The project manager must deal with five different groups of people: upper management, subordinates, interface personnel, functional managers, and people outside the firm. The degree to which the project manager can influence each of these groups will have a bearing on the success or failure of the project. To influence an individual or group, the project manager must exert some type of power so that the necessary concessions or cooperation can be obtained. An idea of the types of power available and the degree to which they can be used is shown in Figure 1.

Legitimate forms of power (formal, reward, and penalty) are types of power the project manager has because of his or her position in the company. While this power can be exerted over subordinates, this type of power is very limited in it's acceptance and often does little to influence behavior.

Expert and referent power, on the other hand, are people types of power and are obtained by the amount of knowledge an individual has obtained and his or her personality. These types of power can be used by the project manager to influence even those people not associated with the project but who the project manager needs support from to gain acceptance of certain areas of the project. Expert power also can be gained from the project manager's knowledge of the project as a whole, because few others know or have access to the information necessary to successfully coordinate the project.

The Relationship Between the Project Manager and the Customer

An important part of the project manager's job deals with satisfying and communicating with the customer. This is a key step since, in many cases (especially in terms of large-scale projects), there would not even be a project without customer demands for a product or service. In gaining the acceptance of a project by a customer, the project manager must be able to sell himself/herself to the customer. The project manager who is a good salesperson may get the customer to select the approach toward the project that is most beneficial to the interests of the company and the project itself in a way that makes the customer feel as if the alternative was chosen without any influence from the project manager.[18]

Being a good salesperson is only part of the task the project manager must complete to keep the customer happy. A good project manager will also keep the customer informed on the technical status, budget status, and schedule status of the project.[19] The project manager is the primary source of information

Figure 1. Group Power Exerted On

	Group Power Exerted On				
Type of Power	Upper Management	Subordinates	Inteface Personnel	Functional Managers	Outside Forces (Customers, Government)
Formal	None	Substantial	None	None	None
Reward	Some	Some	Some	Very little	Very little
Penalty	None	Some	Some	Very little	Very little
Expert	Substantial	Substantial	Substantial	Substantial	Substantial
Referent	Substantial	Substantial	Substantial	Substantial	Substantial

for the customer or client because top management is usually busy worrying about other areas of the organization. In this situation the project manager is the representative for top management and should strive to develop a friendly, honest, and open relationship with the customer.[20] The project manager/customer relationship is an example of how the project manager must be a good communicator and use his or her leadership ability to represent the firm and his or her project in the best way possible. The customer can help solve many of the project manager's problems if kept properly informed and up-to-date.

Project Manager and Conflict Management

For a project to run smoothly, the project manager must be able to deal with conflict as effectively as possible so that the time normally spent in controlling conflict can be spent doing the far more useful goal-oriented project work.

Conflict is inevitable in any situation involving more than one person because of differences in personal goals, functional goals, competitive uses of resources, and different viewpoints (between management and subordinates), but it is especially prevalent in the project situation.[21] There is room for conflict when there are several projects or functional groups in need of the same resources, when there are overlaps in scheduling, and when there are necessary interactions between project and functional groups.[22] There is always a possibility for conflict when several people from different functional backgrounds come together to work on a project. The loss of the autonomy they had when the individuals worked together in their functional surroundings is bound to cause conflict, and the project manager should be ready for this so that he or she can work toward a solution of the problem.[23]

The amount of power the project manager has will affect his or her ability to influence personnel in the project. A project manager with only referent or expert power is less likely to receive a favorable response than someone who also has legitimate power over his or her project personnel.[24] Conflict is not always bad, and in some cases can even be beneficial because it shows that the people are thinking, brings up new ideas, and promotes innovation. However, the wrong type of conflict can hurt the project because it slows down the decision making process, reduces communication, and reduces efficiency.[25] The project manager, according to style of leadership, can be either aggressive in the resolution of conflict (active participation) or a compromise (passive) in the settling of conflict. But whatever method used to approach conflict, the project manager should be aware of the signs that can cause conflict in the project.

Common Sources of Conflict

An effective project manager seeks ways to resolve conflict; but before he or she can deal with conflict, he or she should be aware of the signs or sources of conflict that might be evident in his or her project. Some of the project-oriented sources of conflict are:

1. Conflict over project priorities—differing ideas concerning the sequence of necessary tasks and activities.

2. Conflict over administrative procedures—differences concerning responsibilities, reporting relationships, paperwork requirements, and administrative priorities.

3. Conflict over technical options and performance tradeoffs—differences concerning specifications, technical tradeoffs, and other technical issues.

4. Conflict over manpower resources—competing demands for limited manpower, which is often controlled by supporting functional groups.

5. Conflict over cost—differences in views concerning fund allocation and cost estimates.

6. Conflict over schedules—disagreement concerning project schedules and event sequences.

7. Personality conflict—differences in viewpoints and goals that are related to differences in people.[26]

These are a few of the major sources of conflict that a project manager may influence. Although this list is not inclusive, it gives the project manager some idea of the areas in which conflict is likely to occur. The sources of conflict that usually create the most tension are program priorities, personnel resources, technical issues, and scheduling problems. The sources of high-intensity conflict will be different considering the type of project, its organizational climate, and the phase it has achieved in its life cycle.

Types of Conflict Resolution

As mentioned before, conflict causes problems, which basically slows the project's completion. There are several ways to resolve conflict. Five methods, in particular, have been proven through research to occur in projects.[27] The method most often used by project managers to solve conflict is confrontation, where the two parties work together toward a solution of the problem.[28] Compromise is second in importance. This is a method in which both sides give and take, such that each wins or loses a few points.[29] Smoothing is the third most important method, where differences between the two groups are played down and the strong points of agreement are given the most attention.[30] The next method in use is forcing, in which the project manager uses his or her power to direct the solution. This is a type of win-lose agreement where one side gets its way and the other side does not.[31] Finally, and probably the least used of the methods in the resolution of project conflict, is withdrawal, where one or both sides withdraws from the conflict.[32]

There are several other methods of conflict resolution, but the five previously mentioned are the most used by the project manager. It is important that the project manager be aware of the situations that cause conflicts and the methods that can be used to resolve them. Many things can be learned about conflict management in the classroom and in workshops, but it is important to note that nothing can substitute for experience in resolving conflict. It is also important that the project manager realize that different methods of resolution should be used at different stages of the project process and by or with different individuals. The project manager should carefully consider all alternatives to choose the best for the situation. He or she must, in short, manage the conflict situations in the project.

The Functions of a Project Manager

To define what a project manager is, one must first determine the functions that a project manager is expected to perform during the course of a project. During a regional seminar of the Project Management Institute (Houston, 1976), there were several functions listed as important to the project manager.[33] These functions were planning and scheduling, performance analysis, progress reporting, maintaining client/consultant relations, project trend analysis, cost trends analysis, logistics management, cost control, organization and manpower planning, maintaining the technical/business interface, contract administration, controlling materials and manpower, estimating, and procedure writing and administration.[34] Some other qualifications for a project manager include being a good communicator who works well with others, a qualified negotiator, and a good salesperson.[35] This list is by far not inclusive of all of the functions of a project manager, but it does provide a good starting point from which to determine many of the specific tasks involved.

The following are some definitions of the terms listed above.

1. *Contract administration.* Managing or supervising the execution of a contract with the person or persons that supply the goods or services for the project. The definition given by Houston was taken to mean the administration of contracts, both in the project sense and in terms of those contracts with suppliers of goods and services.

2. *Technical/business interface.* The interaction of the project's technical requirements with the business aspect of the company.

3. *Client/consultant relationship.* The relationship between the client or customer and any third party to the project such as consultants, subcontractors, government officials, and others.

4. *Procedure writing and administration.* The preparation/tailoring, updating/revision, and administration of procedures for various parts of the project's execution.

A list of qualifications and desirable traits for the project manager was published in the *Project Management Quarterly*, to include:
• Works well with others.
• Is experienced in his or her area of technical expertise.
• Has some supervisory experience.
• College education in a technical field.
• Is familiar with contract administration.
• Is able to accurately present company's position.
• Should be profit-oriented.
• Should be a qualified negotiator.[36]

The qualifications may be different for different types of managers, but all sources agree that a successful project manager must be able to work well with others. It is also desirable for the project manager to have a broad base of knowledge, whether developed through education, experience, or a combination of the two. The narrow, technically-minded specialist is notable for consistently failing at the job of project manager.

The Roles of the Project Manager

The project manager must fill several roles in the completion of a project. First of all, as previously mentioned, the project manager must fill the role of an integrator.[37] This role is important because the project manager is the only person who is able to view both the project and the way it fits the overall plan for the organization. It is also important in that the project manager must coordinate all of the efforts of his or her project team into a working unit. He or she must also explain and integrate the project with members outside the project team who may or may not be within the organization.[38] The role of the integrator can be thought of as being inclusive of all parts of the job, but there are other specific roles the project manager must become involved in while completing the project.

The project manager must be a communicator—to upper management, to the project team, and to members outside the project who have an interest in the project's results.[39] This is an important role because, with all of the information coming to the project manager from many different sources in many different forms, the project manager who fails to decipher and pass on the appropriate information on time can become the major bottleneck in the project. The communication process is not always easy because the project manager may find barriers to communication exist, such as a lack of clear communication channels and problems with technical language that must be used. The project manager has the responsibility of knowing what kind of messages to send, knowing who to send the messages to, and translating the messages into a language that all can understand.

A third role the project manager must fill is that of a team leader.[40] In terms of leadership ability, this not only applies to the formal or legitimate authority of position a project manager might use in the organization, but also to the expert and referent type of power that would be used in the informal organization. The project manager must be able to solve problems as they arise, guide people from different functional areas, and coordinate the project to show his or her leadership capabilities. In order to gain this broad experience as a leader, it is important, but not imperative, that the project manager have been a line supervisor at one time so that he or she will have the broad experience of managing people.[41]

Another role that is important for a project manager to fill is that of a decision maker.[42] The specific decision may vary according to the type of project and the stage of the project's life cycle at which the decision must be made, but in any event the project manager must make them. Key decisions include allocation of resources, the costs of performance and schedule trade-offs, and changing the scope, direction or characteristics of the project.[43] The decision making process is certainly not a unique role to project managers, but it is a very important one that could have important consequences on the project as a whole.

The fifth role that a project manager might be expected to fill would be that of a climate creator or builder. It is important that the project manager attempt to build a supportive atmosphere so that the project team members can work together and not against each other.[44] The project manager should seek to create a supportive climate to begin with so that some negative forms of conflict and unrest can be avoided.

The previous section has explained many of the roles and functions the project manager would be expected to perform during the course of a project. An effective project manager will recognize these functions and do everything possible to understand how they apply to the overall project.

PART II

The Education and Experience of the Project Manager

One of the most important areas for the prospective project manager, yet a nebulous area, is the amount of education and experience necessary to be a successful project manager. Research to this point is sketchy and scattered. This part of the monograph will take the material discussed in Part I and expand upon it to provide a concept of the education and experience desired to be an effective project manager.

Experience and Education Requirements for the Project Manager

Probably two of the most important areas dealing with the project manager are how much education is required for the project manager to do the job and how much experience or on-the-job training someone should have before he or she is chosen to manage a project. Complicating this topic is the fact that, to some extent, experience can substitute for education and vice versa. The critical issue is that all of those who have been identified as *good, effective* project managers have had both education and experience. Generally speaking, most project managers have a technical undergraduate degree that generally provides a great deal of knowledge and some experience in a specific technical field, but only limited knowledge of other technical fields. The ability to manage can be gained through experience and/or education in a management area. While experience is irreplaceable as a learning tool for managing people in a project, the manager should also acquire some knowledge of the management field in a more formal educational experience. Assuming that the project manager has a broad understanding of at least one technical field, he or she needs to add to this some general knowledge of other relevant technical fields and some detailed knowledge of the major functional managerial areas so that he or she may better integrate the human resources and the different technical areas of the project. This business or management knowledge is frequently gained through graduate education in business (frequently a master of business administration degree).

Although many project managers do have a technical undergraduate degree, it is also possible for a person to become a project manager by simply working his or her way up through the ranks and gaining experience as he or she goes. This is decidedly the exception, however, rather than the rule. In light of this fact, it is important to note what a project manager should be expected to get from formal education or workshops and what he or she should gain through experience.

Recognizing that project managers should have a good mix of education and experience, one should also be aware of the two areas from which project managers originate.[45] First of all, many project managers come from the ranks of senior functional or line managers. Others develop through the project management route itself, starting as a member of a project team and moving to assistant project manager or even to administrative assistant. This is the route many of the college graduates take when entering the project area to gain the added experience needed to manage a project.[46]

The knowledge a project manager can gain from education falls into two areas: formal college education and informal, specialized training sessions. The following are important areas of education for the project manager, grouped under the most effective source of instruction for the material.

Formal Education
- Psychology
- Computer applications
- Statistics
- Technical writing
- Labor relations
- Law
- Economics
- Personnel
- Accounting
- Merchandising
- Contracting and procurement
- Organization theory

Informal Workshops
- Visual/graphics and communication
- Negotiation
- Conflict management
- Personnel management
- Organizational relationships (practice)
- Working well with others
- Group dynamics
- Leadership techniques

Knowledge gained in the areas listed under formal education are for general application to situations that might occur in an organization and can generally be explained best in theoretical terms. Workshop education, on the other hand, will aid the project manager in learning techniques that are best applied in specific situations. The project manager should be educated in both settings so that he or she can function most effectively in a working situation.

Some specific tools that the project manager should gain from the educational process (through formal education and specialized workshops) for use on the job include the techniques of CPM, PERT, computerized accounting, materials control, inventory and inventory control, purchasing, manpower and other resource leveling, MIS/operations research, and forecasting.[47] These techniques can be learned in theory in a classroom setting. With a better understanding of the theory of these tools, the workplace application can be made much easier, with better results, while specific applications can be developed in short training programs and workshops. In a PMI-sponsored survey conducted by Cook and Granger,[48] it was shown that many colleges and universities throughout the United States have courses relating to the principles of project management within their curriculum (more often in engineering than in business schools). The type of knowledge most likely to be gained by the prospective project manager in these courses involve specific dimensions such as planning, leading, and controlling—little emphasis is placed on organizational relationships, communications problems, and the problem of integrating personnel into a project team.[49] With more emphasis being placed on the human element of the project, it will become necessary for the project manager to mesh his or her technical skills with an understanding of people so that a profitable working relationship can be found.

The other learning device used to teach the prospective project manager is experience working in the functional and project areas of the organization. Some of the types of knowledge and skills that can be gained through this type of experience include the following:

Skills Gained Through Experience
- Safety considerations and methods
- Technical knowledge and experience in an applied sense
- Labor relations, particularly union/management practices in the specific company/industry
- Personnel management techniques used in the specific company/industry
- Data collection and evaluation as it is currently performed
- Time and motion study techniques
- Training methods
- Procurement practices
- Public relations practices
- Negotiation techniques
- Ability to work well with others
- Supervisory experience
- Contract administration as practiced.

Some of these items can also be gained through education because it is necessary to acquire both theoretical and practical knowledge to be proficient in the application of the skills. An important factor that should also be mentioned here is that, when one of the areas listed above is learned by experience, there is little discrimination between good and poor practices. The manager learns what is done in his or her company/industry and picks up the bad habits as well as the good. After a few years, it is critical to supplement this experience with formal education designed to provide a broad base of knowledge to put experience into perspective and to evaluate the practices in terms of results.

The most successful project managers usually (not always) work their way up from assistants in the project office to full-fledged project managers,[50] supplementing that experience with formal education frequently taken in part-time night programs. This process usually takes several years, but the prospective project manager will know when he or she is capable of taking an overall view of the project and when he or she has developed a working knowledge of all the disciplines necessary to complete a project.[51] Although the experienced functional manager may, in some cases, become a most effective project manager, difficulties are frequently experienced in placing the various aspects of the project into perspective. Such individuals must guard against a tendency to favor one aspect of the project over another.

The decisions project managers make tend to reflect the similarity or differences in their education and experience. A study done by Barndt indicates that in some cases differences or similarities in education and experience cause similarities and differences in decisions made.[52] The role of the project manager is to "direct and integrate resources in the development and production of a system while meeting performance, schedule, and cost objectives."[53] To be able to accomplish these goals, the project manager should be technically competent and have a broad knowledge of managing a project. A project manager will only be able to do this if he or she has many of the functional qualities of education and experience mentioned previously.

In the broadest sense, a project manager's education, both formal and informal, is a continuous process. To put this educational process on a general time scale, refer to Figure 2. The time span for each of these areas can be shorter or longer, depending on the individual. The pattern is shown by extensive research to be quite consistent, however. Some task or career assignment goals for the potential project manager are shown as follows:

Development Phase	Production Phase	Supervisory Phase	Career Diversification Phase
(0–5 years)	(5–10 years)	(10–15 years)	(15–20 years)
Technical skills are used and polished	Project engineer, supervisor stage	Project manager	Executive

This chart also gives an idea of the career path for a potential project manager, starting with the development phase to the final career diversification stage.

The previous figure and chart give some idea of the time it takes for an effective manager to gain the knowledge of the organization necessary to

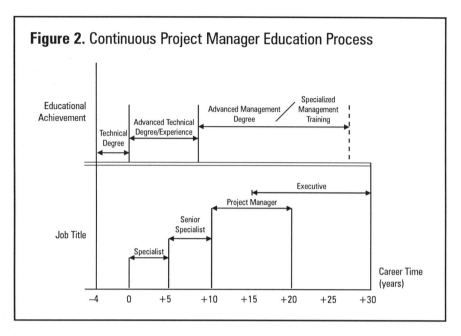

Figure 2. Continuous Project Manager Education Process

become a project manager. As mentioned before, it is not always necessary for the project manager to have this amount of experience to become an effective project manager. However, those effective project managers that have less than the 10 years' experience recommended tend to be the exception rather than the rule. Given the level of experience necessary to be an effective project manager, it is also necessary to look at the education required to be an effective project manager. The table below gives some indication of the desired level of education for the project manager.

The Project Manager—What is His or Her Future?

The future is something that many people try to predict with little, if any, success or certainty. Yet with the past effects of project management on organizations and a more complex future ahead, it seems safe to assume that project management will definitely be a growing part of future organizational structure.[54] The organization of the future will be one where long, vertically oriented bureaucracies will change in form to horizontally structured organizations. These will urgently require the knowledge of project managers to carefully integrate the pieces.[55]

As mentioned previously, the project manager has many functions that must be completed during the course of a project. Some of these functions are exclusive to the project manager; others are not. Like the typical functional

Table 1. Desired Level of Education for the Project Manager

| | | | **Education | | | | | |
| | | | Academic Full-Time | | | Continuing | | |
Definition	Level	High School	BS	*MBA/MS	PhD	*MBA/MS	PhD	Non-Degree
Specialist	4	R	D/R in future	—	—	—	—	D
Senior Specialist	3	R	D/R in future	—	—	—	—	D
Project Manager	2	R	BS + some experience 10 years R	R/D	—	R/D	—	D
Executive	1	R	BS + more experience 20 years R	R/D	D	R/D	D	

R = required; D = desired

*An MBA is required in the future if the project manager or executive already has an MS in a technical area. An MS degree in management, however, is considered the equivalent of an MBA degree for project management purposes and, in some cases, may provide a more relevant educational experience.

**Though this discussion of education and experience, some qualifications for project managers are suggested, but further research and analysis must be done before these could be considered as requirements. If the project manager is to be successful, it will usually require a strong educational background and several years of experience to achieve the status of an effective project manager.

manager, the project manager must continually throughout the project accomplish all four of the management functions: planning, organizing, leading, and controlling. The leadership and control functions have probably been emphasized the most and certainly are important, but so are the planning and organizing functions. Without these, the project would probably fail. The situations these functions are used in are much different from the standardized situations of functional managers.[56] A project manager faces constant change, which makes the employment of these functions much more difficult. It also makes the functions that a project manager must use during the project more difficult. The project manager must also have a wide degree of technical knowledge so that he or she may deal with various specialized personnel within the project team.

The project manager is an important part of the "parent" organization because he or she serves an interface purpose between the project and upper-level management, between subordinates and interface personnel, between the functional managers, and among people outside the firm (customers, clients, consultants, etc.). Along with the interface process, the project manager must also serve to integrate the project with other functions within or outside of the organization. The project manager thus serves as a receiver and transmitter of information from sources inside the project to those outside the project.

A project manager serves five roles in the process of managing a project. He or she fills the roles of integrator, as mentioned before, communicator, decision maker, team leader, and climate creator. Another important aspect of his or her position is that of a conflict manager. The project manager must learn to deal with conflict that might arise between the project team and the functional areas, or among the members of the project team itself, and resolve this conflict so that the project may proceed on schedule.

Once the many functions a project manager must complete during the course of a project have been agreed upon, it is important to know where the necessary knowledge will come from. The first area in which a project manager typically learns of the functions he or she will be expected to know is from education in a college or workshop setting. Many of the degrees held by prospective project managers are in technical areas; but if a prospective project manager were to get an advanced degree in the area of business, he or she would then gain the management background to go along with the technical knowledge needed to manage a project. However, education alone is not enough. A project manager should also have broad experience working in the organization so that he or she may learn about the people and the structure of the organization and thus be better able to manage and use the functions necessary to complete the project.

When all of these things are considered, it is safe to assume that the project manager definitely has a key place in the organizations of the future. These "movers and shakers," as they are sometimes known, get things done in a way that is often unsettling to many of the functional managers, but the important thing is that they get them done. The role of the project manager is to direct and integrate resources in the development and production of a system, while at the same time meeting performance standards, schedule dates, and cost objectives.[57] The project manager may be a little different in the approach to a problem, but the organizations of the future will be dependent upon the manager's ability to make those resource allocation and controlling decisions and to implement them smoothly.

Endnotes

1. John R. Adams, Stephen E. Barndt, and Martin D. Martin, *Managing By Project Management*, Dayton, Ohio: Universal Technology Corp., 1979, p. 15.
2. Ibid., pp. 15–16.

3. Harry Devlin, "Project Management and the Planning Process," *Project Management Quarterly,* 4 (3), September 1973, p. 16.

4. Ibid., p.16–18.

5. Adams, et al., p. 81.

6. Ibid.

7. Linn C. Stuckenbruck, ed., *The Implementation of Project Management: The Professional's Handbook*, Reading, Mass.: Addison-Wesley, 1981, p. 142.

8. Ibid., p. 143.

9. Ibid.

10. Ibid.

11. Ibid.

12. Ibid.

13. Ibid.

14. Ibid., p. 144.

15. Ibid., p. 145.

16. Ibid., p. 146.

17. Ibid.

18. Larry Bennington, "A Project Management Case Study," *Project Management Quarterly,* 3 (2), June 1972, p. 14.

19. Stuckenbruck, *The Implementation of Project Management*, p. 149.

20. Ibid.

21. Adams, et al., p. 143.

22. Ibid.

23. Ibid.

24. Ibid.

25. Ibid., p. 144.

26. Ibid.

27. Ibid., p. 145.

28. Ibid.

29. Ibid.

30. Ibid.

31. Ibid., p. 146.

32. Ibid.

33. "The Project Management Practitioner: What Does He Do? What is the Future?" Regional Seminar, Houston Chapter, Project Management Institute, April, 1976, p. 33.

34. Ibid.

35. Donald H. Henderson, "Career Blueprints for Project Managers," *Project Management Quarterly,* 3 (2), June 1972, p. 11.

36. Ibid., p. 12.

37. Adams, et al., p. 131.

38. Ibid.

39. Ibid., p. 132.

40. Ibid.

41. Henderson, "Career Blueprints for Project Managers," p. 12.

42. Adams, et al., p. 133.

43. Ibid., p. 135.

44. Ibid., p. 133.

45. Linn C. Stuckenbruck, "The Effective Project Manager," *Project Management Quarterly,* 7 (1), March 1976, p. 26.

48. Ibid.

47. "The Project Management Practitioner," p. 38.

48. Desmond L. Cook and James Granger, "How Well Educated is Your Prospective Project Manager?" *Project Management Quarterly,* 6 (2), June 1975, p. 26–28.

49. Ibid., P. 28.

50. Stuckenbruck, "The Effective Project Manager," p. 26.

51. Ibid., p. 27.

52. Stephen B. Barndt, "Some Formal Education and Experience Background Implications for Project Managers," *Project Management Quarterly,* 6 (4), December 1975, p. 37.

53. Ibid., p. 35.

54. David I. Cleland, "Project Management in Industry: An Assessment," *Project Management Quarterly,* 5 (2), 3, September 1974, p. 21.

55. Ibid.

56. David H. Morton, "Project Manager, Catalyst to Constant Change: A Behavioral Analysis," *Project Management Quarterly,* 6 (1), January 1975, p. 26.

57. Barndt, "Some Formal Education and Experience Background Implications for Project Managers," p. 35.

References

Adams, John R., Stephen Barndt, and Martin D. Martin. *Managing By Project Management.* Dayton, Ohio: Universal Technology Corp., 1979.

Archibald, Russell D. "A Questionnaire on Project Management for Use in Manager Indoctrination and Training." *Project Management Quarterly,* 4 (3), September 1973, pp. 9–14.

Barndt, Stephen E. "Some Formal Education and Experience Background Implications for Project Managers." *Project Management Quarterly,* 6 (4), December 1975, pp. 35–40.

Bennington, Larry. "A Project Management Case Study." *Project Management Quarterly,* 3 (2), June 1972, pp. 14–16.

Cleland, David I. "Project Management in Industry: An Assessment." *Project Management Quarterly,* 5 (2), September 1974, pp. 19–21.

Cook, Desmond L., and James Granger. "How Well Educated is Your Prospective Project Manager." *Project Management Quarterly,* 6 (2), June 1975, pp. 26–28.

Devlin, Harry. "Project Management and the Planning Process." *Project Management Quarterly,* 4 (3), September 1973, pp. 16–18.

Gemmill, Gary R., and Hans J. Thamhain. "The Effectiveness of Different Power Styles of Project Managers in Gaining Project Support." *Project Management Quarterly,* 5 (1), January 1974, pp. 21–25.

Henderson, Donald H. "Career Blueprints for Project Managers." *Project Management Quarterly,* 3 (2), June 1972, pp. 11–13.

Morton, David H. "Project Manager, Catalyst to Constant Change: A Behavioral Analysis." *Project Management Quarterly*, 6 (1), January 1975, pp. 22–32.

O'Brien, James J. "The Project Manager: Not Just a Firefighter." *Project Management Quarterly,* 5 (2), September 1974, pp. 16–18.

Stuckenbruck, Linn C. "The Effective Project Manager." *Project Management Quarterly,* 7 (1), March 1976, pp. 26–77.

Stuckenbruck, Linn C., ed. *The Implementation of Project Management: The Professional's Handbook.* Reading, Mass.: Addison-Wesley, 1981.

"The Project Management Practitioner: What Does He Do? What Is The Future?" Regional Seminar, Houston Chapter, Project Management Institute, April 1976.

An Organization Development Approach to Project Management

John R. Adams,
C. Richard Bilbro
and
Timothy C. Stockert

Introduction

Project managers are frequently of two minds when they attempt to conceptualize their field. The typical approach of new project managers is to concentrate on the technical details of the results their project is attempting to produce. While this must always be a concern of the project manager, the successful and more experienced individual soon recognizes that the most time-consuming and significant concerns facing project managers are managerial issues, issues which determine whether or not the project organization will survive and flourish within the larger organization. Most projects must, after all, function within and as part of a larger, ongoing traditional bureaucratic organization, regardless of the technology involved or the sector of our society within which that organization lies. We must ultimately recognize that projects can function only within the parameters allowed by the larger, "parent" organization, and those parameters are managerial by nature. It is therefore the managerial concerns in the project manager's tasks that provide the unifying aspects of a profession that spans essentially every conceivable technical, service, governmental, and industrial field.

For most project managers, these managerial issues create a real challenge. Prepared for the most part with a good technical education related to the type of work their project is trying to accomplish and with several years of work experience and excellent performance ratings within the specialization area, the project manager is frequently ill-prepared to deal with general, broad, managerial issues. The term "technical" here is used in the broad sense to represent any form of specialized education, from theater arts through engineering and the hard sciences to social welfare. It is no wonder that such managerial concepts as organization development, along with their relationships to project management, have long gone unnoticed.

From the standpoint of the broader organization, the introduction of projects into a previously traditional, bureaucratic organization creates a lasting shock wave of change that has a major impact on the way work gets done. Communications must now travel horizontally, not just vertically. The bureaucratic cornerstone of "one man, one boss" is no longer true. A new type of manager, the project manager, now exists within the organization and must be dealt with. Worse yet, the "project managers" have no well-defined basis of authority; they typically have no one they can hire or promote, and yet they seem to generate just enough support to accomplish whatever it is they seem to want done. People can work directly with other people on the same level, cutting across organizational lines without getting prior permission from the "boss." In other words, the whole working world changes and people "act funny." The one thing that seems clear is that friendships and personal relationships seem to be much more important in this new organization than they were in the past. It is much more difficult to rely on the vertical hierarchy to decide what must be done. More people seem to be involved in making decisions and providing direction.

These types of changes are typical of an organization undergoing "organization development." Organization development is an organization behavioralist's approach to changing an organization, generally from a vertical, bureaucratic structure to one more involved with participation, joint decision-making, and team building. As a field, organization development has been around since the early fifties, but until recently it has had the reputation of being an impractical, "touchy-feely" pseudo-science with little practical application. Yet, organization development has developed some very practical and useful methods for modifying and improving the way work gets done in an organization. As a field, organization development has concentrated on—and become quite good at—evaluating the current status and managerial culture of an organization, and establishing some defined target specifying the culture that management would like to see in the organization at some time in the future. Generally this "target" or goal is related to a participative form of management with distributed decision-making, an organization with horizontal as well as vertical dimensions of communication. Typically, organization development has not earned a high reputation for achieving that goal.

Project management, on the other hand, has been little concerned with identifying the overall goal. The project manager generally assumes that someone else established the goal, and then authorized the project as a means of accomplishing the goal. Project managers may refine and detail the desired goal, but generally project management organizations have earned their reputation by developing detailed plans for goal achievement and then implementing those plans and "getting the job done."

The potential match between these two fields is obvious when they are described in this way. However, those practicing project management have until recently generally been educated as engineers and "hard" scientists. Organization development personnel, on the other hand, have been educated in psychology, organization behavior, and management. It is therefore not surprising that these two groups of professionals have failed to recognize the relevance of one to the other, since by education each was developed in a different direction, directions that made it very difficult for one group to understand and value the potential contributions of the other.

This monograph reports on one approach for marrying these two fields, drawing on the strengths of each to overcome the weaknesses of the other. From the viewpoint of the project manager, organization development offers a means for overcoming that most difficult of all problems—getting project management instituted in a previously (and perhaps currently) bureaucratic organization. From the viewpoint of the organization development specialists, project management represents the methods they have been searching for to "get it done." The result of this marriage is a complete process for creating and implementing change within an organization, change that will result in a more participative form of management facilitating the team building and horizontal communications so essential to the effective conduct of projects.

To explain this marriage the authors assume that most readers have a general understanding of the typical project management process. In this monograph, then, we approach the issue of installing project management into a bureaucratic organization from the organization development specialist's viewpoint. This is consistent with the purpose of the PMI monographs, which is to review a general academic field (team-building, contracting/procurement, organization development) that is relevant to the project manager's work, and then point out how the project manager can use the material from this field. To that end, this monograph first reviews the need for organization development and project management, pointing out the increasing rate of change our society is experiencing in this era, and reviewing the process each individual must go through in order to accept each defined, needed change. Next, the type of person needed for what organization development calls the "change master," and what we would call the "project manager" is reviewed. In either case, this person is the entrepreneur, the change agent, the individual who develops and implements the new way of accomplishing work. This person is the project manager. Finally, the monograph presents a unique, pioneering, development program, successful in one major industrial company which is designed to institute project management into a previously highly traditional and bureaucratic organization in order to carry out the organization development objective of creating a more open, participative, team-oriented, and effective organization climate. The authors believe the reader will find that organization development is highly relevant to the project manager, and that the project manager would be well advised to take the time necessary to learn and understand the basic tenents of organization development.

Creating a Project Management Organization

During the last decade, the business literature cited by consultants and business executives, as they design and install changes in the way work is done within organizations, has experienced a major growth in the number of writers who discuss the need for and/or use of project management and organization development tools, techniques and methods. This increase in interest about these two fields of study can be related to the amount of change being forced upon organizations. Writers such as Rosabeth Moss Kanter, Alvin Toffler, and John Naisbitt have documented this change and its impact on organizations. Overall, their work demonstrated a dramatic increase in the number of decisions managers and employees need to be involved in. Beginning in the mid-1970s and continuing to the present, organizations have experienced a dramatic need for increased flexibility among the managers and employees involved in producing goods and services. To be competitive in our capitalistic society, organizations must not only have a good product they also must be able to deliver that product within specific dimensions of quality defined by customers in ways management never considered useful or important in the past.

Project Management and Organization Development

One need not look too far to see examples in contemporary America or in the world for this need for flexibility. The automobile industry, utility companies, the heavy industries of American business are all undergoing change at so rapid a rate that new organizational design concepts, or paradigms, are required. As these changes impact employees, managers find themselves at an introspective crossroad for examining their leadership style and their ability to encourage and nurture change within an organization. In this context, the methodologies of project management and organization development have increased in importance since they offer the knowledge and skill base managers need to control and implement change. More specifically, these two fields of study are becoming more interesting to managers primarily because they suggest ways of redesigning organizations that make it possible to process decisions quicker, analyze information at a more rapid work rate, and incorporate budget and time constraints in a manner that is otherwise not possible.

As a result of these changes, project management is becoming less of a methodology for controlling work and more of a philosophy of life for managers. As managers seek new organizational tools and methods for increasing their flexibility, they are turning more and more to the concepts of project management as a philosophy by which they can redesign organizations to meet the extreme demands made of them. Less and less managers are viewing project management as computers or software packages or bargraphs. They are beginning to view project management as an organizational design and philosophy by which they can enlist the support of employees and organize work so that the barriers of limited time in which to accomplish tasks can be overcome.

Simultaneously, organization development as a field of study is gaining more importance in the world of management. With all the changes occurring in the way work is done, organization development has become the methodology by which these changes are incorporated into an organization so that employees and managers do not become burned out and customers do not become disenchanted with the quality of the organization. The use of organization development methodologies and tools as a strategy for implementing change within an organization is a fairly new paradigm for most managers. It represents a shift from the control and inspection management philosophies of the past to a more developmental and nurturing philosophy of the present. Managers are rapidly recognizing that it is impossible to control and inspect quality into the work or the organization, and next to impossible to gain commitment simply by demanding loyalty. As a result, managers in increasing numbers are relying on leadership styles that encourage employees to accomplish work with limited budgets and time constraints. Such leadership styles do exist. They rely on developing commitment and participation so that employees work smarter.

What managers have learned over the last few years, as this need for flexibility in the organization has occurred, is that they need to spend time building the organization by improving their inter-workgroup communications, installing new types of work control systems, and building strong interpersonal relationships. This is familiar territory for project managers, who for years have been deeply involved in developing teamwork and supportive personal relationships among the project team members and the functional or line managers who must support the project. By spending time developing these aspects of their organization, all managers can empower their organizations to accomplish work through cultural means, as opposed to through evaluative control techniques which assess whether or not employees meet expectations. Further, the expectations themselves are increasing as more and more employees are asked to participate in developing decisions and sharing responsibility for what the organization is to accomplish. This shift has created a whole new paradigm for managers and is the focus of many contemporary books such as *In Search of Excellence, Managerial Breakthrough, Intrapreneuring,* and *Passion for Excellence.* To meet this challenge for being flexible, managers have turned to two previously somewhat neglected fields of study, organization development and project management, as resources they can use to achieve the results required.

Of course, not everybody has recognized these fields of study as providing important new and practical management concepts for contemporary organizations. Managers still frequently believe that project management cannot be installed, or that it is simply a collection of computer programs and planning techniques for dealing with technical issues. Managers also frequently believe that organization development is a "touchy-feely" science that has very little practicality and deals in a world of concepts and theory. In the experience of the authors, neither of these perceptions are uncommon nor to be unexpected. Nevertheless, there is an increasing recognition of the need for organizations to deal effectively with the issue of implementing change.

Change

Since project management and organization development both deal with implementing change in an organization, let us pause for a moment and review

<figure>

Figure 1. Conflicting Views of Change

Traditional View	Contemporary View
• Caused by trouble makers	• Inevitable as organizations react to external pressure
• Bad	• Often beneficial
• Results from poor planning and mistakes in the initial organization design	• Natural result of evolution and growth
• Creates problems and difficulties by displacing experienced personnel	• Provides opportunities for indiviudal participation and involvement
• Disrupts the status quo	• Provides for calleges and growth
• Should be avoided	• Should be welcomed
• Must be controlled and suppressed	• Can and should be managed
• Best implemented by "Getting It Over Quickly"	• Requires time for individual acceptance

</figure>

what we know about change, or at least the major implications of change for large and traditionally bureaucratic organizations.

There are really two basic but opposing views of change, as shown in Figure 1. The traditional view sees change as being primarily negative. Since the traditional organization is established to control people and processes in getting work accomplished, the need for change is viewed as representing a failure of the control process and hence of the organization itself. Change is seen as being bad, caused by "trouble makers," the source of many problems and difficulties experienced by workers and managers alike. People must be retrained as a result of change or they grow obsolete and can no longer perform the useful jobs they have learned and become skilled at over the years. As a result, change should be avoided if possible and carefully controlled and suppressed if it can't be avoided. If change is inevitable, it is best accomplished by having the senior managers decide on the best method for dealing with it, issuing the necessary orders, and then implementing the change immediately. This traditional attitude seems to be:

> *"Get it done" so the pain doesn't last too long and we can get back to work as usual. After all, if we announce an upcoming change ahead of time, we'll generate all kinds of resistance, sabotage, and other aberrant behavior, making the change all the more difficult. If people have to be fired, retrained, or moved to different jobs, it is only humane to put them out of their misery as quickly as possible.*

The contemporary view, on the other hand, sees change in a positive light. While it is recognized that change can be disruptive, it is also recognized as inevitable in modern organizations that must exist in a rapidly changing environment where many unpredictable external pressures require a reaction from the organization if it is to survive. The fact that changes allow the organization to survive means that change is often beneficial. Not only does it frequently create better ways of doing things, it also opens up opportunities for both organization and individual growth, making an otherwise stable and boring situation interesting and challenging. Change can create new jobs, modify old jobs for the better, and provide the opportunity for many more members of the organization to participate in finding a better way to work. Thus change should be welcomed. If properly planned for, if it is managed as a logical and structured process, if it is introduced over a reasonable period of time that allows people to adapt to their new working conditions, then change can clear the way for creating a much more interesting and pleasant place to work.

One thing we can be certain about is that no one ignores change. In today's business world, change has become a way of life, and emotions run high when changes are being planned and announced. There are likely to be many who resist the change, because they see some threat to the way they have become used to things being done. There are likely to be few strong supporters of the change, for those who see a potential benefit to themselves are unsure whether or not the benefits will actually materialize, and are therefore typically hesitant to declare themselves and work openly to create the change. What is needed is a process for implementing change, a process that recognizes the natural resistance and uncertainty of those to be affected by the change, and provides the time necessary for the individuals affected to work through their fears and understand the benefits to be gained from the change. This process of change is shown in Figure 2.

Figure 2 represents the change process as a continuing cycle of moving from stability through awareness and the exploration of options to the implementation of new working conditions, and on to a new (if temporary) plateau of stability. It is important to understand that this change cycle applies equally to both the organization and the individuals within the organization.

- **Quadrant I** in the chart represents stability and control, the situation in which the bureaucracy is most comfortable. Both the organization and the individuals in it know their jobs and are reasonably well satisfied with the status quo. Life is comfortable. Unfortunately (or fortunately, depending on the viewpoint), in today's business world this situation doesn't last too long. Somehow the need for a change is inserted into the otherwise stable situation! Individuals and the organization alike skip immediately into Quadrant II.
- **Quadrant II** represents the growing awareness of and the emotional reaction to the change. Individuals typically become emotionally involved in resisting the change. They "place blame" (It's Bill's fault! If he hadn't come up with this foolish proposal I wouldn't have to spend the next three

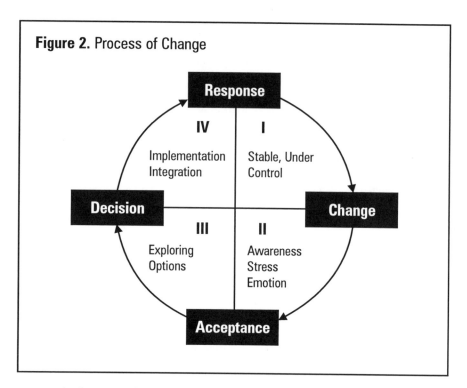

Figure 2. Process of Change

Response

IV | I

Implementation Integration | Stable, Under Control

Decision | Change

III | II

Exploring Options | Awareness Stress Emotion

Acceptance

months learning that new computer program. And those paper pushers in Corporate can't recognize when something is going well ...") and "seek justice" ("It's certainly not my fault. I'm not an expert on the micro-computer. I requisitioned that new computer for our office two years ago, and it hasn't shown up yet ..."). Generally, they work through the stress and anger that typically follows the announcement of a needed change, until eventually they accept the fact that the change is coming, it's needed, it's inevitable, and it may even improve the way things get done. It is only when this point is reached that progress can be made toward implementing the needed change.

• At this point the participants can begin to analyze the change and determine how it can best be implemented. **Quadrant III** represents the problem solving process, where the situation requiring the change is examined and possible options for implementing an appropriate response are evaluated. Hopefully, some logical process will be followed to identify the feasible alternatives, evaluate the pros and cons of each, and select the approach which will best meet the needs of the individuals and the organization concerned. Finally an alternative is selected: that is, a decision is made as to how the need for change will be implemented. At that point it is time to determine how the decision will be implemented.

- **Quadrant IV** represents the process of implementing the change that has been decided upon and integrating the new methods into the normal way work gets done in the organization. These implementation activities finally result in the actual response to the need for change that was originally defined, and the organization settles down into a new routine, a status quo, a new stability—that is, until the next need to change is identified. Thus the cycle continues.

Every individual and every organization involved in any change must go through this cycle, but some will go through it easily and quickly, while others will stumble through with agonizing slowness. There are many reasons for this difference, not the least of which involves the magnitude of the change and its criticality to the jobs of the individuals concerned. It is clear, however, that generally high levels of stress are associated with change. The levels of stress and the resistance to change are increased as the time to react to a given need for change is reduced, while both the stress and the resistance are decreased as individuals are developed to better anticipate and prepare for change. This implies some clear guidelines for the leader who is concerned with implementing and managing the change. In particular, the leader must make the time available to develop his or her subordinates and create a working climate of trust and supportive interpersonal relationships if the organization is to adapt to needed changes in a reasonably smooth and productive manner.

Developing Organizations With Project Management

There is a new model of organization design, however, for managers who perceive project management and organization development as extremely useful managerial tools. These managers are actively creating more time to spend with their employees to discuss how to manage change, enhance the organization, and improve their organization design and management processes. These managers are paying the price up front so they can create a more flexible and dynamic culture within their organizations. As a result, they typically succeed whereas others do not. Their employees are usually more happy, more willing to go the extra mile, more accepting of high performance standards, and more focused on quality and customer satisfaction.

Unsuccessful managers deal with project management and organization development in a different way. Their paradigm, based largely on the successes of the past, is represented by a high need for control and inspection. Their philosophy is to analyze work tasks to a point that is totally understandable and to hold people accountable for only that portion of the work assigned to them. As a result, they typically do not accomplish anything fast enough to address the organizational issues with which their employees are frustrated. The result is reduced motivation and productivity. These managers typically view organization development and project management as:

- Only tools and techniques to be used in simplistic ways to control and inspect
- Computer-based control mechanisms, as opposed to a way of life or philosophy
- Work management trivia, rather than a means of empowering their employees to deal with psychological contracts among and between individuals organized by project management systems
- Installation of new ideas by an expert consultant and sending out a memo explaining how things should be done, as opposed to training and developing an organization to meet expectations.

We may be in a leadership crisis in America. This perception is supported by writers such as William Macabe and Tom Peters, who view "leadership" as a totally different concept from "management." They propose that for organizations to be dynamic and flexible, employees need direction from a leader who views organizations in a philosophical and abstract sense, as opposed to a manager who perceives it in terms of situational requirements and control. To the authors, this is the challenge of contemporary management.

The ability to understand why organization development and project management are important entities in terms of creating flexibility within an organization, and the ability to assess the leadership required to use these tools adequately and effectively, are two of the greatest challenges facing contemporary organizations. Managers can no longer be selected solely on experience and knowledge. Contemporary managers are more likely to be selected because of their ability to understand how to get people involved and committed to the expectations of an organization. This is extremely difficult for some individuals to accept. It means changing one's views of the organization. The old views involved analysis, detailed breakdown of tasks and jobs, and careful control of activity. They involved sending employees off to be trained in management and teaching them that if they do what the organization says and don't cause trouble or controversy, they are likely to be rewarded by promotion and higher salary. In the rapidly changing business environment of today, this approach is no longer appropriate. Organizations operate on controversy and confrontation and are more focused on negotiation as the methodology for getting work done.

Most contemporary organizations, finding themselves in a position requiring flexibility of employees, have moved toward selecting people for management positions because of their demonstrated leadership abilities as opposed to their management experience. These individuals are the ones who recognize that project management and organization development are part of their job role as managers, not simply managerial toys. These individuals typically view organization development and project management as:

- A philosophy of organization design by which an organization becomes participatory in nature and evokes commitment and loyalty

- The guide by which an organizational culture and climate is defined and nurtured
- The theory and concepts by which organizational tools and mechanisms of management are designed, developed, or selected
- The definition by which good management is characterized and succession planning for management is determined
- The guidelines by which a strategy for dealing with the future can be created
- The theory by which abstraction can be analyzed and specific work plans can be created.

Summary

The world of management has changed dramatically over the last decade. The view that managers are controllers, inspectors and evaluators has changed to one that identifies managers as being developers of people, cheerleaders and motivators, as well as performance generators who set high performance standards for quality. Nowhere can a description of this change be better defined than in Tom Peters' book, *Passion for Excellence.* In the book, he clearly illustrates what is occurring in American business.

It is the belief of the authors that as we move toward the latter part of the 1980s and into the 1990s, managers will see this new paradigm more clearly and organizations will select more people for leadership positions based on this new paradigm. As a result, greater use of project management and organization development methodologies will occur. Managers will be more focused on managing change so that change can be healthy and supportive of performance requirements. The future looks bright not only for these two fields of study but also for the organizations and the leaders who will use them for the betterment of their organizations.

Leading the Change Process

The change process discussed in Section II (See Figure 2) involves major challenges to those who must lead it to install an effective and efficient project management organization. Managing this change process is in itself a challenge which typically requires the establishment of a project and a project manager, whose task it is to modify the organization and develop effective project leaders and project team members. Others have called this project manager a "change master," and it is his or her responsibility to implement major changes in the organization in a way that results in success. In this section the change master and his or her responsibilities are examined along with an analysis of a process most appropriate for the change master to use in accomplishing this task.

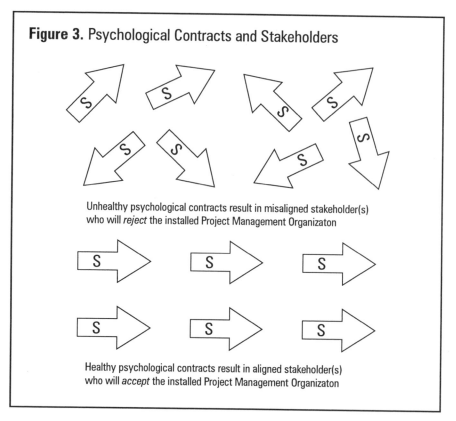

Figure 3. Psychological Contracts and Stakeholders

Unhealthy psychological contracts result in misaligned stakeholder(s) who will *reject* the installed Project Management Organizaton

Healthy psychological contracts result in aligned stakeholder(s) who will *accept* the installed Project Management Organizaton

Challenges

Most likely, the project management organization to be installed must reside within the bureaucracy of the parent organization. This bureaucratic power base may have existed for an extended period of time, in many cases for several decades. In such a situation, the values, beliefs and attitudes of the people within the parent organization are based on the traditions of maintaining the status quo. Most people are comfortable and will, in all probability, resist any changes that might result in installing a new or different way of doing work. The reasons for this resistance were discussed in Section II. The concern here is how to deal with this resistance.

Psychological Contracts

Two basic questions must be answered by any individual who is faced by a new change or proposal that requires his or her participation. The answers to these questions constitute an unwritten agreement between the individual and the change master, an agreement that is no less powerful than a contract in terms

of personal commitment and individual participation, in spite of the fact that it is unwritten. The understanding that develops between the individual and the change master is called a psychological contract. The questions that constitute this contract, and must be continually reevaluated and assessed as the change is installed, are:
- What's in it for me?
- Do you mean me any harm?

Each individual who must support the installation process will need answers to these questions in order to maintain a healthy psychological contract. There must be something in it for the individual (the job will become easier, better, or more challenging; there will be a chance for growth or increased pay, etc.) and the change master must mean the individual no harm (at least in the long run) in order for the individual to support the change. Without systematic, visible and candid responses to their need for this information, people will find it very difficult to align themselves with the changes brought about by the installation process.

A strategy must be adopted by the project leader to build a coalition of acceptance by those "significant others" who are the stakeholders in the project management organization (see Figure 3). This strategy will focus on the project leader as a change master. It will suggest that developmental leadership should be used in order to create a healthy, productive, and team-driven project management organization.

Psychological Contracts and Stakeholders

Unhealthy psychological contacts result in misaligned stakeholder(s) who will *reject* the installed project management organization.
Healthy psychological contracts result in aligned stakeholder(s) who will *accept* the installed project management organization.

A Change Master's Strategy[1]

Response: A change master's strategy for installing a project management organization means responding in a proactive fashion with regard to the status quo conditions. (See Figure 4.) The need for change and an awareness of why a project management form of organization must be considered the best alternative for dealing with productive changes in the organization must be clearly communicated to all stakeholders (project team members, line managers, staff, contractors, auxiliary agencies, etc.). This communication can be very threatening to many of the stakeholders because they may not feel deviations in the "status quo way-of-doing-things" are that critical. Further, the fact that things need to change may be taken as an indication that things

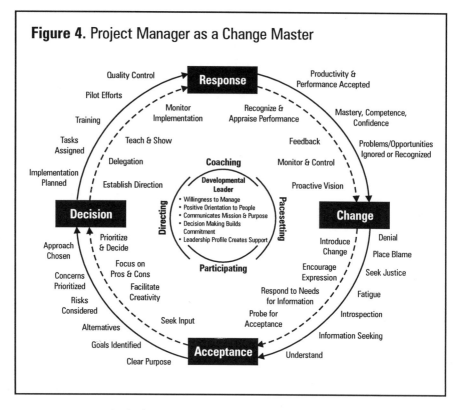

Figure 4. Project Manager as a Change Master

weren't going right before. At any rate, the vision of the future that the project leader has as a change master must be shared. This is a difficult and oftentimes painful realization for those who must change their way of doing things. How can a project leader take people from where they are now to where they need to be in the future?

Change: The change itself should be introduced to the project team by all the project leaders, and all participants should be encouraged to express their concerns about the need and the method planned for meeting that need. (See Figure 4.) It is quite normal for individuals to deny the need for a change, to place blame on someone else for upsetting their organizational environment, and to seek justice themselves as having done no wrong. The project leader should understand that in order to maintain the psychological contracts of the individual stakeholders, responding to needs for information is critical. The change should be fully explained and justified. Other alternatives that were considered should be discussed, and the reasons they were eliminated should be brought out and evaluated. This openness will ensure that the individuals' needs for information are met. Providing this information and generating an open discussion is the key to helping the stakeholders understand and accept the reality of change as the installation of the project management organization proceeds. This acceptance sets the stage for a planned and logical approach to determining how to deal with and implement the change itself.

Acceptance: Hopefully, at this juncture of leading the installation process, the project leader will have achieved acceptance of the changes by the majority of stakeholders. (See Figure 4.) Each stakeholder, by this time in the change process, should have gained enough awareness and understanding to begin clarifying the purpose, goals, objectives, alternatives, and risks involved in choosing the best balanced approach for implementing the project management organization. Each individual by this time will have determined whether or not he or she will participate and cooperate in instituting the change. Hopefully, the majority will be willing to participate in making the new methods work, for their psychological contracts will be such that there will be "something in it for them," and "no harm will be intended." The objective of using a logical, structured approach, of course, is to integrate project management methods into the ongoing work of the parent organization.

This approach cannot be effectively accomplished without the guidance and leadership of the project leader. As change master, he or she must create a climate of trust, must elicit commitment and involvement from the stakeholders. By definition, only those who choose to participate will become effective stakeholders. Those who refuse will either continue to withdraw or eventually join as the change process continues. Seeking the input of these stakeholders by espousing the philosophy that "none of us is as smart as all of us" will facilitate creativity, generate teamwork and participation, and result in development of synergistic options to be considered for the final decision concerning how to implement the project management organization.

Decision: The decision to install a project management organization should now have the support of most of the stakeholders, the key actors in this new organization. (See Figure 4.) The best balanced approach for this decision has been chosen. It has been accomplished by exercising developmental leadership on the part of the project leader. He or she must now establish direction, delegate tasks, teach and demonstrate to others how this new organization will function, and monitor the implementation process.

This requires that the installation of the project management organization be carefully planned by all those who must support and participate in the work. The stakeholders' input is critical. Tasks need to be assigned to those who will accomplish them, and dates need to be set. Training will serve to minimize confusion and maximize commitment to the changes that are being integrated into the parent organization. As efforts extend beyond the initial "start-up" or "pilot" activities, it is important for everyone to be sensitive to the quality control aspects of the installation process. Where are we now? Where do we need to be? What's going on now? What needs to be going on? Key questions such as these need to be asked frequently, and asking them requires that the change master and the stakeholders come full circle in the change process. It is the answers to these questions that determine the need for further changes, and the cycle continues.

As depicted in Figure 4, the change process is dynamic and iterative. Now that the project management organization has been installed it must be sustained and maintained. For this to be accomplished, changes are inevitable; consequently, the change master and the team must continue this iterative process of:

• Responding to the problems and opportunities that will occur
• Recognizing the changes that cause the problems or opportunities to occur
• Accepting of those changes that require attention
• Implementing decisions after careful analysis and best balance solutions are chosen.

What does it take to facilitate this dynamic process of installing a project management organization? The key concern in selecting a project leader who will function as a change master must be to identify those key characteristics that seem to be present in most (if not all) of those who are recognized as "developmental leaders," for there are very few individuals who can successfully lead the change from a bureaucratic to a project management form of organization. In the remainder of this section, the key behavioral dimensions of the change master are reviewed in the hope of providing some guidance in the selection of this individual.

Figure 5 focuses on the five key components of developmental leadership. These components are:

• A willingness to manage
• A positive orientation to people
• The skill to communicate mission and purpose
• A decision-making technique that builds commitment
• A leadership profile that creates support.

The project leader as change master must possess these developmental leadership attributes in order to install, as well as sustain and nurture, the project management organization. Under each of these components shown in Figure 5 are key questions which those selecting the change master should ask to determine which candidate best reflects these developmental leadership attributes.[2]

A Willingness to Manage

The project leader functioning as a change master is a unique individual that must possess a desire to influence and lead others in the change process that installs and maintains a project management organization. At the same time, the change master must remain objective and focused on the positive benefits the company will achieve as a result of this change process. The change master must also retain a positive attitude about the change he or she is institut-

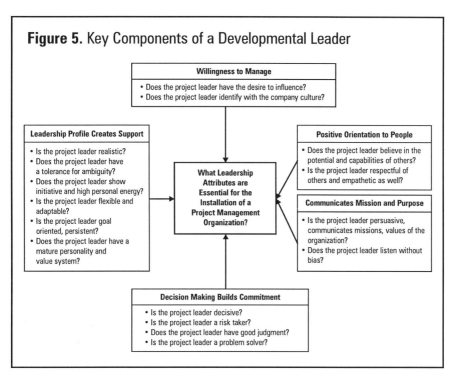

Figure 5. Key Components of a Developmental Leader

Willingness to Manage
- Does the project leader have the desire to influence?
- Does the project leader identify with the company culture?

Leadership Profile Creates Support
- Is the project leader realistic?
- Does the project leader have a tolerance for ambiguity?
- Does the project leader show initiative and high personal energy?
- Is the project leader flexible and adaptable?
- Is the project leader goal oriented, persistent?
- Does the project leader have a mature personality and value system?

What Leadership Attributes are Essential for the Installation of a Project Management Organization?

Positive Orientation to People
- Does the project leader believe in the potential and capabilities of others?
- Is the project leader respectful of others and empathetic as well?

Communicates Mission and Purpose
- Is the project leader persuasive, communicates missions, values of the organization?
- Does the project leader listen without bias?

Decision Making Builds Commitment
- Is the project leader decisive?
- Is the project leader a risk taker?
- Does the project leader have good judgment?
- Is the project leader a problem solver?

ing, for this is necessary if others are to be influenced to support the change. It is also critical that the project leader identity with the culture of the organization since he or she is likely to have a large influence on the culture that will exist in the future, and this new culture must continue to support the overall, superordinate goals and objectives of the company-at-large.

A Positive Orientation to People

A project organization is not a set of tools and techniques for accomplishing a specific goal. Rather it is the set of roles and relationships that pulls a group of individuals together into an effective, operating team. No resource is as complex and as necessary as the people needed to get the work done. A project leader needs to sense the feelings, attitudes, and needs of those people who make up the project organization, as well as those who must support it. As a change master, the project leader should have "unconditional positive regard" for the people involved in and affected by the change being instituted, a genuine liking and respect for the individuals with whom he or she works. This requires a project leader that has personal attributes that reflect genuine sensitivity, respect, and empathy for those individuals whose contributions are critical to the success of the project organization. It is through this positive orientation toward the project contributors that he or she is able to challenge them and empower them to reach their highest potentials through their contributions to the project goals.

The Skills to Communicate Mission and Purpose
It is important that the project leader have a clear vision of the mission and purpose of the project organization. It is more important, however, that he or she, as change master, communicate that mission and purpose to all the others affected by the change. This requires a persuasive and "humanistic-helpful" thinking style that understands and accepts the values of the project organization and is quick to listen without bias to all people, inside or outside of the project organization, whose contributions and support will help guarantee the success of the project organization.

A Decision-making Technique that Builds Commitment
The change master needs to be willing to make a decision and stick by it in the process of instituting the change, even though others may question the decision and apply pressure to get it revised. In doing so, the risks must be evaluated and balanced, with the potential for gain exceeding (hopefully, by several times) the potential for loss. The risks will always be present. The project leader, distinct from others, recognizes the risks and accepts them willingly. He or she must use a logical and detailed analysis in selecting the alternative approach that will be used to achieve the needed change. In other words, the change master uses a systematic, visible and candid problem-solving approach to making the decisions needed to implement the project organization.

A Leadership Profile that Creates Support
Finally, the successful change master will demonstrate those qualities typically associated with high leadership potential. Such characteristics as initiative, energy, persistence, goal orientation and maturity have long been identified with leaders in our society. Realism is a less commonly recognized attribute, but the change master must clearly be a realist to identify and work only for what is achievable in the organization. He or she must also be willing to reject objectives and approaches which cannot be justified due to limited, incomplete, or ambiguous information. The result is a foundation of stability that others can turn to for guidance, support, direction, and motivation as the project management organization is implemented and the change process progresses.

Leadership Skills
The 16 attributes listed in Figure 5 are reflected in the five components of a developmental leader cited in Figure 4. A change master will lead the installation of a project organization by embracing all 16 of these developmental leadership attributes. He or she will also recognize that installing and nurturing a project organization involves a change process and demands "situation-

al leadership skills," skills that allow the leader to change the approach as the situation demands. The project leader as change master develops a "sixth sense" for knowing when in the change process it is appropriate to lead by:

- Pace setting
- Participating
- Directing
- Coaching.

All of these styles of leadership are appropriate if and only if, they are introduced at the right point in the change process, applied to the right people who need that particular style of leadership to function at optimum levels at that specific time, and used in response to the correct situational stimuli. The remainder of this monograph examines some of the situational differences faced by the change master, and reviews some of the options available to him or her in exercising that "sixth sense" of project leadership.

Maintaining and Nurturing a Project Management Organization

Part II presented change as a process of creating and project management as a strategy for creating an institutionalizing change in an ongoing bureaucratic organization. Part III presented the change process as it relates to psychological contracts and the developmental leadership needed to meet the challenges of introducing project management into an ongoing bureaucratic organization in which the managers and employees have grown "comfortable" with the status quo. Introducing project and change management into such an organization provides a shock to all members who are affected by the change. The normal reaction is a feeling of "this too shall pass," an attitude that can be expressed by the phrase, "if we can just live through all this foolishness, things will soon return to 'normal,'" or "once we get this new system implemented, we'll be able to relax and enjoy life again." In other words, the members of the organization look forward to returning to "Quadrant I" of the change cycle shown in Figure 2, a comfortable state of maintaining the status quo, where the organization is under control and there is a shared understanding among all its members about what work is to be done and how it is to be accomplished.

The fact is that introducing project management into an organization is not a one-time change that members of the organization can get used to and integrate into the earlier ways of accomplishing work. In today's society there is nothing to indicate that the need for change is a one-time phenomenon, or that the rate of change is likely to slow down in the future. Rather, there is every indication that change and the resulting need for a project management type of organization has become the pervasive way of life for

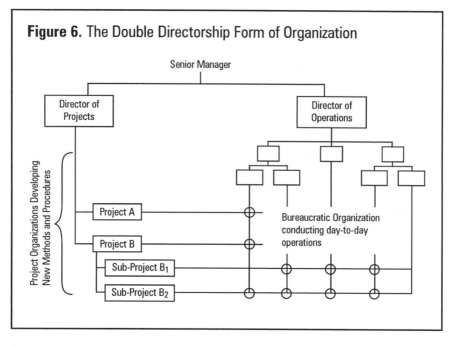

Figure 6. The Double Directorship Form of Organization

Senior Manager

Director of Projects

Director of Operations

Project Organizations Developing New Methods and Procedures

Project A

Project B

Sub-Project B₁

Sub-Project B₂

Bureaucratic Organization conducting day-to-day operations

future successful organizations. The task is not to establish one or several projects, develop and institute new ways of accomplishing work, and then stabilize the new methods in a revised but still bureaucratic organization: the real challenge is to institutionalize the process of project management so that the organization can continue to change and adapt to whatever demands are placed upon it. To accomplish this the project management approach and philosophy must be nurtured and maintained within the organization, for it is project management that provides the means by which that change takes place.

More and more senior managers are finding that the major demands on their time no longer come from problems involved with keeping the "normal operation" going. The more critical and time-consuming aspects of the job are now frequently generated by projects that are developing and instituting changes in the way the organization will function in the future. The logical response to this situation is for the senior manager to reorganize in a way that allows more concentrated managerial attention to be devoted to project issues. Depending on the nature of the organization, either a double or single directorship (as shown in Figures 6 and 7, respectively) is becoming more common. Both of these organizational forms have the major advantage of allowing the senior manager to concentrate more attention and time on project issues.

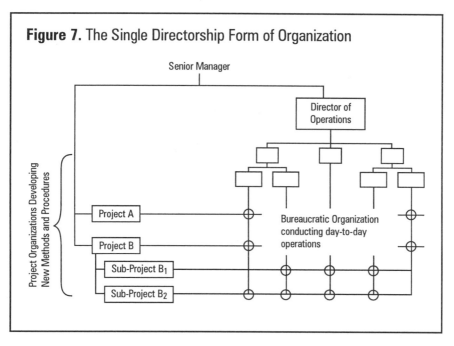

Figure 7. The Single Directorship Form of Organization

The Challenge of Maintaining a Project Management Organization

Maintaining and nurturing project management requires that all members of the organization become oriented to the process of change as implemented through projects, and to the fact that change has become a continuing fact of life within the organization. It is no longer sufficient that the project manager become the "change master" as discussed in Part III of this monograph. In a continuing project management organization, the change master's strategy must be rolled down through the organization to include all levels of management (see Figure 8). The senior level of management recognizes and accepts the need for change first, then explores their options, decides on a course of action, and responds by implementing their chosen action. Implementing this change, however, inevitably requires that the members of the next lower level of management (middle management) revise the way they perform part of their jobs; for a senior management level, "change" typically means that the organization must either begin to do something new or else it must do something it is now doing in a different way. This demand for change in turn places the middle managers in "Quadrant II" and requires that they work through this same process of acceptance, decision, and response. This process repeats itself at each level as the change rolls down through the organization. Maintaining a project management organization, then, means maintaining an organization that is in a constant state of flux, with different levels

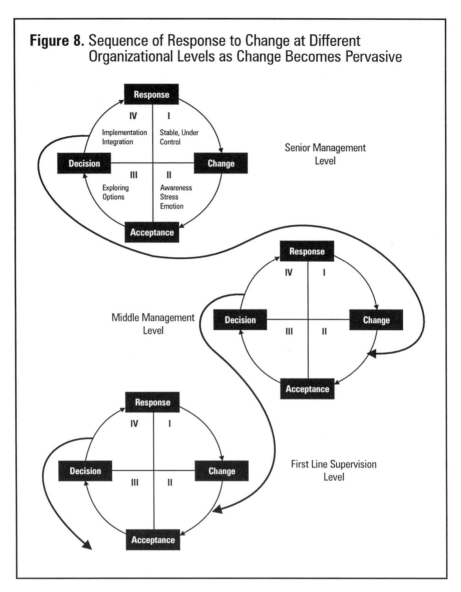

Figure 8. Sequence of Response to Change at Different Organizational Levels as Change Becomes Pervasive

of the organization continually at different stages of accepting a variety of changes that in themselves continually change. During all of this, the normal day-to-day work of the bureaucratic organization must still be carried out, for it is this work that produces the income and profit that makes the whole process possible. Maintaining a productive and effective organization in such a situation is clearly a worthy challenge for any manager.

Figure 9. Comparison of Characteristics for Bureaucratic and Project Organizations

Characteristic	Bureaucracy	Project
Organizational Structure	Standardized Policies, Rigid Organizational Relationships	Flexibility, Teamwork, Change to Meet Current Needs
Individual Response	Compliance to Directives and Policies	Participation in Developing Action Plans
Individual Performance	Standardized Performance and Monetary Rewards	Psychological Contracts, Commitment, and "Tailored" Rewards
Personal Relationships	Formal, Impersonal	Systematic, Visible and Candid

The nature of this challenge is also clear. In essence, all levels of the project management organization must resist the natural tendency to revert to bureaucratic methods of work. Several of the relevant differences between these two forms of organization are noted in Figure 9. Where the bureaucracy would impose standardized policies and rigid organizational relationships, project managers must maintain the flexibility of organization structure necessary to create unique teams of individuals to deal with anticipated needs for change. Where the bureaucracy would issue directives and expect an immediate and complete compliance, project managers must elicit participation in developing an appropriate action plan in response to a needed change. Where the bureaucracy would expect and demand minimum standards of performance from its members, project managers must create psychological contracts with their team members, which demand performance and commitment far above the minimums necessary to "get by" but at the same time provide the unique, differential rewards expected by the individual in return for exceptional performance.

It is important to note that these rewards are likely to involve recognition, or the chance to perform challenging work, or the freedom to decide how to perform work, or the opportunity to take on added responsibility and participate in another project effort, rather than the usual monetary rewards favored by the bureaucracy. In a project organization, the reward for doing well in one project is frequently the opportunity to participate in or manage another project. Most important, the bureaucracy would favor distant and impersonal relationships among superiors and subordinates, with a clear distinction being maintained between those who make decisions and those who carry them out. Project managers, on the other hand, must foster teamwork and involvement through systematic, visible, and candid relationships among team members, relationships that are designed to elicit a far greater contribution from each participant than would "normally" be expected. Project managers must thus maintain a working climate within a bureaucratic environment that is markedly different from that normally encountered within a bureaucracy. To do so requires commitment and an expenditure of energy far above those normally demanded within bureaucratic organizational structures.

Maintaining a Project Management Organization

It is hard to tell the "truth" about organizational changes, and thus to learn what "really" makes them happen ... Generally, ... by the time high-level organizational odometers are set at zero to record a change, a large number of other—perhaps less public—events have already occurred that set the stage for the "official" decision process, that indeed make it possible. ... Most of us begin recording of "history" at the moment at which we become conscious of our own strategic actions, neglecting the groundwork already laid before we became aware of it. What seems to us the "beginning" is, in another sense, a midpoint of a longer process, and not seeing this "prehistory" we may not understand the dynamism of the process already in motion. ...[3]

Maintaining a project management organization means maintaining an ongoing openness to change throughout the organization. Implementing a given change means "rolling it down" through the organization as described in Figure 8. In the dynamic sense, however, an ongoing project management organization is experiencing a complex system of changes with each identifiable "project" at a different stage in this "roll-down" process. There are definite limits to the amount of this change that the individuals in an organization (and hence the organization itself) can stand within any given time period. Increases in the "amount" or "rate" of change are reflected in increasing levels of stress across the organization. Unlimited change translates into chaos, where nothing—not even the "normal' work—gets accomplished. Very limited or no change translates into maintaining the status quo, a situation we have referred to as a "control" orientation to management represented by the traditional bureaucracy. Maintaining a project management organization, then, implies evaluating the organization as a whole, determining the level of stress that the individuals involved can sustain, and then controlling the rate at which individual changes are introduced and rolled down through the various organizational levels. It is a process, a process that is ongoing, which—once set into motion—has no beginning or end, but which really reflects an attitude of openness and acceptance among the members of the organization.

Orienting for Project Management

While the individuals in the organization have limits to the amount of change and stress they can withstand in a given period of time, their tolerance levels can be raised through an appropriate program of training and development. This training program parallels the development program necessary to produce effective project managers and project team members, while the intensity and level of detail within the training increases markedly as the individual moves from an "uninvolved" organization member to a project team member to a project manager. All members of the organization need to understand why this rapid change is necessary, the part they are expected to play in the ongoing process of change, the effect the changes are likely to have on their jobs and careers, and some of the methods being used to implement the changes. The purpose of all this is to reduce and control the amount of resistance to change by the organization's members. The essence of this organizational development program is to create the appropriate psychological contracts that will answer in a positive way for each individual the two questions likely to be uppermost in their minds:

- "What's in it (the change process) for me?," and
- "Do you mean me any harm?"

There are, in general, three phases to the organizational development program needed to generate these psychological contracts. Phase one is designed to develop the basic skills needed to participate and contribute to the change process. Phase two is designed to bond the participants more closely together and generate a consensus toward involvement in the change process. Phase three is designed to involve the participants in the changes themselves, equipping participants with an understanding of the change process and of the attitudes necessary to maintain the process.[4]

Phase One—Basic Skills

Three areas of formal instruction are needed, depending on the skills brought to the program by each participant. (a) Instruction in the principles of project management, emphasizing the rational problem-solving and decision-making approach used by the project manager, provides the perspective and the tools needed for clear thinking and a productive, logical approach to creating the needed change. The instruction is designed to demonstrate a systematic way of appraising situations, analyzing problems and decisions, and preventing the possible occurrence of future problems. (b) Training in the principles of human behavior, emphasizing the teamwork and small group dynamics critical to managing any project, provides the insight that is essential to solving problems and designing systems that will work in the "real world," as opposed to those that can function only in the abstract. Designing workable systems to implement organizational change is possible only to the extent that the project managers understand people's needs, expectations, wants, attributes, motivation, and how they respond and communicate. (c) Studies of the causes and methods of organizational resistance to change allows individuals to understand why any change from the status quo may be perceived by others at the various levels of the organization as a threat, a genuine source of anxiety and fear. This understanding is essential for those who must plan for and design changes, as well as for those who are expected to accept and implement the new methods and practices.

Phase Two—Team Building

Experiences in this part of the organization development program are particularly appropriate to those on the project teams, but are useful to those in the organization at large as well. Here the members are bonded closely together as a functioning team, each with their own part to play, but each striving to achieve a goal greater than the individual's benefit. The participants must build confidence in themselves and in each other, and reach a consensus on how to go about accepting and implementing changes in the way work is performed. As a result of the team-building effort, the organization should be more aware of its abilities, better prepared to participate in determining how to adapt to and implement changes, and more receptive to information about the need for change.

Phase Three—Enlightenment

This phase prepares the organization's members by providing an understanding of the change process itself and of various methods for implementing change within bureaucratic organizations. By analyzing actions occurring in their own organizations and evaluating the results, participants are able to determine effective methods of dealing with the stress and fear of change, both on the individual and the organizational level.

Although these phases of the organizational development program are necessarily presented sequentially, there is no need to "complete" one phase before entering another. Indeed, the same training program or experience may well contribute to all three phases of the program for a given individual. The depth and detail of training provided to each individual member or managerial level of the organization should be determined by:

- The extent to which the change(s) will affect them and their jobs/careers
- The extent to which they are expected to participate on the project teams that are planning and implementing the changes, and
- The extent to which they are expected to take responsibility for identifying the need for change and determining when the organization must react to a specific threat or opportunity.

The Project Management Organization Development Program

A complete program of project management organization development, then, involves a continuing process of providing training, professional development, and process consulting opportunities for each organization that is willing to accept them. When organizations exercise these opportunities they will inevitably maintain the process (a) by which the need for change is recognized and accepted, (b) by which the method of dealing with the needed change is developed and planned, (c) by which the change is implemented, and (d) by whom those responsible are provided with recognition, rewards, and an opportunity to develop their change management (project management) skills further. One such program developed and used in a major U.S. industrial organization is presented in Figure 10 and described below.

Figure 10 really presents an integration of the organization development (OD) process for introducing change into an organization with an extensive program for training and developing project managers. The entire process assumes that senior management has recognized a need to make their organizations more flexible and has turned to their organization development specialists for assistance in carrying out this change. Thus it is the organization development specialist who is the "point man," the leader in instituting project management in an organization.

The process is most appropriately applied at the division, department, or perhaps section level of a parent organization, depending on the size of the managerial unit. From our experience, the process works best in those organizational units that are:

- Small enough so that each employee can have a good idea of the way the organizational unit is structured and the overall mission of each major component
- Small enough to be within the capacity of one or two organization development specialists and the training unit to deal with, yet
- Large enough to provide a good mix of capabilities, and levels of motivation and initiative among the employees, along with perceived opportunities for development and advancement without waiting for someone to "die or retire," and

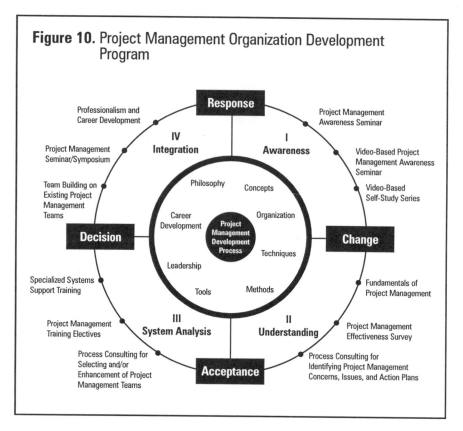

Figure 10. Project Management Organization Development Program

- Large enough to be able to draw upon its own resources and modify its own structure to create project teams for managing the implementation of change.

Overall, we have found that this process works best on managerial units of between roughly 200 and 600 or so employees.

The idea is to create a project management type of organization within one of these relatively small managerial units, and let that unit demonstrate that it is more effective, can deal with change more easily and thus respond to needed changes more quickly, and that it is a more interesting and pleasant environment to work in—morale is high. The more self-contained and isolated the unit is the better, particularly if there are other similar units to which performance can be compared, for then the change process itself and the results of that change process are readily apparent to other units of the parent organization. One such "success story" typically results in so many demands for similar programs in other managerial units of the company that the available organization development personnel must carefully limit the number of units they work with at any one time. Thus, in the electric utility industry with

An Organization Development Approach to Project Management

which the authors are familiar, the process might be applied at a power plant, or within an engineering unit, or perhaps with a customer group.

Organization development specialists typically work as "internal consultants" in large organizations. They are called on by a managerial unit's senior managers to help deal with some specific problem or concern. They must build a high level of rapport and trust with the senior manager, and demonstrate that the project management program will be of value to the unit. Since we are dealing with the entire structure of the manager's organization, and are also planning to commit a considerable amount of resources to creating this change, the initiation of the process must be carefully planned. It cannot be rushed. Frequently, the ability to develop an assistance program depends on just how much "pain" the manager (client) is in, and it may take several months or more of increasing pressure, stress, and "pain" before the client sees this change as really necessary. The major asset of the organization development specialist at this point is patience. Figure 10 illustrates what happens next.

Quadrant I

At this point, the client is in "Quadrant I" of the change process but is approaching "Quadrant II" that is, the organization is in a stable situation, but pressures are mounting that demonstrate a need for change. As this pressure (the pain) mounts, the organization development specialist introduces the concept of project management as a possible means of adjusting to the pressures. This can begin with as simple a process as giving the manager a good introductory book on project management. At this point most managers do not feel they can commit three or four days to a training program, but they may be willing to watch a couple of hours of video tapes. Frequently, as the pressures rise, managers will commit to a short, one-to-two day "Video-based Project Management Awareness Seminar" for their immediate subordinates, and hopefully for themselves, the "executive team" of the managerial unit. This seminar draws on a variety of video-tape-based teaching materials (not the project management video training programs we see advertised today, although they are available and short segments of them may be used in these sessions), integrated with explanations of the materials and carefully structured discussions of how project management might apply in the manager's unit. Should the manager be interested, a more standard one-to-two day "Project Management Awareness Seminar" can be used to introduce a group of the unit's personnel to the concept of project management, In general, the idea here is to present project management as a way of dealing with the increasing pressure and stress which signifies that a major organizational change is needed. We are really taking the senior manager around the full "cycle of change" to the point where he or she accepts the change to project management. This immediately places the rest of the organization, at least that level of the organization directly in contact with the senior manager and the executive team, into "Quadrant II."

Quadrant II

In Quadrant II, the purpose is to allow personnel to work through their natural resistance to change. The approach is to help them understand both the need for change and the use of project management to implement that change. The "Fundamentals of Project Management" are taught in a five-day seminar designed in itself to simulate a project and demonstrate how the project is planned and carried out. The objective of this project is for all participants to satisfactorily complete the course, with the participants themselves forming their own teams and determining how best to complete a series of training modules which actually cover the content materials. The trainers actually work as "facilitators," making suggestions and demonstrating how what the participants are doing is related to the project management concepts they are learning. This seminar is limited to between 16 and 24 participants. It requires three facilitators, and a supporting administrative assistant to maintain and control nearly $10,000 worth of training materials and equipment. The results, however, have been extraordinary in providing both an awareness and an understanding of the technical and behavioral dimensions of project management as a philosophy. Of course, several such seminars may be needed depending on the size of the managerial unit involved.

The seminar is supported by a "Project Management Effectiveness Survey" designed to evaluate the unit's current effectiveness in dealing with work that would normally be accomplished by projects—work that involves creating change within the organization. The results of this survey can also be used as part of an ongoing process consulting program within the managerial unit, with the organization development specialists and facilitators (the same ones who conduct the Fundamentals of Project Management seminars, and hence know the individuals within the unit) working with the unit's personnel to point out how project management might be useful in specific situations, to help build action plans for instituting projects, to assist in the team-building process, and to help allay fears of inadequacy. As more members of the managerial unit move through the Fundamentals seminar, a "critical mass" is generally reached which represents acceptance on the part of the managerial unit as a whole that project management as a way of life is being instituted within the unit. The organization development specialist's job then becomes one of supporting members of the unit as they initiate the project management process itself.

Quadrant III

At this point the task of the organization development specialist becomes analytical and supportive. The unit's personnel themselves must design their own project management organization in order to have the commitment to "make it work," The organization development specialist evaluates the progress being made and offers assistance in selecting project team members, developing participation, and conducting team-building sessions. Where individuals or small groups may need specialized training, either technical or process in nature, the organization development specialist can arrange to have it provided. This training could take any form, from sending an individual off-site to a standard course to bringing in a consultant to aid in developing computer applications. The key is that support is made available as it is needed to assure the project teams can function effectively in their new roles.

Quadrant IV

Finally, as the concept of project management takes hold and proves itself, recognition and rewards must be provided for those who have taken the lead in instituting the process. This particular company offers a variety of opportunities for professional development to its project managers and team members. It supports member- ship in the local Project Management Institute (PMI) Chapter, and annually sends several of its project managers to the Annual PMI Seminar/Symposium. The company conducts its own "project management symposium," at which successful project managers discuss what is happening in the company, how change in being implemented, and how it will affect the work of the organization. Promotions and advancements are noted. In general, project managers and project management are recognized as making significant contributions to the well-being of the company, and individuals are provided with the opportunity to further develop their project management and general management skills.

Summary

The program described may seem idealistic. It is not. It exists because of a very real need, and it is implemented because a few thoughtful, farsighted managers saw a need to do work differently in today's environment than it was done several decades ago. Developing and implementing the Project Management Organization Development Program took several years to accomplish, and it was feasible only because two or three organization development specialists were able to develop the trust and confidence of a few senior managers. These senior managers then risked both their careers and a large amount of the company's resources to demonstrate that the project management approach would improve the effectiveness of their managerial units. This proved to be the case. As a result, project management as a philosophy is rapidly spreading throughout the organization.

The key lesson to be learned here, however, is that the entire process was made possible through a team-building process between organization development specialists and project managers. Each brings the inherent strengths and weaknesses of their fields into the process, but with a careful integration of the talents of both, and the overall product becomes greater than either could generate alone. Project management is perhaps the best method for managing and controlling the change process, while organization development may well hold the key for defining the need and orchestrating the implementation of project management. It would appear to be in everyone's best interest for project managers to learn some of the skills of organization development, while organization development specialists achieve some level of expertise in the process of project management. The results of working together, as demonstrated in this monograph, may well yield results that neither could obtain alone.

Endnotes

1. The authors would like to express their sincere thanks to the Edison Electric Institute Training Task Force for being allowed to modify and adapt some of their "Emerging Executive: Developmental Leadership for the '80s and '90s" materials for use in this PMI monograph.

2. These attributes are not new and are supported in other research work that has appeared in PMI publications. For example, see Neal Thornberry and Joseph Weintraub, "The Project Manager: What it Takes to be a Good One," *Project Management Quarterly*, 14 (1), March 1983; or John R. Adams and Brian Campbell, "Roles and Responsibilities of the Project Manager," a handbook published by the Project Management Institute, Drexel Hill, Penn., July 1982.

3. Rosabeth Moss Kanter, *The Change Masters*, New York: Simon and Schuster, 1983, pp. 182–183.

4. See for example, John J. Nora, C. Raymond Rogers and Robert J. Stamy, *Transforming the Work Place*, Princeton, N.J.; Princeton Research Press, 1986, pp. 56–58.

References

Glasser, W. *Positive Addiction*. New York: Harper and Row, 1976.
Iaccoca, L. *Iaccoca, An Autobiography*. New York: Bantam Books, 1984.
Jacques, E. *A General Theory of Bureaucracy*. New York: Halsted Press, 1986.
Juran, Joseph M. *Managerial Breakthrough*. New York: McGraw-Hill, 1964.
Kanter, R.M. *The Change Masters*. New York: Simon and Schuster, 1983.
Kepner, Charles H. and Benjamin B. Tregoe. *The New Rational Manager*. Princeton, N.J.: Princeton Research Press, 1981.
Kidder, T. *Soul of a New Machine*. Boston, Mass.: Atlantic Monthly Press, 1981.
Levinson, H. *The Great Jackass Fallacy*. Boston, Mass.: Division of Research, Graduate School of Business Administration, Harvard University, 1973.
Maccoby, M. *The Leader*. New York: Simon and Schuster, 1981.

Naisbitt J. *Megatrends*. New York: Warner Books, 1982.

Nora, J.J., C.R. Rogers, and R.J. Stramy. *Transforming the Work Place*. Princeton, N.J.: Princeton Research Press, 1986.

Peters, T. and N. Austin. *A Passion for Excellence*. New York: Random House, 1985.

Peters, T. and R. Waterman. *In Search of Excellence*. New York: Harper and Row, 1982.

Pinchott III, Gifford. *Intrapreneuring*, New York: Harper and Row, 1985.

Toffler, A. *The Third Wave*. New York: Morrow, 1980.

Team Building for Project Managers

Linn C. Stuckenbruck
and
David Marshall

Introduction

Most books on project management tend to be highly prescriptive—they provide recipes or cookbooks for effective project management. The emphasis is on the tools and techniques. "If you do this and use these tools, project management will work." However, even the best projects using the best tools are not immune to failure. In most cases when projects are in trouble, the problem is more basic—the problem is getting the team members to work together and provide outstanding group performance.

Why Team Building?

Team building is necessary because not all teams are winners, at least not right away. A football team is certainly the most publicized example of a team effort, and everyone knows that poor teamwork is the principal reason that teams are losers. Some of the symptoms of bad teamwork on a football team are indicated in Figure 1. A project team is exactly like a football team in that it will not be a winner unless it is a truly coordinated team effort. The total team effort is much more than the sum of the efforts of its individual participants.

Project managers have a variety of management functions, and most of these functions are exactly the same as those of any manager in any organization. However, the project manager has several unique responsibilities that most line or disciplinary managers do not encounter. Projects exist to accomplish complex tasks which cannot be handled by lone individuals. Also, by definition, projects are usually jobs that are accomplished only once, have limited duration, and are accomplished by a multidisciplinary team. The project manager will, therefore, find that the project team consists of a diverse collection of individuals with widely differing backgrounds, abilities, needs, and disciplinary interests. The project manager implementing a new project starts with team members who are unfamiliar with the project goals, and whose capabilities are unknown to the project manager. This is particularly true if the project is organized in a matrix mode where the two-boss problem makes it very difficult to obtain real commitments from team members who may only work for the project part time, and who may have little interest in the project's goals. Project managers will recognize that they have a great need for team building, and that they have very little time to conduct a team-building program. Therefore, team building should become very high on a project manager's priority list in that it should start with the project's implementation and should continue throughout the entire life of the project.

Figure 1. Why Some Football Teams Are Losers

- The "star" wants all the glory.
- Others are jealous of the "star" and don't provide the best support.
- The team doesn't really believe that it can win.
- The team does not have a common goal—winning.
- Some people just don't get the word—"We've got to do it better."
- Some team members never really grasp their assignments.
- Others are afraid of the coach, and avoid asking needed questions.
- The coach is considered to be a dud.
- The coach's decisions are ignored.
- The coach doesn't believe in himself.
- "If it was good enough for Rockne, why change?"
- "We lost the first game, so we're dead."
- The center thinks that the quarterback is a "nerd."
- The team doesn't analyze and learn from last week's mistakes.
- "I'm only doing this for the money."
- "It's all Joe's fault."
- "I don't have to remember signals, I'm only a lineman."
- "Joe's a dirty player."
- "I can't wait to get traded to the Bears."

What is Team Building?

When a new project is started, there is a great need to get everyone on the project team going in the same direction and aimed at accomplishing the same project goals. Basically the problem is that everyone on the project team sees the project in terms of their own particular discipline and background, and they will tend to go in different directions, often suboptimizing in their solution of project problems. The project manager must get the individual team members to view the project from the "big picture" perspective, and to concentrate on overall project goals. Obtaining this team spirit and team commitment is what team building is all about.

Team building has been described as "the process of planned and deliberate encouragement of effective working practices while diminishing difficulties or blockages which interfere with the team's competence and resourcefulness."[1] In other words, team building is the process of getting a group of diverse individuals to work together effectively as a team.

Team Building for Project Managers

What is a Team?

It would be correct to say that any group of people working together constitutes a team. The group of people may only be working at the same place—
their goals and objectives may be very different. An *effective* team would be
better described as any group of people who must significantly relate with
each other in order to accomplish shared objectives."[2] Teams have also been
described as collections of people who must rely on group collaboration if
each member is to experience the optimum of success. An *effective* team has
also been described in the following ways:

- It is group of people who share a common goal, and are striving to get a
  common job done.
- It is a group of people who enjoy working together, and enjoy helping one
  another.
- It is a group of people who have made a commitment to achieve the goals
  and objectives of the project by accomplishing their particular portion of
  the project.
- It is a group of very diverse individuals having all kinds of different disciplinary and experiential backgrounds who must now concentrate on a common effort.
- It is a group of people who have great loyalty to the project as well as loyalty and respect for the project manager, and have a firm belief in what the
  project is trying to accomplish.
- It is the attainment of a team spirit, and high team morale.

An effective team is all of these things, but only a group of people that combines effective job performance, high morale, and exceptional creativity can
meet the criteria to be an effective project team.

In order to ensure that the group is truly an effective team working toward
the same goals and objectives, the team members must have an overpowering
reason for working together. They must need each other's skills, talents, and
experience in order to achieve their mutual goals. In order to achieve these
team goals, the project must have a charter to provide the reason for working
together, and the project must provide sufficiently interesting and exciting
multidisciplinary problems to challenge the group and provide the basis for
working together.

Goals of Team Building

A project team is a system, and the basic tenet of systems theory indicates that
the whole is more than the sum of its parts. A team, therefore, is more than
a sum of its individual team members. It has been demonstrated many times
that a well-functioning team can often produce results that far outstrip the
potential output of its individual members. This has been attributed to the

cross-fertilization of ideas that stimulate creativity and innovation. It will happen if the team atmosphere stimulates discussion, constructive criticism, and the building of ideas on ideas. The terms *synergism* and *symbiosis* have been used to describe this effect—i.e., 2 + 2 can equal 5 or more!

What constitutes an effective project team? The characteristics of an effective team are difficult to identify; however, one place to start is with the desired characteristics of the individual team members. It has been proposed that the team members will attain the following characteristics. They:[3] [4]

- Must be interdependent
- Must have a reason for working together
- Must be committed to working together
- Must all be accountable as a functioning unit within a larger organizational context
- Must have a moderate level of competition and conflict.

A team-building program must be designed so that its goals will be the attainment of the above team member characteristics.

An equally important goal of team building is to make sure that every team member is going in the same direction, and that they recognize the same project goals and objectives. Problems arise because every team member sees the project in terms of their own particular discipline and objectives. In addition, everyone has different levels of objectives, i.e., personal, professional, departmental, organizational, company, team, project, etc. A project's team members' effectiveness will depend on the priority that each gives to project objectives. Therefore, a major focus of team building must be on identifying and obtaining consensus on project goals and objectives.

The Need for Team Building

Basically, projects are necessary to solve complex problems, project management is necessary to make projects successful, and team building is necessary to make project management work. Perhaps the basic need for team building is caused by the ever-increasing complexity of all of our technology and our systems, and hence our problems. More and more of our problems, whether they be technical, political or social, are reaching almost insoluble levels of complexity. This has required that such problems be attacked by multidisciplinary teams representing increasingly diverse types of people, and has made team building for managing the process of solving these problems almost mandatory.

How do you know that your particular project needs team building? Every project can benefit from a team-building program. However, some projects need it more than others. Unless a project team consists entirely of people who know each other well from previous project contacts, team building will definitely be indicated. It will certainly be necessary for a major new project, and even more necessary for an initial project in an organization that has not previously used project management. Therefore, the safest approach would be to initiate a team-building effort as part of every new project.

There is a particularly critical need for team building in a matrix organization. Here the two-boss situation results in considerable uncertainty in reporting channels, so that team members are continually pulled from different directions. The result can be conflicting policies and work directions, which can only be resolved by a team-building effort to assure that everyone understands the importance of the project.

When to Use Team Building

Management theory has long advocated the advantages of using team efforts, task forces, managerial teams, and other ways of accomplishing objectives through unity of purpose and group efforts. Sometimes these group approaches work and sometimes they do not. As Douglas McGregor has pointed out—"most so-called managerial teams are not teams at all, but collections of individual relationships with the boss in which each individual is vying with every other for power, prestige, recognition, and personal autonomy. Under such conditions, unity of purpose is a myth."[5] This same comment can be made about project teams. Unfortunately for project managers, however, if their projects are going to be successful, they must attain unity of purpose. Therefore, a team-building effort appears to be essential for the implementation of almost every project.

Fortunately for project managers, the degree of personal self-interest inherent in most managerial teams may be reduced on the project. Project teams are normally made up of specialists whose interests and objectives can more easily be focused on a common goal. But a project team that would not benefit from team building will be very rare, and most teams would benefit from a great deal of intense team building.

Symptoms of Bad Teamwork

What about an ongoing project—a project that has been operating for some time, but is either in trouble or shows signs of impending doom? How does one know whether such a project is in need of team building? To make this determination, look for some of the following symptoms that indicate that bad teamwork exists in the project team:

Frustration—When team members have not made a commitment, are not motivated, and do not obtain satisfaction from their efforts, they will become frustrated. Such frustration will evidence itself in team member's negative attitudes, grumbling, and poor productivity. Another indication is the team commitment and degree of dedication to the project. Is everyone performing to their maximum without watching the clock, or is one likely to be "killed in the five o'clock rush?"

Conflict and unhealthy competition—Competition in every project team should be encouraged, but it must be healthy so that it stimulates rather than stifles team innovation. It is normal to have rivalry between people and between groups working on a project. However, when competition becomes unhealthy or turns to detrimental conflict, it can seriously degrade a team effort. Such unhealthy competition involves intense rivalry or even constant war between individuals or groups, characterized by constant political jockeying for power and advancement. Bickering, backbiting, and "dirty tricks" will be common events.

Unproductive meetings—The principal reason for project meetings should be to focus the collective skills and resources of the project team on the common problems of the project. Unfortunately, many project meetings turn out to be either gripe-session or an occasion for the project manager to "lay down the law." Such meetings are characterized by members of management doing all the talking, with little contribution from the team members. Such meetings can be demoralizing to the project team.

Lack of trust or confidence in the project manager—An excellent working relationship between the project manager and the team members is essential. The team members must have complete trust in the project manager or true teamwork cannot exist. A project manager who has become isolated from the team members, either because of fear or because of communication failure, will be ineffective.

Francis and Young[6] have listed the following types of team problems that can be resolved through a team-building effort:
- Poor recruitment and selection
- Confused organization structure
- Lack of control
- Poor training
- Low motivation
- Lack of individual creativity
- Inappropriate management philosophy
- Lack of succession planning and development
- Unclear aims
- Unfair rewards
- People problems
- Other more important organizational problems require solution
- The wider organization culture not supportive of a team approach to management
- Teams unsuitable or unreceptive

- A team effort undertaken by insufficiently skilled people or with inadequate help.

Wilemon and Thamhain[7] also list the following indicators of teams requiring team development:

- There is excessive "wheel-spinning" within the team.
- Team performance is slipping but no one knows why.
- Decisions once made remain unimplemented.
- Objectives are unclear or they are not accepted by the team members.
- The team leader encounters detrimental surprises.
- Team members are unresponsive or apathetic to the needs of the team or of the project.
- Team meetings are unproductive, full of conflict, and demoralizing.
- Team members withdraw into their own areas of responsibility and avoid needed cooperation.
- Problem-solving activity, like "constructive conflict," is avoided.
- There is poor motivation and apathy.
- Schedule slippages, quality problems, and consequent cost escalations develop.

These lists of criteria indicating a need for team building seem to suggest that team building is a cure-all for all project problems. To a considerable extent this is true—there are very few project problems that cannot be solved by a capable team utilizing its collective knowledge and collaborative skills.

The Limitations of Team Building

The most obvious limitation to team building is that no amount of team building will produce a successful project if the project concept is faulty, or if top management is unsupportive. Two other possible limitations are hopelessly unproductive people on the project team or a hopelessly inept project manager. However, in the absence of these constraints, team building will certainly improve productivity within any project.

Another limitation involves whether the project is new or whether the project manager has inherited a project in trouble. Obviously if the inherited project is in trouble because of poor teamwork, the new project manager's ability to build an effective team may be very limited. There will not be sufficient time to accomplish a great deal of team building. Newly acquired team members may be very discontented and even rebellious, and may have considerable mistrust of the new project manager. Therefore, team building will have to start over from the beginning, and the project manager will face an uphill battle.

Project Team Building

Over the years, projects have become much more complex, more multidisciplinary, and more demanding of innovation and advances in the state of the art. As a result, projects must use a diverse team of specialists who have few common interests. Projects, by definition, demand high job performance since they typically have very tight schedules, budgets, and performance requirements. Experience has shown that superior project performance can only be achieved by a superior team effort.

Many project team-building methods have come from the aerospace industry where temporary task forces to carry out limited-duration projects have become a way of life. This industry, in particular, has encountered great difficulty in bringing together specialists from a number of different disciplines, and getting them to quickly become an effective team. The conclusion has been that devoting time to team building is an absolute necessity.

A great deal has been written about team building from an overall organizational development point of view, but relatively little has been written about team building specifically for project managers. What's different about projects? What specific things should a project manager do to integrate team building into the life cycle of a project? Many project managers have often felt the need for a team-building program, but have been uncertain how to take the first step or have not found the time for it in their "crash" projects. As a result, few projects have experienced anything more than very casual team-building efforts.

Benefits of Team Building to Project Management

However, there are many important benefits of team building for project management. Experience has shown that any organization can receive the following benefits from a team-building program.
- Mutual problem resolution
- Conflict resolution
- Motivated members
- Enhanced creativity
- A created support base
- Interdependence
- Reduced communication problems
- Collective strength
- High-quality decision-making
- Increased job satisfaction
- Synergy

All of these potential benefits will be discussed at same point in the following pages. However, the "bottom line" is that good team building will produce good project teamwork and a feeling of team membership, which will go a long way toward making project work exciting, satisfying, and enjoyable.

Who's on the Project Team?

The basic project team consists of the project manager (and possible assistants) and a group of specialists assigned or recruited for the project. The project can be either a pure project or exist in a matrix; it makes little difference from a team-building standpoint, except that team building is much more difficult in a matrix.

The project team should include everyone who will significantly contribute to the project, both managerial and non-managerial people, whether they are full-time or part-time. The project team will obviously include all of the technical people responsible for the project's efforts toward research, design, development, procurement, production, and testing. It is less obvious which of the many supporting and service functions involved with the project should be represented on the project team. This problem has no direct, easy answer, and often depends on whether there are available representatives from the support organizations who have both the time and inclination to become significantly involved with the project. However, there are certain supporting service functions which should definitely be represented on the project team, including Contract Administration and Purchasing. Representatives from other supporting groups, such as Quality Control, Finance, Logistics, should be sought when their function is vital to the project or is desired by the customer. Team members are expected to attend all project meetings and to participate in project decision-making. Therefore, care should be taken in making sure that the team does not have any non-performing members.

There is often considerable uncertainty as to how far to go in requesting managerial representation on a project team. Should top management be represented? No, it just does not seem to work. Occasionally a top management steering or advisory group puts its representatives on project teams. Such persons seem to function primarily as observers rather than as true team members. In a matrix a more important question is, should all involved line or disciplinary managers be members of the project team? It would be an excellent idea to make them formal team members since "involvement enhances commitment," and getting the line managers involved is the best way to obtain their wholehearted support. However, this seldom works because most line managers do not have either the time or any real interest in a project that is not in their immediate field of expertise, and in most cases they will choose not to become actively involved.

The Role of the Project Manager

It is generally accepted that the project manager is the one person responsible for the project team's guidance, motivation, output, and control. This statement implies that the project manager is all of the following:

- Leader
- Project's technical director
- System integrator
- Project planner
- Project administrator
- Team's communications expediter
- Mender of fractured relationships
- Team's "den mother."

After reviewing this list of responsibilities, one can only conclude that the project manager should be either a superperson or that the project manager's job is virtually impossible. On top of all of these responsibilities is added the task of team building. The effective project manager makes team building a part of each of the above aspects of his or her job.

The project manager is the officially designated team leader. However, the project team may or may not immediately accept his or her leadership role. Whenever a new project is formed, members seek to clarify their true roles relative to the project and their relationships with others in the team organization. The most important of these relationships will be with the project manager who will sometimes be regarded as a "father figure" and sometimes with considerable suspicion or even animosity. In either case, project managers will be tested in a thousand ways to determine the real extent of their power and authority.

Team members will carefully watch and evaluate the project manager's performance. Unless their respect and loyalty is gained, the team members are quite likely to sabotage the project manager's leadership, and team building will be less effective. Small groups or cliques may develop which may give first priority to parochial interests rather than to overall project interests. In other words, the role of true team leader must be earned. Only project managers who enjoy the unqualified respect and loyalty of their project teams are in a good position to successfully develop a superior project team. Therefore, a major component of any team-building effort should be an intense effort on the part of the project manager to early develop a superior rapport with the project team.

Ground Rules for Project Team Building

Before initiating a team-building program, project managers must recognize that they have a difficult task ahead of them. To make the task easier, the team-building process should be based on the following simple ground rules:

- Start early.
- Don't stop—continue team building throughout the life of the project.
- Recruit the best possible people—hopefully, team players who are compatible with each other.
- Make sure that everyone is on the team that needs to be.
- If there are people on the team who don't want to be there, find out fast and get rid of them.
- Obtain team agreement on all major actions.
- Recognize the existence of team politics—but keep out of it.
- Remember that a project manager is a role model—practice what you preach.
- Teamwork cannot be forced—you can lead a horse to water, but you cannot force it to drink.
- Don't hesitate to delegate—it's the best way to assure commitment.
- Don't try to manipulate your project team members.
- Regularly review and evaluate team effectiveness.
- Be aware of what is going on—watch for "teamwork disrupters."
- Recognize that team building takes time.
- Plan and use a team-building process.
- Don't be afraid to ask for help—find a team-building expert.

The Team-Building Process

An effective project team is not born spontaneously; it must be created. It is true that team building will occur naturally as people work together toward a common goal. However, such natural team building will only occur very slowly, too slowly to be of much value in the hectic pace of today's projects. Therefore, if an effective team is to be created early in the project life cycle, the project manager must place a high priority on initiating and implementing the team-building process. In other words, the effective team doesn't just happen, it must be made to happen through effective team building. There is little disagreement among the experts regarding this statement. However, there is little agreement as to what constitutes a good team-building process.

The team-building process could consist of a special program of activities and exercises carried out either before or during the early stages of a project. Since project team members can seldom be brought together before the actual implementation of a project, team building is most often integrated into the normal ongoing project activities. Unfortunately, there is seldom time for academic exercises in the hectic pace of a project; therefore, team building must be incorporated into everyday project activities such as meetings, task assignments, planning, and even informal discussions.

The responsibility for team building falls squarely on the shoulders of the project manager, for he or she is the only person in the position of being able to ensure that team building occurs and that it is effective. Team building will only be effective when it is carried out under the direction of a strong leader who in this case must be the project manager.

There are many ways to get team building started, and many actions that the project manager can take to encourage team building. The approach will differ greatly depending on the type of project, the managerial style of the project manager, and on the specific types of people on the project team. Woodcock[8] has suggested that successful teams have undergone a process of team building which has dealt with each of the following nine aspects of its functioning and performance:

- Clear objectives and agreed goals
- Openness and confrontation
- Support and trust
- Cooperation and conflict
- Sound procedures
- Appropriate leadership
- Regular reviews
- Individual development
- Sound intergroup relations.

If any one, or more, of these key aspects of team performance is not developed, the team may fail to achieve its full potential. Wilemon and Thamhain[9] have developed a model which they refer to as a multidimensional framework to guide the project team development process. This team development model indicates that the team development process is composed of the following tasks and goals:

- Recruiting of team members
- Climate setting for team development
- Goal setting
- Role clarification
- Procedure development
- Decision-making
- Control.

The team-building process discussed in the following pages was used in the aerospace industry, and incorporates most of the aspects of team building covered in the above references. This team-building process consists of the following actions or steps that must be carried out by the project manager, although not necessarily in this sequence:

- Plan for team building.
- Negotiate for team members.
- Organize the team.
- Hold a "kick-off" meeting.

- Obtain team member commitments.
- Build communication links.
- Conduct team-building exercises.
- Incorporate team-building activities into all project activities.

Each of these actions are discussed in more detail on the following pages.

Plan for Team Building

Where should team building start? The first task of every project manager initiating a new project is to complete a project plan; therefore, it is the logical place to start team building. The four aspects of the project plan that are particularly important because of their team-building implications are the *what*, *how*, *when*, and *who* of the project. These aspects of planning are of greatest importance to team building because they constitute the basis for the job assignments that must be made as soon as the project team is organized. It is essential for good team building that everyone clearly understands their team task assignments and responsibilities. This portion of the planning effort can easily be forgotten in the early rush to get a project moving. It is also unfortunately true that not all project managers are good planners. Planning is very difficult work. Each portion of the project plan should be written with the aim of providing as much impact as possible on the team-building process.

What—The project goals and objectives must be well planned because they become the basis for team goals and objectives. Both sets of goals and objectives must be consistent and compatible. It must be recognized that team members have their own sets of goals and objectives. Therefore, it is important that the project team goals reinforce rather than hinder the individual team members' efforts to attain their personal goals.

How—Project procedures and controls must be carefully planned and documented. How can the project goals and objectives be best accomplished using the team effort? What types of project monitoring and control tools and procedures will work best with a team effort? Will these tools be an aid or a hindrance to helping people work together? Will they encourage the growth of a team spirit? Project procedures should be written with the objective of making them a basic part of the team-building program.

When—Project schedules should be prepared with people in mind. Often teams work best under pressure, but not if the deadlines are impossible.

Who—Project roles must be carefully and thoroughly thought out as an aid in selecting the right people for each job assignment. For which assignments will it be essential to obtain team players? What types of assignments might be safely given to a "loner" or a person who might be disruptive to the team effort? How can a non-conforming "genius" be best utilized? Finding the right people for the important roles of subunit or task leaders within the framework of the overall project must be carefully planned. Are adequate people available within the organization or must some key people be hired? This is the time to decide what kinds of people are needed, and to determine if there are specific people within the company or organization who are the very best for each particular assignment.

Negotiate for Team Members

Obtain the most promising project team personnel that can be found. Candidates should be chosen primarily because of their potential to contribute their technical or other expertise to the project, and secondarily because of their potential to be effective team players.

Unfortunately, project managers do not always have the luxury of personally hand-picking only the very best people for their projects. Even in a pure project organization, the project manager may not have complete freedom of choice; some team members may be inherited, and new hires may not always work out as anticipated. In a matrix the problem is exacerbated because personnel are often assigned to the teams by functional or line managers on the basis of who is immediately available. The project manager may have to exert considerable effort to have any influence at all on the selection process. The project manager who settles for "second best" will only be making team building more difficult. The effective project manager should make "very large waves" in an effort to get exactly the right people for his or her project team. However, getting everyone that you want is unlikely.

Organize the Team

This is the time to convert preliminary or proposal plans to a project plan—plans must now become actions. Promises made and goals set by various team members in the rosy optimism of proposal preparation must now be made to come true. The project manager must organize a group of diverse individuals into an effective project team. In this organization all the people who must work together as a team now meet face-to-face, many for the first time.

Organizing the team means that specific assignments to specific people must be made as indicated by the project action plan. Work authorizations will be prepared for each of the work packages in the work breakdown structure and assigned to specific people or groups of people. Now the project plan and the people have been integrated as a group with a job to do, and they have been given specific responsibilities and accountabilities. This is the time to prepare a responsibility matrix or a linear responsibility chart and circulate it to the project team. The next step is getting the individuals to work together as a team.

Hold a Kick-Off Meeting

Often the first action in a new project, and one absolutely critical to the team-building process, is to hold a kick-off meeting. The principal purpose of a kick-off or start-up meeting is to get the project started on the right foot. However, its secondary purpose, often the most important, is to initiate the active team-building process. It is here that, for the first time, all of the individuals involved in the project are brought together in one place. The project manager should take advantage at this situation to get everyone involved in the project and to build a unity of purpose for the accomplishment of the project goals.

Is it always necessary to have a kick-off meeting? Probably not, but something is definitely necessary to get all of the factions in a project together and a meeting is the simplest, most practical way to do it. However, it need not be a formal meeting with a formal agenda if the major purpose is only to get all of the team members to know each other. It can be as simple as an informal group meeting for an hour or so, or as elaborate as a weekend retreat at a resort or a hotel. A social event at a local "watering hole" often serves the purpose of developing a team spirit, or a social event can be used to supplement a formal meeting. In most cases an informal get-together will not eliminate the need for a formal kick-off meeting.

A kick-off meeting should have all or most of the following objectives:
- Get team members to know one another.
- Establish working relationships and lines of communication.
- Set team goals and objectives.
- Review project state-of-the-art or status.
- Review project plans.
- Identify project problem areas.
- Establish individual and group responsibilities and accountabilities.
- Obtain individual and group commitments.

The most effective way to make sure that all of these objectives are accomplished is to have a complete and carefully timed agenda covering as many of the above listed objectives as needed. Figure 2 is an example of a project kick-off meeting agenda. The project manager should certainly chair the meeting, but considerable restraint should be exercised to ensure that the meeting is not just a monologue by the project manager. It is certainly important that the team members get to know the project manager, but it is much more important that they get to know each other. It is very important that sufficient time is spent in having the team members introduce themselves and discuss their areas of expertise and what they feel they can contribute to the project. It is also important that the team goal and objectives be openly and completely discussed, and that the project manager attempt to obtain a consensus and a team commitment from the project team. The next most important objective of the kick-off meeting is to start the process of obtaining individual team

Figure 2. XYZ Project Kick-off Meeting Agenda

Project War Room
Oct. 25, 1983

1. Introduction of Team	8:00 – 9:00 A.M.
2. Establish Project Procedures—PM	9:00 – 9:30 A.M.
3. Establish Project Goals—PM	9:30 – 10:00 A.M.
Coffee Break	
4. Establish Individual commitments—	
Team	10:15 A.M. – 12:00 P.M.
Lunch	
5. Review Project Plans	
Review Contractual	
Commitments—PM	1:00 – 3:00 P.M.
Review Proposed WBS—PM	
Establish Accountabilities and	
Responsibilities—PM	
R&D Plans—PI Research	
Design Plans—Project Engineer	
Test & Evaluation Plans—Test Engineer	
Construction Plans—Plant Engineer	
Production Plans—Manufacturing Engineer	
6. Identification of Problem Areas—	
PM	3:00 – 4:00 P.M.
7. Establish Meeting Frequency—PM	4:00 – 4:15 P.M.
8. Schedule Next Meeting—PM	4:15 – 4:30 P.M.
Suggest Agenda Items	

member commitments. This important step will seldom be accomplished in one meeting, but this is the most opportune time to obtain commitments since obtaining them in a public meeting almost assures their fulfillment.

Obtain Team Member Commitments

Obtaining individual team member commitments on their proposed contribution and dedication to the project is a necessary but often frustrating process. Individual team members are often reluctant to make positive commitments, particularly early in a project's life cycle. They prefer to wait until they are sure that they want to stay with the project, or until they have more information, or any one of dozens of other reasons. Therefore, obtaining commitments will be a slow process, but is essential to building effective teamwork. The degree of commitment that will be obtainable will vary widely—from practically no commitment, such as the opportunist who is merely using the project as a temporary stepping stone for advancement, to complete dedication.

Personal commitments from individual team members can best be obtained by getting the people deeply involved in the project. The old cliché that "involvement enhances commitment" is really true. Involvement should begin as early in the project life cycle as possible, preferably long before the actual project start date. It often starts during the proposal or project planning stage. Involvement can also start with an interesting and challenging assignment, which becomes the "carrot on the stick" to draw the person into the mainstream of the project. The project manager then has the challenge of trying to make all project assignments interesting and keeping them challenging throughout the life of the project. Individual team member commitments should involve a *time commitment,* a *role commitment* and a *project priority commitment* if they are involved in other work.

Build Communication Links

Teamwork will not exist without good communication links within and outside of the project organization. Of course, good communication means that everyone is talking to one another, but it should mean more than that. Communication really means that meaningful information is passed from one person to another. The process involves more than the transmittal of facts; it means that each person understands the intent and real meaning of the information being transferred.[10]

One of the team-building responsibilities of the project manager is to build and maintain all communication links. The project manager directly controls many of the outside communication links, such as those with top management, the customer or client, and with other managers in the organization. Project managers must also communicate with their project team. This communication cannot be a one-way street—meaningful information must flow in both directions. If project teamwork is to really be effective, it is very important that communications within the project are functioning to link the various individual team members. The project manager can be an effective catalyst to building these communication links within the project. The team members, however, cannot be forced to communicate. The communications process can be encouraged though, and a climate conducive to good communications can be provided. Project managers can do their part by making sure that the right people interact, and that real communication occurs in all project meetings.

Conduct Team-Building Exercises

Team building can be greatly accelerated by the use of special team-building events, activities, and exercises. Many such "building blocks of effective teamwork" have been described in the literature.[11] These can be very effective, particularly when used early in the project life cycle. Unfortunately, in the punishing pace of an ongoing project there is, seldom much time for academic exercises. Team building is therefore, most practical and most effective when it is integrated into the normal day-to-day project activities.

Utilize Ongoing Project Team Development

Conducting an initial project team-building program is a major step in the right direction. However, it must be recognized that team building is a continuous process throughout the life of a project. One major concern is to keep up the momentum and morale of the team, particularly during very long projects. The direction of the effort cannot be allowed to slip away from the project goals. In addition, there will be periodic infusions of new personnel who must be integrated into the existing project team. At a major project milestone where the project enters a new phase and the emphasis is drastically changed, such as a transfer of the project from Research to Design or from Development to Manufacturing, the key members of the team may change completely. Occasionally even the project manager may be replaced because of the change in project emphasis. In any case, a continued or a renewed team-building effort will be indicated.

Team building can be made an important part of almost every project activity, particularly meetings and group or individual counseling sessions. Ongoing team development involves using every possible opportunity during the life cycle of a project to promote and enhance team building. Opportunities will arise every time a project manager interacts with a team member, particularly during informal conferences. Such conferences are excellent opportunities to discuss the importance of team effort, and to emphasize the importance of the personal and organizational interfaces that the particular team member is responsible for.

A major opportunity for ongoing project team building occurs every time that the project manager holds a scheduled or unscheduled meeting. Every project meeting can be a team-building meeting. During the life cycle of a project, the project manager will have a wide variety of different types of meetings, such as:
- Staff meetings
- Planning meetings
- Scheduling meetings
- Replanning sessions
- Technical reviews
- Status reviews
- Design reviews
- Budget reviews

- Failure reviews
- "Budget violator" meetings
- "News flash" meetings
- "Get-well" meetings
- Top management briefings
- Customer briefings and audits.

For the most part these meetings will be under the direction of the project manager, and all can be used to some extent as team-building meetings. To this end the project manager can take a number of actions that will ensure that each meeting will have a significant team-building content. Every meeting should be a team meeting—not the project manager's meeting, and the team members should be the principal participants. The following are some suggested actions aimed primarily at getting team members more intimately involved and more team conscious:

- Introduce new team members.
- Recognize special project performance.
- Keep the team informed on late developments—both good news and bad.
- Keep the team informed on client and customer actions and thinking.
- Report project follow-on potential.
- Bring in special outside speakers and presenters to emphasize project importance and bring in an outside viewpoint—top management, customer, client, etc.
- Provide exposure for team members by giving them major roles in every meeting.
- Get project and team recognition by having representatives from the media and authors of in-house publications attend meetings.

Probably the most important responsibility of project managers involves their handling of project team problems in meetings. Technical difficulties, slipping schedules, and budget overruns must be discussed as team problems, without accusations or "finger pointing." By getting the entire team deeply involved, the problem can be approached as a team issue, with no uninvolved bystanders on the sidelines. Everyone needs to be working on the problem, and there will be a great deal of peer pressure applied to reluctant team members to be more innovative and productive.

Getting the Team Members to Work Together

The greatest challenge and also the greatest source of satisfaction to a project manager is the achievement of a smoothly functioning and effective project team. In attempting to develop such a team, the project manager may find that the integration of a team-building program into the normal activities of the project is not enough. The team may still not be working well together, and the project manager recognizes that more drastic steps need to be taken. This chapter is designed to provide more detailed information in a number of specific problem areas, and the following topics are discussed with the aim of providing the project manager with additional team-building tools.

Diagnosing Team Strengths and Weaknesses

Before plowing full speed into a team-building program, the project manager should carefully consider the strengths and weaknesses of the existing project team. The assessment of a project team's potential effectiveness, however, can be a rather futile exercise if done during the early stages of a project. As the capabilities and personalities of the team members become more apparent, diagnosing the overall team strengths and weaknesses becomes easier. Team building must capitalize on the team's strengths while at the same time trying to correct the weaknesses.

The process of diagnosis can be made a part of the team-building process by having the project team consider the question—What is hindering our project team effectiveness? A short "brainstorming" session on this subject often serves the desirable purpose of making the team members aware of factors which may be hindering project team effectiveness. Awareness is always the necessary first step toward correcting any problem. There are excellent questionnaires that can be very helpful in both diagnosing and obtaining awareness of team problems (Schein[12] and Woodcock[13]).

Team weaknesses may be manifested by any one or many of the following types of group or individual team problems:
- Passive, non-participative team members
- Indifferent, uninvolved team members
- Lack of commitment
- Lack of imagination and creativity
- Inadequate lower-level leadership
- Unwillingness to make decisions
- Unwillingness to acknowledge or face up to problems
- Tendency to overrule dissenters
- Distrust among team members
- Fear of authority
- Fear of criticism
- Fear of expressing negative reactions
- The NIH (not-invented-here) syndrome
- Ineffective meetings.

Typical strengths that are frequently apparent early in the growth of the team environment include:
- Total involvement in the project
- Good team empathy and trust

- Faces up to problems
- Makes decisions
- Fully supports decisions once made
- Willingly accepts leadership responsibilities
- Discussions free and uninhibited
- Welcomes other viewpoints
- Tolerant of deviate thinking
- Flexibility in work roles
- Seeks better ways of doing things
- Welcomes innovative and creative ideas
- Members developing professionally.

Wilemon and Thamhain[14] have approached the problem of team strengths and weaknesses from a different viewpoint and have identified the following barriers to project team development:

- Differing outlooks, priorities, interest and judgments of team members
- Role conflicts—ambiguity over who does what
- Project objectives/outcomes not clear
- Dynamic project environment—continual change causes disruption
- Lack of team definition and structure—responsibilities not clear
- Team personnel selection—no input into the selection process
- Poor credibility of the project leader
- Lack of team member commitment
- Communication problems
- Lack of senior management support.

The above reference also discusses a number of suggestions that can be used by project managers for either minimizing or eliminating these barriers to project team development.

Relieving the Team's Anxieties

How does a project manager make team members feel that they are really a part of a team effort? Obviously the team members must be made to feel at home and comfortable, reasonably secure, confident that they have good leadership, comfortable that their career objectives are being met, and that they have a significant role in an important project effort. Project team members will normally feel considerable anxiety concerning their projected roles in the project. The greatest anxiety usually concerns how their individual goals and objectives will fit with those of the project. The challenge to the project manager is to relieve these anxieties. Project team members come to a new team expecting to find immediate answers to such questions as:

- What are we here to do?
- How shall we organize ourselves?
- Who is in charge?

- Who cares about our success?
- How do we solve problems?
- How do we fit in with other groups?
- What benefits do team members get from the team?
- Will I be able to achieve my personal goals while working on this project?
- Will this project help me develop professionally?

Project managers can best relieve these anxieties by clearly spelling out each team member's role in the project effort, and indicating exactly how their career and other goals will be advanced while working on the project.

Building a "Team" Climate

A really effective project team is a highly motivated group of people. However, the achievement of a highly motivated project team doesn't just happen spontaneously; it must be made to happen. It is the project manager's responsibility to ensure that the team is provided with the leadership, resources, tools, support, and the right "team" climate necessary to encourage innovation and a dedicated team effort.

To achieve these goals there are a number of specific actions as well as a management philosophy that project managers can use to help in achieving this "team" climate. In the life cycle of the usual crash project there may be little time for specific actions such as holding social gatherings for the team, or taking team members to lunch. However, there should always be some time to apply a management philosophy of participation, which will encourage a "team" climate. The traits of such a participative manager are:

- Be accessible.
- Be open.
- Be honest.
- Keep promises.
- Do not play politics.
- Practice what you preach.
- Manage by walking.
- Encourage frank discussions.
- Delegate where appropriate.
- Encourage professional development.
- Hold off-site meetings.
- Participate in and hold social gatherings.
- Lunch with key personnel.

Getting people to work together by issuing a directive or by giving orders will not do it. Just going through the steps in a team-building program will not do it either. What is needed is to motivate the team to work together with a dedicated unity of purpose directed toward accomplishing the project goals and objectives. A "team" climate must be achieved where there is a feeling of group membership, and a feeling that "we can do it together." This must be accomplished before going on to the next step—obtaining a group commitment.

Achieving a Group Commitment

Obtaining personal commitments from individual team members is usually relatively simple. A clear and interesting job assignment, with lots of personal contact and discussion, should be sufficient to get most people thoroughly involved and committed. Obtaining a group commitment is quite another matter, primarily because everyone must agree as to what the project wants to achieve. Obtaining a group consensus is difficult because each team member may perceive the project's goals and objectives subtly in very significantly different ways. Even when team members have publicly agreed on project goals and objectives, their individual priorities may differ widely. Some people may hold personal reservations on the practicality or feasibility of portions of the project effort. Differing perceptions of the project tasks may also result in overlapping responsibilities or gaps in the effort. The project manager may not even be aware of these differences in perception unless considerable effort is expended to make the team aware of such problems and to face them as a group effort.

A real group commitment can only be obtained if the team members not only agree on what the project wants to achieve, but also identify with these goals and objectives because they have helped develop them. The project goals and objectives need to be thoroughly discussed and completely understood by everyone, and a real consensus and commitment needs to be obtained from the team if they are to complete the project as planned. Obtaining this group commitment is an essential prerequisite for outstanding project teamwork.

Motivating the Team

A thoroughly committed team will inevitably be a very highly motivated team. However, motivation must be continually nurtured and cultivated or it will wither. Motivation begins with the individual team member who first must be encouraged to participate in the team effort, and then encouraged to be individually innovative and productive. Team building will not be completely effective until the team members are motivated to put in the necessary time and effort.

Perhaps the most effective motivator is the importance of the job or project. Experience has shown that team building is most successful when the project team is faced with a substantial and very important job to be accomplished. The team has a great need to be very effective, and the team members will be challenged to work together. This explains much of the success of various aerospace projects, which provided unlimited challenge and almost mind-boggling goals. The obvious motivational action would be to ensure that everyone on the project team is aware of the great importance of the project to the company, national security, the space effort, etc.

But what of the thousands of projects with somewhat less ambitious goals? Such projects must have been of importance to someone, or the projects would not have been initiated. It may be somewhat difficult for some people to become excited about a new project for the improvement of a dog food. However, the improved product may be essential for the survival of the company, and for the existence of the team members' jobs. Such knowledge can be the best of all possible motivators.

There are a variety of other possible situations and actions that an alert project manager can use as motivators, most of which are discussed in other sections of this monograph, however, the most important are the following:

Present the challenge. Team members will respond positively to an exciting and challenging problem or situation. The challenge of the untrod path and the excitement of the unknown will provide more than enough motivation for most people.

Give regular review and feedback. Experience has shown that team members who believe that they have real and open communication with their project managers are the most motivated and most satisfied with their work.

Use the team reward system. Company benefits and perks are important motivators, but special project rewards such as visibility to top management and recognition for outstanding performance may be even more important to many team members.

Encourage professional development. An excellent "carrot" to motivate professional and technical people is to appeal to their interest in personal development by providing opportunities to write professional papers, attend educational classes and seminars, and to learn new skills. Opportunities for career path guidance can also be provided by the project manager.

Encourage competition. Healthy competition and even a little conflict will provide considerable motivation. Competition has been demonstrated to be a powerful stimulant in motivating people to be more innovative.

Provide a good environment. The project should be known as a good place to work. The environment should be friendly, and the emphasis should be on rewarding people for doing a good job rather than on punishment for substandard work. The project manager should make every effort to ensure that everyone has all of the tools and support necessary to do a superior job.

Building Effective Team Communications

A basic prerequisite for a smoothly functioning project team is that there be effective communication within the team and between the team members and all important outside contacts. Communication does not necessarily take place whenever someone speaks or writes a memo to someone else. There must also be understanding or there is no communication. One of the hazards of project management is the delusion that all communication links are functioning effectively just because people are talking to one another. As indicated by Fulmer, "One of the most common pitfalls of communication is the assumption that because a message was sent a message must have been received."[15]

Most of the responsibility for building and maintaining real communication links falls on the shoulders of the project manager. Recognizing that even though the needs of the project team members will vary widely, there are six possible areas of action that a project manager can use to enhance project communications and team building. Each of the following actions will be discussed separately:

- Be an effective communicator.
- Be a communications expediter.
- Get rid of communication blockers.
- Use a "tight matrix."
- Have a "war room."
- Make your meetings effective.

Effective communications. Most project managers spend approximately 90 percent of their working hours engaged in some form of communication: conferences, meetings, writing memos, reading reports, and talking with team members' top management, customers, clients, subcontractors, suppliers, etc. As least one-half of a project manager's communication time will be with team members, and this time can be a vital portion of the team-building process. It is important that this time be well spent, since it is so essential for effective team building.

Of course, project managers must be good communicators. But this does not mean that they be orators or spellbinders, but it does mean three things:

- They must recognize the importance of the interpersonal communication network within the project team, and encourage, not inhibit, informal communication between team members.
- They must recognize the importance of human relations to the success of communication flow and team building. Effective communication will not be achieved if there is not harmony and trust.
- They must recognize that communication is a two-way street. The project manager does not just give orders; the project team must understand, participate, and agree before teamwork is achieved. Feedback in both directions is necessary for team building and is vital for a continuing team effort.

The communications expediter. Effective project managers function as communication expediters in that they help to bring people together and initiate relationships which become communication links. Part of the job is establishing both formal (reporting and responsibility) and informal communication channels. Effective formal communication channels alone are not sufficient to assure a smooth working team, particularly in a matrix where there is considerable ambiguity concerning who reports to whom. Of much greater importance is the informal communication network within and outside of the project team. Project managers can never be certain that real communication always exists. They can determine where coordination will be essential for project success, however, and they can initiate any necessary dialogue. Sometimes just getting people to talk to each other can be difficult, particularly during the early stages of a project when people do not know each other. However, understanding the necessity for effective communication in team building, project managers must function as communication expediters to make sure that the right people talk to each other.

Communication blockers. Too many innovative ideas are smothered by negative thinking before they are given any chance to prove their worth. It is much easier to think of dozens of reasons why something will not work than to figure out how to make it work. People who are prone to this type of thinking, particularly if they overdo the "devil's advocate" role, will act as communication blockers and seriously impede the process of team building. These people announce their presence by their typical negative responses when something new is suggested. The following types of responses have been termed "idea killers:

- It's been done before.
- It will never work.
- The boss won't like it.
- That's interesting, but ...
- It will never fly.
- It will cost a fortune.
- Let's be realistic.

If there are too many such communication blockers, and their way of thinking cannot be changed, perhaps less troublesome team members should be found.

The tight matrix. This is an organizational option that can be used to improve communications and teamwork in a matrix. The term "tight matrix" refers to a matrix where all of the team members are brought together in one location. Normally, all or most of the team members in a matrix have their offices and do most of their work in their functional departments, and only go to the project office when attending conferences or meetings. Therefore, bringing all of the project personnel together physically to work in the same area can be a drastic action. However, it can also be extremely effective in facilitating better communications and rapid team building. The effectiveness of the tight matrix has been demonstrated by studies indicating that communication decreases rapidly as distance between the two parties increases. The tight matrix effectively prevents dilution of the project effort by decreasing outside distractions and by focusing the efforts of the entire team on the same problems.

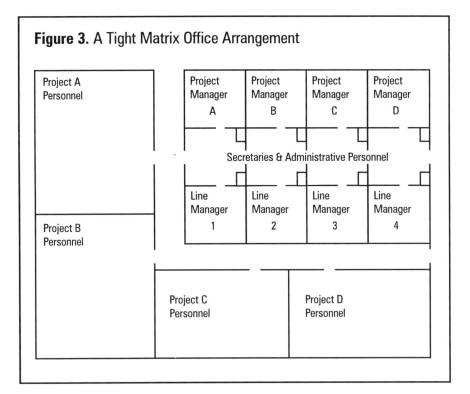

Figure 3. A Tight Matrix Office Arrangement

| Project A Personnel | Project Manager A | Project Manager B | Project Manager C | Project Manager D |

Secretaries & Administrative Personnel

| Line Manager 1 | Line Manager 2 | Line Manager 3 | Line Manager 4 |

Project B Personnel

Project C Personnel

Project D Personnel

Unfortunately, a tight matrix is unworkable for many projects because the team members can work more effectively in their own disciplinary environment. This is particularly true of scientists, engineers, and other specialists who require special facilities and support from their own discipline. It is also difficult, but not impossible, for people working part-time for a project to adapt to a tight matrix. In addition, both line managers and top management may strenuously object to moving people temporarily from their departments. The tight matrix has been used very successfully in construction, product development, public works, and in other similar projects. Having the designers with their drafting boards and computers working next to the manufacturing engineers almost guarantees that communication will occur. Thus, when the product is designed, manufacturing will be able to produce it.

A tight matrix may not be the team-building solution to everyone's problems, but it should be considered when drastic steps are indicated. An office arrangement for a tight matrix as used by a utility company for its construction projects is shown in Figure 3.

The war room. An important consideration useful for the purpose of strengthening project communication and teamwork is having a single location where the project team or any portion of the team can get together for any purpose. This office or conference room has long been referred to by project managers in the aerospace and defense industries as the "war room." Also, referred to as the control room or the project information room, it is a location designated by the project office as the point of contact where all of the members of the project team can meet to discuss their common problems. For very small projects the project manager's office will suffice, but an auditorium may be needed for a very large project.

The "war room" should be a room that is only used by the particular project. Therefore, the room can be used at any time of the day or night by any group of project team members. In addition, the room can be used as a repository for project artifacts, models, records, and almost anything that serves as an indication of project teamwork. Of even more importance, the room can be used for maintaining up-to-the-minute wall charts of project technical performance, schedules, and cost status. Input-output charts can thus be immediately available for use by the project manager or by any team member. No one can fall back on the excuse that they did not know what was going on.

Effective meetings. The most important project communication activity is its meetings. A meeting could be defined as an occasion when three or more people get together, formally or informally. However, the most important project meetings are those convened for a specific purpose, whether they be impromptu or regularly scheduled. Because of their characteristic team effort, most projects have many more meetings in a week than would line managers with equivalent-sized departments. Meetings are almost the only way that project managers can efficiently and effectively reach every member of a project team. It is possible to reduce the number of meetings, but only by greatly increasing the need for time-consuming and inefficient one-on-one discussions. As projects become larger, the difficulty involved in making individual contacts increases dramatically. Most project managers agree that a cohesive team effort can only be built and maintained by means of meetings, meetings, and more meetings.

Meetings are essential for team building because they serve to draw a group of diverse people together for a common purpose. Most of the important objectives of team efforts are the result of meetings—group decision-making, group problem-solving, and achieving a group consensus. Much of the project manager's two-way communication with the project team must, of necessity, occur at meetings. Such meetings must accomplish their purpose of providing truly effective communication if team building is to succeed.

Most organizations have meetings which are regarded only as a good time to take a nap. Poorly conducted meetings only dampen inspiration and enthusiasm, and often serve only as a forum for furthering the personal and organizational aspirations of the more aggressive participants rather than furthering group goals. Such meetings are regarded as a chore rather than looked forward to as an opportunity to contribute to project progress.

The challenge to the project manager is to ensure that all meetings are properly conducted, and that they hold the attention and interest of all participants. Many authorities have published "do's and don'ts" for conducting effective meetings. These rules can be summarized in the following guidelines, which are most applicable to the needs of project managers:

- *Establish a meeting policy.* The project procedures guide should establish the way in which all meetings will be conducted.
- *Only call a meeting if there is a real need.* Meetings should only be held to solve problems, to make group decisions, to exchange information, to explain policy or procedure changes, or enhance team building.
- *Make the purpose of the meeting very clear.* Every meeting must have a purpose and stated objectives which must be made clear to the project team.
- *Prepare an agenda.* An agenda must be carefully thought out and organized, even if the meeting is an urgent "fire drill" to make an instant decision. If possible an agenda should be distributed a day or more before the meeting to permit team members to prepare for it. An agenda is essential as a communication tool because it keeps the meeting on the subject and forces the project manager to thoroughly prepare for the meeting.
- *Follow the agenda.* Start the meeting on time, follow the agenda only as rigorously as needed, and end the meeting on time.
- *Encourage participation.* Without extensive team participation, team involvement and team building will be nonexistent. An excellent way to start a project meeting is to obtain agreement on the agenda. It provides still another way to obtain team member involvement and commitment.
- *Team building.* Use all meetings as part of a team building program. In addition to team-member involvement, every meeting should be used as a forum for team members to receive recognition for their important contributions to the project effort.
- *Issue minutes.* It is important to make a formal record of all decisions made, action items discussed, task assignments made, and commitments obtained during the meeting. Minutes should be brief, to the point, and should be issued the day after a meeting.
- *Follow-up.* Make sure that the meeting is not a waste of time. Follow-up on all task assignments and action items coming out of the meeting.

Developing Team Problem-Solving Capabilities

Problem-solving capabilities involve the same two components of the thinking process that constitute any intellectual effort—analytical ability and innovative or creative ability. People with analytical skills are relatively easy to find. Most people delight in taking problems apart and diagnosing the causes of a problem. However, finding people who can conceive innovative and imaginative solutions to problems is quite another matter. Truly creative people are rare indeed, and since IQ is primarily a measure of analytical ability, it is difficult to really be sure that a person is creative.

A large, complex project must be carried out by a multidisciplinary team since the system under development will cross many disciplinary boundaries. Dependence upon a single individual "genius" to provide most of a team's innovative spark may result in suboptimized problem solutions. Inevitably, specialists will try to solve every problem within the context of their own particular discipline. Therefore, since most project problems and most of the problem solutions are multidisciplinary, they must be solved by a group or team effort.

However, there is considerable controversy regarding whether groups can really be innovative, or whether innovation is primarily a trait of the individual. The argument is that a true imaginative leap into the unknown can only be made by an individual; therefore, the ability of groups to arrive at creative solutions to problems has been severely questioned. For instance, Janis[16] criticized what he termed "groupthink," and demonstrated that there are strong pressures within a group to conform to group norms at the expense of critical and innovative thinking. "Powerful social pressures are brought to bear by the members of a cohesive group whenever a dissident begins to voice his objections to a group consensus."[17] It is vital that a project manager be alert to the possibility that "groupthink" can occur, and that a team can become too cohesive and too amiable. As long as there are "devil's advocates," critical evaluators, and an occasional infusion of "new blood," groupthink can be controlled.

Since projects by definition are team efforts, project managers have little choice but to concentrate on obtaining group creativity. Fortunately, an effective project team is usually an innovative team if the team climate, its motivation, and its leadership are all outstanding. However, there are a number of things that project managers can do to provide an innovative climate. Certainly the project manager can encourage team discussion of different viewpoints, and bring out into the open disagreements, objections, and doubts. The synergism resulting from a team effort, and the cross-fertilization of ideas from discipline to discipline is what project teamwork is all about. The project manager can best serve as a catalyst to stimulate this cross-fertilization.

Project teamwork has a major advantage over individual effort in that there are as many points of view and as many possible sparks for new ideas as there are people on the team. One never knows from whom the key idea will come which will lead to a problem solution. In addition, the other team members, through discussion and constructive criticism, will have a much greater chance of synergistically building on a tentative or even on an impractical idea to make it a winner.

Providing an Effective Team Reward System

People are motivated in direct proportion to the value which they feel is being placed upon them; and the only demonstrated indication of this value is the rewards given them. Money is by far the most important aspect of any reward system, but if there are wide ranges in the pay structure it can actually be a demotivator. If team members feel that they are not being paid as well as their counterparts in other organizations, or if they feel that certain "stars" are overpaid, then team building may be difficult. Project teams must be staffed by very effective people, which implies that they be well paid. It is well to remember the old cliché—"If you pay peanuts you get monkeys."

Money, however, is not the only effective reward. There are a number of other more subtle "perks" that can be put into the total team-reward package. The list could be endless, but the following types of rewards are most often seen as significant components of a reward system:
- Private office
- Office with a carpet
- Office with a door that can be closed
- Use of a company car
- Assignment of a secretary
- Freedom from time clocks and timecards
- Assigned parking space
- Company-provided medical examinations
- After-hours educational reimbursement
- Attendance at in-house training sessions
- Stock purchase options
- Holidays and vacation benefits
- Health insurance.

Some of these benefits are a part of a company's standard benefit plan; others can, in some cases, be implemented or requested by the project manager.

The use of cash incentives to reward outstanding individual performance is very desirable, but should be used only when there is a team consensus that it is merited. Team incentive rewards are even more effective motivators. However, few organizations have the procedures or the special discretionary funds set aside to implement such incentive plans. Therefore public recognition and outstanding merit reviews may be the only routes open to the project manager. A good rule for project managers is to give the team all of the glory possible during the life cycle of the project; there may be little left at the end.

There may be lots of players on a project team, but there are essentially only two major roles—the team leadership role and the team member role. Each of these roles presents particular problems that may cause serious roadblocks to team building.

Project Team Roles

The Leadership Role

There is no question that the primary role of the project manager is to provide effective leadership to the project team. But questions arise as to the most effective way to provide this leadership so as to obtain the best teamwork.

What is leadership? Is leadership different from management? Most authorities agree that the two words have somewhat different connotations. Slevin[18] believes that there should be no distinction between them because they both involve modifying other person's behavior. Everyone knows that management is "getting things done through other people," but leadership sometimes implies considerably more.[19] Being a good manager as recognized by modern practice does not necessarily mean that one is a leader. Today's hierarchies are full of managers who follow all of the procedures and regulations, and carefully do not rock the boat. "Such employees lead only in the sense that the carved wooden figurehead leads the ship."[20] A leader is someone that people will follow willingly because they perceive that he or she can provide them a means of achieving their own desires, wants, and needs. A good leader influences by example, and by providing a role model for the team members. Since a major goal of team building is to develop the leadership role, a great deal of effort should go into gaining enthusiastic support and trust of the team. In other words, team trust and leadership do not come automatically with the job assignment as project manager. They must be earned as part of the team-building process.

Leadership is easy to define, but it is very difficult to characterize the traits of leadership. To quote Robert Townsend: "How do you spot a leader? They come in all ages, shapes, sizes, and conditions. Some are poor administrators, some are not overly bright. One clue: since most people per se are mediocre, the true leader can be recognized because, somehow or other, his people consistently turn in superior performances."[21] Probably even more relevant is the following bit of project management folklore: "Leadership is getting people to do things for you when they don't work for you?"

Leadership Style

Project managers have a choice in terms of the specific leadership style they can employ. Many managers have a preferred style, while others fit their style to the leadership situation. Leadership styles have been described in terms of the four following possible extremes of the leadership role:

- *Autocratic.* Such managers solicit little or no information input from their group and make the managerial decision solely by themselves.

- *Consultive autocrat.* In this managerial style intensive information input is solicited from the members, but such formal leaders keep all substantive decision-making authority to themselves.
- *Consensus manager.* Purely consensual managers throw open the problem to the group for discussion (information input) and simultaneously allow or encourage the entire group to make the relevant decision.
- *Shareholder manager.* This position is literally poor management. Little or no information input and exchange takes place within the group context, while the group itself is provided ultimate authority for the final decision.

Slevin[22] indicates that "the key to successful leadership is knowing what your dominant style is and being able to modify that style depending upon the contingencies of the various leadership situations that you face." He has also developed a leadership model and a diagnostic tool (the Jerrell/Slevin Management Instrument) intended to provide managers with feedback on their management style.[23]

Shared Leadership

The concept of shared leadership is a useful way for project managers to view their job, if they are going to be really successful in team building. Shared leadership is more than just participatory management; it involves actually letting the project team take over as much of the leadership role as they will accept. The project manager must actually let go of some of his or her authority, and by sharing it with the project team, the project manager becomes more of a team member and the team members assume more of the leadership role. This increases the willingness of the team to participate in problem-solving and decision-making and to accept responsibility for the success or failure of the project. Effective project managers realize that shared leadership will take some of the load off their backs, and will bring about a team commitment and a feeling of ownership. In other words, it is the shortest route to true teamwork. The modern view of management has changed significantly in recent years.

The modern manager has shifted from dealing with problems on a one-on-one basis to solving more problems collectively, involving everyone who has a contribution to make in either solving a problem or implementing actions. In this context, the manager is a coach, a facilitator, a developer, a team builder.[24] Perhaps the best analogy is that of the project manager to a coach. The success of a football team will depend on more than just obtaining the 11 best players in the country. Their individual skills will not be enough unless the players work together well as a team. The coach can tell the team exactly what they must do, but unless there is shared leadership with the players, they are unlikely to be winners.

Leadership Challenges

Occasionally project managers will find that there will be challenges to their leadership role, particularly during the early stages of a project. If the team or some of its members do not feel that the project manager is qualified either as a technical leader or as a manager, there may be covert challenges to his or her leadership. For instance, highly skilled technical specialists may question a project manager's credibility in daring to presume to lead them in what they perceive to be purely a technical problem. Such a challenge is usually temporary, but can significantly retard the team-building process. The management performance of a project manager will also be closely observed by the project team. The first of the many inevitable conflict situations can make or break a new project manager. If the situation is not well handled, the project manager's leadership will be seriously weakened.

Conflict Management in the Team

The high-pressure project environment is conducive to the production of intense conflict. Therefore, a major responsibility of the project manager is to be continually alert for possible conflict situations, and to either avoid or resolve them. A rather minor conflict can almost instantly destroy a team spirit that has taken months to develop. Competition within a project team is inevitable, and cannot be eliminated even if it was thought to be desirable. Rather, competition should be regarded as a desirable asset to an effective team, and should be encouraged. Competition is essential because it produces the energy and the incentives necessary to stimulate innovation and creativity. A competitive spirit within a project team brings out the best individual efforts, and is in fact the very life-blood of a superior team effort. The project manager must walk a fine line in encouraging healthy team competition, while at the same time trying to ensure that it does not result in destructive conflict.

Team Conflict Avoidance

Conflict within a project team can best be avoided by careful planning so as to side step the problem before it becomes a problem. Generally there will be two types of possible project team problems—personality clashes (people problems), and disagreements over some aspect of the project. It is almost impossible to forecast what kind of chemistry will develop between any two people, but a little planning will help to team up the most compatible people. The obviously abrasive or obnoxious people can be eliminated or put where they can do the least harm, and the eccentric people can be teamed up with the most understanding.

There are innumerable aspects of the project work effect that can bring about internal disagreements and lead to conflict, such as technical options, who should do what, and who has the greatest need for equipment or facilities. Such potential conflict situations can usually be avoided if the project manager takes the following precautions, which should be a part of normal team building:

- Be certain that the project team members are informed exactly where the project is headed, and that they clearly understand the project goals and objectives.
- Carefully plan the effort so that very clear task assignments can be made without ambiguity or overlapping responsibilities.
- Make work assignments as interesting and challenging as possible, and provide a stimulating work environment.
- Keep team members completely informed of all key decisions, changes in project goals or objectives, and changes in schedules or budgets.
- Get top management involved so that the project team knows that the entire organization is committed to and supports the project.

In other words—keep the communication links working and conflict will be minimal.

Dealing With Outside Conflict

The temporary nature of projects and the relatively low power level of many project managers make conflict inevitable. Most troublesome, particularly in a matrix, is the necessity for obtaining personnel and other types of support from functional managers' organizations. Functional managers are often reluctant to deal with "body snatchers," as they often view the project managers. The most frequent contacts with the world outside the project are made by the project manager, and many of these contacts will be with functional managers. The functional managers may take a dim view of the project managers' desire to pick their own people, and functional managers are not always particularly sympathetic to project urgency.

Thamhain and Wilemon[25] studied seven categories of conflict issues that can arise in a project environment, and they observed that the greatest intensity of conflict was definitely between project managers and functional departments. They found that schedules, project priorities, and manpower resources caused 50 percent of all conflict in the seven categories, but that conflict existed in all seven areas in the following rank order:

- Conflict over schedules
- Conflict over project priorities
- Conflict over manpower resources
- Conflict over technical opinions
- Conflict over administrative procedure
- Conflict over cost objectives
- Personality conflict.

Conflict can also occur between project team members and people outside the project. Individual disagreements with support personnel outside the project can also be disastrous to project teamwork. The most effective precaution is to avoid adversarial relationships with any group outside the project. As a "team spirit" develops, it is inevitable that a "we versus them" attitude builds up in the team. A little of this attitude is necessary for team building, but it can easily turn to conflict. The customer, top management, line management, or any other portion of the outside organization becomes "them" or "they"— the enemy. It then becomes too easy to blame "them" for every problem that arises, resulting in further conflict.

Conflict Resolution

Much of a project manager's success in team building and in managing a project often depends on his or her ability to cope with conflict. Project managers can use any conflict resolution style which works for them, but as Thamhain and Wilemon[26] have shown, some styles work better than others. Social science researchers[27, 28, 29] have categorized five distinct modes of conflict resolution:

- *Withdrawal*—retreating from an actual or potential conflict situation.
- *Smoothing*—emphasizing use of agreement rather than emphasizing differences of opinion.
- *Compromising*—searching for solutions which bring some degree of satisfaction to both conflicting parties.
- *Forcing*—pushing one's viewpoint at the potential expense of another.
- *Problem-solving*—treating conflict as a problem to be solved by examining the alternatives.

Withdrawal is seldom a good solution to a project manager's problems. It never solves anything, but is often useful because it may provide a cooling off period during which a better solution may be found. Smoothing allows the work to go on and can soothe ruffled feelings and defuse conflict; however, it seldom solves anything. Both withdrawal and smoothing are only temporary solutions to problems. Permanent solutions to problems can be reached only by using compromising, forcing, or problem solving.

A project manager's style of conflict resolution can have far-reaching effects on team building and on project success, so care should be taken to use an appropriate style. For instance, a research study suggests that "a forcing and withdrawal mode appears to increase conflict with functional support departments and assigned personnel while confrontation, compromise and smoothing tend to reduce conflict."

What Happens When the Problem is the Project Manager?

Unfortunately, sometimes the problem blocking the attainment of team building and effective teamwork turns out to be the project manager. The project manager is not just the leader but also a key member of the team. Therefore, in this crucial dual role it is rather easy for some personal trait or management style to rub someone the wrong way. Almost any number or personal character of behavioral traits may endanger the team-building process. The project manager may be perceived by the team to be:

- Overbearing
- Uncooperative
- Cold and unapproachable
- Timid and reserved
- Naive
- Afraid to take action
- Untruthful
- Untrustworthy
- Manipulative
- Overly critical
- Vindictive
- Closed minded
- Technically incompetent
- Lacking management skills
- Unprofessional
- Overly concerned with buttering up top management
- Paternalistic or willing to show unwarranted favoritism.

The project manager's management and leadership style may also be a block to team building. The project manager may lean a little too far toward authoritarianism, and be prone to "laying down the law." It is also very easy to go too far in the direction of participative management. In attempting to gain the good will and cooperation of the team, a project manager may be perceived as a weak manager and lose the control and respect of the project team.

Whether any of these traits or behavior patterns are real or not does not really make any difference as long as they are the perceptions of the project team. Actually, the perceptions may be only an indication that the project manager is trying too hard. These perceptions are particularly troublesome if the project manager does not realize that he or she is the problem. Team members are usually quite unwilling to make the project manager aware of the problem for fear of a negative reaction.

The Team Member Role

The only thing that a newly appointed project manager can count on is that the project team will consist of almost every conceivable type of individual. Their personalities and their effects on other people will be entirely different from person to person. Each will have their own distinctive ways of making an impact on project communications and decision making. In general, however, team member roles will be either constructive or destructive in terms of their contributions to the project team effort.

Figure 4. Constructive Team Roles

- *Initiators*—"Let's do this ..."
- *Information seekers*—"Don't we have some better information?"
- *Information givers*—"My experience is ..."
- *Encouragers*—"That was of great help ..."
- *Clarifiers*—"I believe that we are saying ..."
- *Harmonizers*—"I believe that we are all saying the same thing."
- *Summarizers*—"I feel that we can now come to an agreement on this."
- *Gatekeeper*—Helps others participate: "We haven't heard from the back of the room."

People who accept constructive role functions are highly valued, and should be encouraged. They are particularly useful in meetings to make problem-solving and decision-making truly effective. Figure 4 identifies constructive behavioral functions or roles that are possible in a project team. Figure 5 also identifies a variety of possible destructive roles that can be found in a project team.

Many people function in more than one of these roles at different times, while others may exhibit only a single behavior. Most constructive and destructive roles will be found in most project teams, although fortunately, most people are constructive. The effective project manager must be capable of dealing with both types of behavior, either using them or, in the case of excessively destructive roles, getting rid of them. Most destructive behavior, if allowed to continue, could seriously endanger a team-building effort. Do not overlook the role of devil's advocate. It can be an invaluable role in project problem solving if it is not too negative, and does not obstruct team building and the project effort.

Summary

Team building can well be the most important aspect of the project manager's job. There is no way that today's complex, high-performance, multidisciplinary projects can succeed if they do not have outstanding teamwork. Teamwork will not come automatically, but rather must be developed, principally through the team-building efforts of the project manager. A team-building effort should be started as early in the life of a project as possible, and should be continued until project termination.

The team-building process must be a simple, practical method of achieving a feeling of team membership and a unified team spirit. This process must not

Figure 5. Destructive Team Roles

- *The aggressor*—Criticizes and deflates status of others.
- *The blocker*—Rejects the views of others.
- *The withdrawer*—Holds back and will not participate.
- *Recognition seeker*—Seeks attention by monopolizing discussions.
- *Topic jumper*—Continually changes subject.
- *Dominator*—Tries to take over discussion.
- *Devil's advocate*—Brings up alternative viewpoints. Can be positive or very negative.

interfere with the project effort, or cause schedule or budgets to slip; therefore, the process must be integrated into the everyday activities of the project. Team building can be made an important part of almost all project activities, particularly meetings and informal conferences. The project manager must assume the role of orchestrating the team-building process. Calling in a consultant can be a great help, but nothing will work more effectively than integrating team building into the project effort. No one can do this as well as the project manager who has the ultimate responsibility for the success of the project.

Endnotes

1. Mike Woodcock and Dave Francis, *Organization Development Through Teambuilding*, New York: John Wiley and Sons (Halsted Press), 1981, p. 3.

2. Ibid.

3. A.J. Reilly and J.E. Jones, "Team Building," *The 1974 Annual Handbook for Group Facilitators*, San Diego, Calif.: University Associates, 1974, p. 227.

4. H.B. Karp, "Team Building From a Gestalt Perspective," *The 1980 Annual Handbook for Group Facilitators*, San Diego, Calif.: University Associates, 1980, p. 157.

5. Douglas McGregor, *The Human Side of Enterprise*, New York: McGraw-Hill, 1960, p. 228.

6. Dave Francis and Don Young, *Improving Work Groups: A Practical Manual for Team Building*, La Jolla, Calif.: University Associates, 1979.

7. David L. Wilemon and Hans J. Thamhain, "Team Building in Project Management," *Proceedings of the Eleventh Annual Seminar Symposium*, Drexel Hill, Penn.: Project Management Institute, 1979, pp. 373–380.

8. Mike Woodcock, *Team Development Manual*, New York: John Wiley & Sons (Halsted Press), 1979, p. 7.

9. David L. Wilemon and Hans J. Thamhain, "A Model for Developing High Performance Project Teams." *Proceedings of the Fifteenth Annual Seminar/Symposium*, Drexel Hill, Penn.: Project Management Institute, 1983, p. III–H–1.

10. Frank A. Stickney and William H. Johnson, "Communication: The Key to Integration," *Proceedings of the Twelfth Annual Seminar/Symposium*, Drexel Hill, Penn.: Project Management Institute, 1980, p. I–A–1.

11. Wilemon and Thamhain, 1979, *Proceedings*, PMI.

12. Edgar H. Schein, *Process Consultation: Its Role in Organizational Development*, Reading, Mass.: Addison-Wesley, 1969.

13. Woodcock, pp. 22–28.

14. Wilemon and Thamhain, 1979, *Proceedings*, PMI.

15. Robert M. Fulmer, *The New Management*, New York: Macmillan, 1974, p. 299.

16. Irving L. Janis, "Groupthink," *Psychology Today*, November 1971.

17. Ibid.

18. Dennis P. Slevin, "Leadership and the Project Manager," in *Project Management Handbook*, Edited by Cleland and King, New York: Van Nostrand Reinhold, 1983, pp. 567–580

19. Harold Koontz and Cyril O'Donnell, *Management: A Systems and Contingency Analysis of Managerial Functions*, New York: McGraw-Hill, 1976, p. 587.

20. Laurence J. Peter and Raymond Hull, *The Peter Principle*, New York: William Morrow and Co., 1969, p. 54.

21. Robert Townsend, *Farther Up the Organization*, New York: Alfred A. Knopf, 1984, p. 123.

22. Slevin, p. 574.

23. Thomas V. Bonoma and Dennis P. Slevin, *Executive Survival Manual*, Belmont, Calif.: Wadsworth, 1978.

24. William G. Dyer, *Team Building: Issues and Alternatives*, Reading, Mass.: Addison-Wesley, 1978, p. xi.

25. Hans J. Thamhain and David L. Wilemon, "Conflict Management in Project-Oriented Work Environments," *Proceedings of the Sixth Annual Seminar/Symposium*, Drexel Hill, Penn.: Project Management Institute, 1974, p. 87.

28. Ibid.

27. P.R. Lawrence and J.W. Lorsch, *Organization and Environment*, Boston, Mass.: Harvard Business School, 1967.

28. R.R. Blake and J.S. Mouton, *The Managerial Grid*, Houston, Texas: Gulf Publishing, 1964.

29. Thamhain and Wilemon, p. 89.

References

Benningson, Lawrence. "The Team Approach to Project Management." *Management Review*, January 1972, pp. 48–52.

Bonama, Thomas V., and Dennis P. Slevin. *Executive Survival Manual*. Belmont, Calif.: Wadsworth, 1978.

Dyer, William G. *Team Building: Issues and Alternatives*. Reading, Mass.: Addison-Wesley, 1978.

Francis, Dave, and Don Young. *Improving Work Groups: A Practical Manual for Team Building*. La Jolla, Calif.: University Associates, 1979.

Fulmer, Robert M. *The New Management*. New York: Macmillan, 1974, p. 299.

Janis, Irving L. "Groupthink." *Psychology Today*, November 1971.

Karp, H.B. "Team Building From a Gestalt Perspective." *The 1980 Annual Handbook for Group Facilitators*. San Diego, Calif.: University Associates, 1980.

Koontz, Harold, & Cyril O'Donnell. *Management: A Systems and Contingency Analysis of Managerial Functions.* New York: McGraw-Hill, 1976, p. 587.

Lawrence, P.R., and J.W. Lorsch. *Organization and Environment.* Boston, Mass.: Harvard Business School, 1967.

Mahoney, Francis X. "Team Development." Amacom, *Personnel* Series of articles in September–October 1981 to July–August 1982 series.

McGregor, Douglas. *The Human Side of Enterprise,* New York: McGraw-Hill, 1960, p. 228.

Merry, Uri, and Melvin E. Allerhand. *Developing Teams and Organizations.* Reading, Mass.: Addison-Wesley, 1977.

Morton, David H. "Project Manager, Catalyst to Constant Change: A Behavioral Analysis." *Project Management Quarterly,* 6 (1), March 1975, pp. 22–23.

Peter, Laurence J., and Raymone Hull. *The Peter Principle.* New York: William Morrow and Company, 1969, p. 54.

Reilly, A.J., and J.E. Jones. "Team Building." *The 1974 Annual Handbook for Group Facilitators* San Diego, Calif.: University Associates, 1974.

Rogers, Lloyd A. "Guidelines for Project Management Teams." *Industrial Engineering,* Vol. 12, December 1974, pp. 12–19.

Schein, Edgar H. *Process Consultation: Its Role in Organizational Development.* Reading, Mass.: Addison-Wesley, 1969.

Slevin, Dennis P. "Leadership and the Project Manager." *Project Management Handbook.* Edited by Cleland and King, New York: Van Nostrand Reinhold, 1983.

Solomon, Lawrence N. "Team Development: A Training Approach." *The 1977 Annual Handbook for Group Facilitators.* San Diego, Calif.: University Associates. 1977, pp. 181–193.

Stickney, Frank A., and William H. Johnson. "Communication: The Key to Integration." *Proceedings of the Twelfth Annual Seminar/Symposium.* Drexel Hill, Penn.: Project Management Institute, 1980, p. I–A, 1–13.

Thamhain, Hans J., and David L. Wilemon. "Conflict Management in Project-Oriented Work Environments." *Proceedings of the Sixth Annual Seminar/Symposium.* Drexel Hill, Penn.: Project Management Institute, 1964, pp. 85–96.

Townsend, Robert. *Further Up the Organization.* New York: Alfred A. Knopf, 1984.

Wilemon, David L. "Project Management and Its Conflicts: A View from Apollo." *Chemical Technology,* September 1972, pp. 527–534.

Wilemon, David L., and Bruce N. Baker. "Some Major Research Findings Regarding the Human Element in Project Management." *Project Management Handbook.* Edited by Cleland and King. New York: Van Nostrand Reinhold Co., 1983, pp. 623–641

Wilemon, David L., and Hans J. Thamhain. "Team Building in Project Management." *Proceedings of the Eleventh Annual Seminar/Symposium.* Drexel Hill, Penn.: Project Management Institute, 1979, pp. 373–380.

Wilemon, David L., and Hans J. Thamhain. "A Model For Developing High Performance Project Teams." *Proceedings of the Fifteenth Annual Seminar/Symposium.* Drexel Hill, Penn.: Project Management Institute, 1983, pp. III-H. 1–12.

Woodcock, Mike. *Team Development Manual.* New York: John Wiley & Sons (Halsted Press), 1979.

Woodcock, Mike and Dave Francis. *Unblocking Your Organization.* La Jolla, Calif.: University Associates, 1978.

Woodcock, Mike, and Dave Francis. *Organization Development Through Teambuilding.* New York: John Wiley & Sons (Halsted Press), 1981.

Conflict Management for Project Managers

John R. Adams
and
Nicki S. Kirchof

Conflict in Organizations

One of the primary, underlying reasons conflict exists in organizations today is the tremendous amount of change that has occurred in the workplace in recent years. In order to survive in today's environment, organizations need to adapt rapidly to change. "The Industrial Revolution was characterized by the development of the factory system of production,"[1] which led to the division of labor and our modern, large-scale bureaucracy. Production systems were established to produce goods in the "most efficient" manner, and a change in that system was allowed only after extensive testing proved that the new method provided important and measurable improvements in efficiency. In this environment, change occurred very slowly. Organizations were highly structured and roles were clearly defined. In the past 30 years, however, there has been a revolution in popular concepts of organization which has led to the development of new organizational structures. This revolution has occurred primarily as a response to a rapidly changing environment which demanded dynamic organizations that could adapt to change. Some factors that have led to this "dynamic" environment are technological advances, new concepts of education, increased leisure time, and major societal concerns over environmental and energy issues.[2] Because of automation and other technological changes, new types of managerial occupations have developed along with changes in supervisor/subordinate relationships (Ritzer, 1977). The revolution in education has led to an abundance of educated people and positive implications for the professionals, but negative implications for the semi-skilled worker. Increased leisure time is an outgrowth of technological advances and the increase in the percentage of educated people. These changes lead to conflict as people disagree on how organizations should adapt and as they see the results of that adaptation benefiting or hurting their status and prospects.

Another basic cause of conflict, which stems from the change that now seems to constantly surround organizations, is the incongruence of goals and objectives of the organization employees. Typically, the organization's goals and objectives are formulated by top management along with the purposes, values, and missions pursued by the organization. Employees have to abide by these goals and objectives to remain loyal to and employed by the firm. However, the firm's goals and objectives may differ markedly from the individual employee's personal goals and objectives, a situation which can cause extensive conflicts. Fifty years ago, the classical management organization, as shown in Figure 1, was found to be satisfactory for control of the organization's activities.[3] Conflicts were at a minimum, since employees were able to set and pursue long-range objectives consistent with those of the organization.[4]

The increased rate of change demanded a more dynamic organization. Projects and project teams were developed to deal with, manage, and create change. The goals of individuals and organizations became even more incongruent as

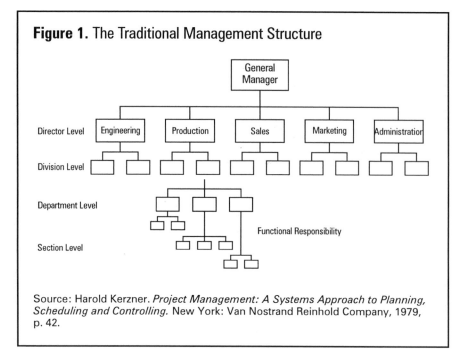

Figure 1. The Traditional Management Structure

Director Level — Engineering | Production | Sales | Marketing | Administration

Division Level

Department Level

Section Level

Functional Responsibility

Source: Harold Kerzner. *Project Management: A Systems Approach to Planning, Scheduling and Controlling.* New York: Van Nostrand Reinhold Company, 1979, p. 42.

the projectized organizational structure evolved (Figure 2). The organization structure became even more complex. Project managers and functional managers competed for authority. "Because the individual performing the work is now caught in a web of authority relationships, additional conflicts came about because functional managers were forced to share their authority with the project manager."[5] Therefore, inconsistent goals between supervisors and subordinates, as well as between individuals and organizations, existed in the projectized environment also, but for different reasons than those of the traditional organization.

These factors of change and incongruent goals evident in the individual/organization and the supervisor/subordinate relationships found within the project lead to high levels of conflict. Thus, the project organization is a major center of conflict. As Butler states:

> ... the conflict specifically associated with project management may be classified into two broad, partly overlapping categories: (a) conflict associated with change; and (b) conflict associated with the concentration of professionals of diverse disciplines in a more or less autonomous group effort which has limited life.[6]

Therefore, conflict readily exists in a traditional organization and is even more evident in projects. Conflict is inevitable in organizations, "... because they have

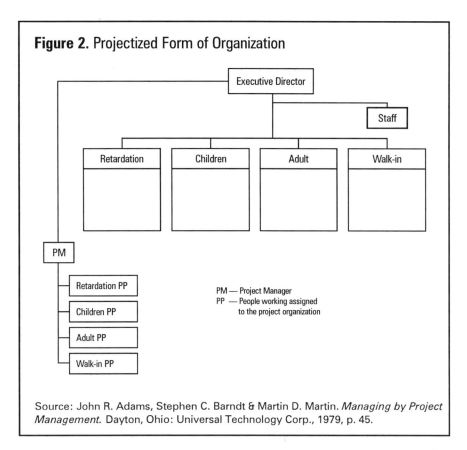

Figure 2. Projectized Form of Organization

Executive Director

Staff

Retardation | Children | Adult | Walk-in

PM

Retardation PP

Children PP

Adult PP

Walk-in PP

PM — Project Manager
PP — People working assigned
to the project organization

Source: John R. Adams, Stephen C. Barndt & Martin D. Martin. *Managing by Project Management.* Dayton, Ohio: Universal Technology Corp., 1979, p. 45.

limited means with which to satisfy the divergent interests of their various publics."[7] Conflict needs to be effectively managed, especially in a project environment, because of the imminent time, cost, and performance constraints imposed on the project effort. The primary responsibility for conflict management in the project lies with the project manager. If the project is to be successful, the project manager must cope with conflict and develop profitable resolutions.

Conflict management is a critical issue for the project manager, for uncontrolled conflict can literally tear the project apart. The purpose of this monograph is to provide the theoretical and practical understanding of conflict and its management needed to enable the project manager to successfully deal with the project's conflict problems.

Figure 3. What is Conflict?

Traditional View	Contemporary View
• Caused by Trouble-Makers • Bad • Should be Avoided • Must be Suppressed	• Inevitable between Humans • Often Beneficial • Natural Result of Change • Can and Should be Managed

Theory of Conflict Management

Conflict is generally defined as "a clash between hostile or opposing elements or ideas."[8] As applied to human behavior it is a disagreement between individuals, which can vary from a mild disagreement to a win/lose, emotion-packed confrontation. There are two basic, but opposing, views of conflict, the traditional and the modern (see Figure 3). The traditional view sees conflict as being primarily negative. In this view, conflict is caused by troublemakers; it is bad; and it should be avoided. The manager who views conflict in this way avoids admitting that it exists, keeps it under cover, and tries to suppress it. The contemporary view sees conflict in a more positive light. According to this view, conflict is inevitable. It is a natural result of change and is frequently beneficial to the manager if properly managed. In particular, an atmosphere of tension, and hence conflict, is essential in any organization committed to developing or working with new ideas, for innovation is simply the process of bringing together differing ideas and perspectives into a new and different synthesis. This latter view is much more realistic in modern organizations. In today's environment, conflict is inevitable because of the various competing unit objectives, personal goals, uses for resources, and divergent viewpoints that exist and must be integrated toward the organization's objectives. It is how the individual manager views and deals with conflict that makes it constructive or destructive for the organization. From the authors' perspective, the primary aim is to manage conflict constructively to achieve the organization's goals. In order to do this, it is necessary to understand the conditions leading to conflict, the potential results of conflict, and the various methods of dealing with conflict in an organizational setting.

In his book, *Interpersonal Conflict Resolution*, Alan C. Filley develops nine conditions which predispose an organization toward conflict (see Table 1).[9]

These antecedent conditions for conflict do not exist separately in any organization. It is the extent to which they exist in combination that creates the conditions for conflict. All of them may exist within a single organization at one time. As stated earlier, conflict is a disagreement among individuals. These antecedent conditions simply set the stage for personal disagreement.

The first antecedent condition is called "ambiguous jurisdictions." This situation occurs when two or more parties have related responsibilities, but their work boundaries and role definitions are unclear. This type of occurrence can be found frequently in both the projectized and the matrix organizational structures because both use the "two-boss concept." "Conflict of interest," the second condition leading to conflict, exists when two or more parties want to achieve different or inconsistent goals and desires relative to each other from their association with the organization. For example, the engineer may wish to build his or her reputation by association with a unique and advanced design, while the manager may be more concerned with completing the job on schedule and at low cost using a standard design. "Communication barriers" is the third condition of conflict. Communication difficulties create misunderstandings and inhibit their resolution by blocking efforts to explain the needs, viewpoints, and actions of those involved in the organization. When there is a "dependence on one party," there tends to be a situation of conflict because one person is dependent on the other to provide needed resources. "Differentiation in organization" exists when different sub-units of the organization are responsible for different tasks. This exists in all organizations. However, in modern organizations dealing with today's complex technologies, there tends to be large numbers of both horizontal and vertical divisions of tasks, creating many specialized groups with their own languages, acronyms, goals, and perspectives. "Association of the parties" is the sixth condition leading to conflict. When people *must* associate together and make joint decisions, conflicts can occur. This situation is especially prevalent when different technical groups have to work together with a variety of management groups. In this case, there may be little of the common ground needed for agreement found in the association. The "need for consensus" follows closely "association of the parties" as a condition leading to conflict. These two conditions are very similar in that, again, people *must* work together. But, when a need for consensus exists, people *must* willingly agree among themselves. There is no decision-maker available, able, or willing to select among several alternatives and enforce the selected solution. When several people from different backgrounds, having different goals, must freely agree on a course of action, the conflict generated can be extremely protracted and difficult to manage. The eighth condition leading to conflict is called "behavior regulations." When the individual's behavior must be regulated closely, as in situations involving high levels of safety and security concerns, high levels of conflict frequently exist as individuals resist the tight boundaries placed on their actions. Their views of what is necessary may differ markedly from that of the organization, and the regulation of activities may inhibit the ease of accomplishing work. As a result, high levels of frustration may exist, leading to extensive conflict. "Unresolved prior conflicts" tend to build up and create an

Table 1. Antecedent Conditions Leading to Conflict

1. Ambiguous Jurisdictions
2. Conflict of Interest
3. Communication Barriers
4. Dependence on One Party
5. Differentiation in Organization
6. Association of the Parties
7. Need for Consensus
8. Behavior Regulations
9. Unresolved Prior Conflicts

atmosphere of tension, which can lead to still more and more intense conflicts. In many cases, the longer conflicts last without a satisfactory resolution being developed, the more severe they become. The use of raw power to "settle" conflicts may also generate more intense conflict at a later time. If one party is unwilling to resolve a conflict, those people involved are likely to generate more difficulties until they may become totally unable to work together. Thus, a failure to manage and deal with conflicts largely guarantees that the manager's job will become more difficult in the future.

These nine antecedent conditions of conflict exist in every organization at all times to a greater or lesser extent. They tend to be more apparent in the project and matrix forms of organization because these organizational structures are frequently used to create change using modern, advanced technology in highly complex and uncertain situations. When these conditions are found, it is up to the project manager to avoid potential destructive results of conflict by controlling and channeling it into areas that can prove beneficial to the project.

Destructive conflict can be highly detrimental to the organization and can significantly alter its productivity. It can drastically hamper the decision-making process, making it long, complex, and difficult. Conflict can also cause the formation of competing coalitions within the organization, thus reducing employee commitment to the organizational goals. In essence, destructive conflict can lead to a number of divisive, frustrating distractions that degrade the effort normally applied toward organizational goals.

In order to avoid these destructive consequences, the manager must channel the conflict in such a way that it is either resolved or used for constructive purposes. There are a number of positive results to be derived from conflict. One of these is the "diffusion of more serious conflict."[10] Games, for example, can be used to control the attitudes of people. Games provide a competitive situation which has entertainment value and can provide tension release to the parties involved.[11] Such conflict processes, which have acceptable resolution procedures already established, can function as preventive measures against more destructive outcomes. Similarly, systems that provide for participation by the members of an organization in decision-making, while positively associated with the number of minor disputes between parties, are negatively associated with the number of major incidents that occur between members of the organization (Corwin, 1969).[12] Therefore, closeness among organization members is a means of channeling aggressive behavior and tends to result in disagreements which, in turn, reduce the likelihood of major fights and disruptions. Another positive value of conflict is the "stimulation of a search for new facts or resolutions."[13] When two parties who respect each other are involved in a disagreement, the process can sometimes lead to a clarification of facts. Conflict can also stimulate the search for new methods or solutions. "When parties are in conflict about which of two alternatives to accept, their disagreement may stimulate a search for another solution mutually acceptable to both."[14] In both cases, the conflict needs to be managed to keep attention on the facts of the situation and to keep the emotional content low.

An "increase in group cohesion and performance"[15] is another potential value of conflict. Conflict situations between two or more groups are likely to increase both the cohesiveness and the performance of the groups in question. In this situation, however, the effects of conflict must be divided into two periods; during the conflict itself, and after a winner and loser have been determined. During the conflict, there is extremely high loyalty to the group associated with willingness to conform to group attitudes and ideas. Little effort is made to understand the opponent, and the opponent's position is evaluated negatively. The level of effort allocated to the group effort is increased. Therefore, in this sense, competition is valuable as a stimulus to work groups. However, when conflicts end, the situation changes. The leader of the winning group gains status. This person's influence tends to continue and be extended. The leader of the losing group, however, loses status and tends to be blamed for the loss. The group atmosphere also changes. There exists a high level of tension, a desire to avoid problems, an intense desire to do better, and highly competitive feelings in the losing group. These factors decrease in the winning group and are replaced by a feeling of accomplishment and satisfaction.[16] The losing group will tend to try harder next time and the winning group will tend to relax. Therefore, during the conflict, there is an increase in group cohesion and performance in both groups. These attitudes can decrease in both groups once the conflict is resolved, but they decrease for different reasons. "The measure of power or ability"[17] is the fourth value of conflict. Conflict can provide a fairly accurate method of measurement. Through conflictive situations, the relative power between two parties may be identified. "Coercion, control, and suppression requires clear superiority of power of one party over another, whereas problem solving requires an equalization of power among the parties.[18] Suppression of one party by another can therefore be avoided by

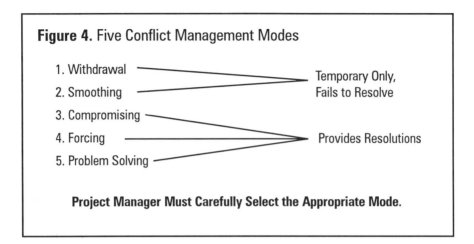

Figure 4. Five Conflict Management Modes

1. Withdrawal
2. Smoothing ————————————— Temporary Only, Fails to Resolve
3. Compromising
4. Forcing ————————————— Provides Resolutions
5. Problem Solving

Project Manager Must Carefully Select the Appropriate Mode.

creating an approximately equal power balance, and this approach usually leads to the use of problem solving methods to resolve disagreements.

The potential results of conflict described above demonstrate that the results of conflict are not necessarily all bad. In fact, conflict is neither good nor bad but can have both positive and negative results for the organization. It really depends on the atmosphere created by the manager as he or she manages the conflict situations in his or her organization. Destructive results of conflict, however, need to be avoided by careful and detailed conflict management.

From a management perspective, there are five distinct methods for dealing with conflict (see Figure 4). The project manager must carefully select the appropriate mode for handling conflict within his or her organization so that an atmosphere conducive to constructive results is developed. The five modes, smoothing, withdrawing, compromise, forcing and problem solving, are defined and viewed in light of their general effectiveness in this section.[19] Later, they are analyzed and reviewed in depth in relation to the project manager's role. *Smoothing* is defined as "de-emphasizing differences and emphasizing commonalties over conflictual issues."[20] Smoothing keeps the atmosphere friendly; but if used too frequently or as the main or only method of dealing with conflict, the conflicts will never be faced. *Withdrawal* can be defined as "retreating from actual or potential disagreements and conflict situations."[21] This method is appropriate only in certain situations; for example, when a "cooling off" period is needed to gain perspective on the conflict situation. Both smoothing and withdrawal are delaying, ignoring tactics which will not resolve the conflict but will temporarily slow the situation down. Note that, if the conflict is not dealt with and resolved in the long run, future conflict will be more severe and intense. *Compromising*, "considering various issues, bargaining, and searching for solutions which attempt to bring some degree of satisfaction to the conflicting parties,"[22] is a situation where neither party can win, but each may get some degree of satisfaction out of the situation. A compromise does hurt; both parties must give up something that is important to them, but compromise does usually provide some acceptable form of a resolution. Forcing and problem solving also provide resolutions. *Forcing* is "exerting one's viewpoint at the potential expense of another party, characterized by a win-lose situation."[23] That is, one party wins while the other loses. Forcing can increase conflicts later as antagonisms build up among the parties involved. It should therefore generally be used by the project manager as a last resort. *Problem solving* (or confrontation) is a mode where the disagreement is addressed directly. It is a process where conflict is treated as a problem. That is, the problem is defined, information is collected, alternatives are developed and analyzed, and the most appropriate alternative is selected in a typical problem solving technique. This method is considered theoretically to be the best way of dealing with conflict because both parties can be fully satisfied if they can work together to find a solution that meets both of their needs. It is a time-consuming process, however, and it requires that both parties desire to solve the problem and are willing to work together toward a mutually agreeable solution. If a solution is needed quickly or immediately, however, the problem solving approach simply cannot work.

Of the five basic modes, some are more conducive to certain situations than others. Problem solving is considered the "best" mode since it can lead to innovative results, capable of satisfying all parties. It does not work in all situations, however, especially when time is critical. Smoothing and withdrawing are delaying actions which cannot resolve the issue. Forcing provides a rapid solution but may make the conflict more intense in the long run. Compromise provides a resolution but rarely satisfies anyone. So, again, it is up to the project manager to identify the type and source of the conflict, evaluate the situation objectively, and select one of the conflict handling modes to solve the issue. In other words, the project manager must manage the conflict situation.

There are other methods the project manager can use in handling conflict. These differ from the five modes of conflict in that they relate more specifically to personal styles of handling conflict. Filley identifies these five styles of handling conflict as:

> ... *high concern for personal goals and low concern for relationships (win-lose); low concern for personal goals and high concern for relationships (yield-lose); low concern for personal goals and low concern for relationships (lose, leave); moderate concern for personal goals and moderate concern for relationships (compromise style); and high concern for personal goals and high concern for relationships (integrative style).*[24]

These essentially "one party" styles of conflict resolution can be related to the five modes as seen in Figure 5. With these relationships in mind, an examination of these personal styles follows. The win-lose style is the "tough battler"

Figure 5. Styles of Conflict Resolution

		Concerns for	
		Personal Goals	Relationships
Force	Win-Lose	High	Low
Smooth	Yield-Lose	Low	High
Withdraw	Lose-Leave	Low	Low
Compromise	Compromise	Medium	Medium
Problem Solver	Integrative	High	High

who seeks to meet his or her goals at all costs.[25] The yield-lose style is the friendly helper, "who overvalues maintenance of relationships with others and undervalues achievement of his or her own goals."[26] The lose-leave style person sees conflict as "a hopeless, useless, and punishing experience."[27] The compromise style person will try to find a position where each side can end up with something. Finally, the integrative style person seeks to satisfy his or her own goals as well as the goals of others.[28] He or she is the problem solver. Like the five modes reviewed earlier, the problem solving and compromise-oriented styles (integrative and compromise) are the most successful styles. The win-lose style, yield-lose style, and lose-leave styles would not be effective because of their extremes. The compromise style and integrative style must be evident in a successful project organization. The first three styles (win-lose, yield-lose, lose-leave) would ultimately lead to project failure, while the last two (compromise, integrative) would lead to project success.

In summary, conflict is inevitable in an organization and is usually considered to be a disagreement among two or more parties. The results can be good or bad for the organization, depending upon how the manager manages the conflict. The antecedent conditions for conflict provide a guideline for managers to follow in predicting the type and intensity of conflict likely to exist in the organization. Destructive conflict can be very detrimental to the organization, and it is the manager's responsibility to control and channel the conflict process for constructive results. The five methods of dealing with conflict and their general effectiveness give project managers some tools with which to manage conflict in their project environments.

Conflict Management for Project Managers

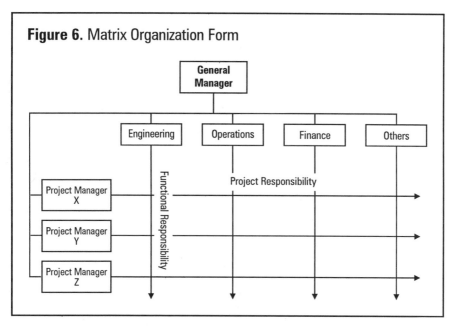

Figure 6. Matrix Organization Form

Conflict in Project Organizations

There are several types of project organizations. The one which seems to create the most conflict is the matrix organizational form (see Figure 6). In this form, "… the project manager actually performs the managerial functions of planning, organizing, and controlling the activities of project personnel, but only with respect to his or her project."[29] The project manager's human resources, however come largely from the functional departments and remain responsible to the functional managers. This situation can frequently confuse those working on the project since they constantly work for two bosses. The result is typically a high level of conflict. The specific sources of conflict derived from this structure are reviewed later in this section. Conditions leading to conflict in this type of organization are examined below.

The antecedent conditions of conflict were previously defined in general terms. They are particularly apparent in the project and matrix organizations. Ambiguous jurisdictions, for example, are especially prevalent in the matrix organization. In this structure, the limits of each party's jurisdictions are purposely ambiguous since each person is responsible to different people for different things. In particular, "the individual working at the interface position has two bosses; he or she must take direction from both the project manager and the functional manager."[30] Thus, the interface person's role is not clearly defined. Even though the roles of the project manager and functional manager are deemed "clear" in this structure, their duties in reality do overlap extensively, and they must often work together to solve problems. This situation can create conflict because functional managers and project managers want something different from the project, and frequently from the organization as a whole. Therefore, because of a lack of clear role definitions, ambiguous jurisdictions exist to a high degree in the matrix and project environments.

Conflict of interest between the parties leads to increased conflict. This statement is especially true in a project environment where there is competition for scarce resources. For example, key personnel must often be shared, particularly in a matrix organization. In this case, there is likely to be continuous conflict between the project and functional managers, both of whom want the services of the best personnel available. Often conflicts of interest exist between an interface individual and a functional and/or project manager. The functional manager and project manager frequently differ in the goals and objectives they have set for the interface person. The interface individual also has goals and desires of his or her own. A three-way conflict is thus frequently generated in both the project and matrix environments.

Communication barriers are the most often discussed condition leading to conflict in matrix and project structures. These barriers exist to a great degree if the parties are separated from each other, either physically or by the timing of their contributions to the project. In a project environment, functional and project managers frequently physically perform their work many miles apart, with the project manager typically located at the project site and the functional manager at the corporate offices. Further, people with different skills are required to contribute to the project at different times. For example, those responsible for carrying out the project are dependent on the planning done much earlier by designers. These space and time separations create natural groupings which promote separate group interests rather than advance a common effort toward joint goals.[31] Again, this concept exemplifies the conflict between functional and project groups, all of which must contribute to the project effort. When participants identify with their own groups rather than the project as a whole, conflicts due to a lack of communication are exacerbated.

"Dependence on one party" can easily occur in a project environment. Typically, the project manager is dependent on the functional manager for interface personnel support. Project managers also depend on the functional managers and the interface personnel for the quality of much of the project work. In turn, the project manager is depended upon for clear, concise work statements and reasonable schedules. "The interface members generally give loyalty to the person signing their merit review,"[32] and this can pose a problem if conflicting directions are given by the functional and project managers. On the other extreme, one of the two managers may fail to define expected performance for their interface personnel, which can lead to frustration and conflict.

"Differentiation in organization" is clearly evident in a project environment. "Conflict will be greater as the degree of differentiation in an organization increases."[33] In a project environment, the number of levels of authority "... create difficulties of communication, conflicts of interest, difficult dependency situations, or jurisdictional disputes."[34] Again, the conflicts generally exist among the functional managers, the project managers, and the interface personnel who are subject to the "two-boss" situation. The general manager (or top management) could be included in this precursor to conflict as well. Top management provides the formal power and authority to both the project and functional managers and hence is responsible for maintaining an appropriate balance. The project manager tends to give his or her allegiance to the project and its goals. The functional managers have the responsibility of maintaining technical excellence on the project and in the ongoing functional work of the parent organization. These different levels, responsibilities, and perspectives clearly create the potential for conflict in project and matrix organizations.

"Association of the parties" is a condition leading to conflict when both parties must participate in decision-making. When two parties must make a joint decision, the possibility of conflict is increased. In a project environment, joint decisions concerning the allocation and sharing of project personnel must be made jointly by the project and functional managers. Similar joint decisions must be made among top management, the project manager, and functional managers relative to all resources. This situation increases the need for close, face-to-face contact among the managers and can thus lead to increased conflict.

The "need for consensus," where all parties must agree on a decision, can be considered an extension of "required association" with the added demand for cooperative results. Different people from different backgrounds, like functional managers whose focus is on long-term results and project managers whose focus is on the short-run project accomplishments, frequently have a difficult time agreeing on critical decisions. Some managers actually resort to voting or coin-flipping to promote consensus.

Behavior regulations put boundaries on acceptable behavior; boundaries which can create conflict. Interface personnel would suffer from this situation. They are subject to the rules and regulations created by both the project and functional managers. Together these can lead to unreasonable controls on the way a job is done. Again, the "two-boss concept" can be seen as leading to high levels of conflict.

The last antecedent condition leading to conflict is unresolved prior conflicts. If the human elements of the project withdraw or smooth over conflict situations, or use power and unsatisfactory compromises to achieve desired results, the conflict in the project can build to very high levels of intensity. The type of conflict resolution method used to solve the prior conflict has a residual effect on the management atmosphere pervading the project. If the conflicts were not satisfactorily resolved in the first place, the conflicts are still there. They continue to affect the management of the project. Because conflict is so common in project and matrix organizations, this antecedent condition also is commonly found in project environments.

All of these conditions exist to a great degree in the project environment. As a result, the potential for conflict is high. Conflict will exist in projects. It is therefore one of the project manager's responsibilities to manage the conflict and to avoid destructive results.

There are some unique conflict conditions in projects of which project managers should be especially aware. These conditions include the high-stress environment, ambiguous roles/responsibilities, the multiple-boss situation, and the prevalence of advanced technology concerns. Projects typically involve high stress because performance is clearly measurable in terms of the project's time, cost, and performance objectives. "In most cases, time is of the essence."[35] The schedule is critical both to integrate project activities and to produce the end product when needed. Thus, pressure to meet the project milestones is very intense. "Many projects are of vital importance to the long-run survival of the parent organization ... and ... are often accomplished for— and are of major importance to—external beneficiaries."[36] The result is a great deal of stress on the project manager to meet the project targets, and the pressure increases dramatically when the slack and contingency disappears, as it always seems to in important projects.

In a project environment, there also exist many ambiguous roles and responsibilities. As reviewed earlier, the ambiguous roles of the project manager, functional manager, and interface personnel can lead to conditions of conflict. These roles are ambiguous because of "... the relatively unstructured and dynamic project organization."[37] Frequently, the project manager and functional manager must share responsibilities. Also, the interface personnel are unsure of their role in a structure where there are two bosses. In a multiple-boss situation, much confusion exists due to the fact that functional managers assign personnel to a specific project and the actual work performed is assigned and controlled by the project manager. Thus, a dual line of authority is imposed on this individual, one emphasizing the short-term task and the other emphasizing the long-term career potential and professional development.[38]

The two-boss employee also experiences high levels of stress and anxiety, along with ambiguity over who the boss really is and who can impose work requirements. The role loses some of its ambiguity as the organization develops, but it never reaches the level of specificity expected in the normal bureaucratic organization.

Advanced technology is another unique conflict condition found in the project environment.

The use of an advanced technology to accomplish a complex task almost automatically increases the level of uncertainty inherent in the work effort, since the fact that it is a new technology implies that its findings have not been tested and proved as have the more stable technologies.[39]

Further, when new technology is used, many of the needed answers are not available and must be developed within the project. This situation also leads to high levels of uncertainty and hence conflict which must be handled.

These four conditions, high-stress environment, ambiguous roles, multiple-boss situation, and advanced technology are inherent in the project form of organization, perhaps more so than in other organizations. In concert with the previously discussed antecedents to conflict, they explain why conflict is so prevalent in project and matrix organizations, and why it is so necessary for the project manager to understand the management of conflict. It is also useful for the project manager to understand the sources of conflict that are particularly relevant to project organizations. The project manager can then prepare to deal with the type of conflict likely to be generated in his or her project.

Thamhain and Wilemon have identified seven major sources of conflict in project environments.[40] Their work, originally performed in a private manufacturing company, has been confirmed in the military by Eschmann and Lee[41] and in the educational environment by Peter Stoycheff.[42] The basic sources of conflict are listed and defined in Figure 7.

Conflict over schedules seems to be the major cause of conflict for all five interface situations of dealing with functional departments, assigned personnel, between team members, superiors, and subordinates.[43]

Conflicts over schedules are simply disagreements concerning the timing, sequencing, and scheduling of project-related tasks; and since there is no single "best" way for any project to be scheduled, it is of little surprise that schedules are perceived as the most significant source of conflict. It has also been determined that the timing and scheduling constraints contribute greatly to the high-stress environment of the project. The second ranked source of conflict is project priorities, which involves a situation where the project participants have different ideas over the sequence of activities and tasks needed to achieve successful project completion[44] This "conflict ... may occur not only between the project team and other support groups but also within the project team."[45] Conflict over manpower resources occurs almost constantly in the project environment.

Conflicts may arise around the staffing of the project team with personnel from other functional and staff support areas, or from the desire to use another department's personnel for project support even though the personnel remain under the authority of their functional or staff superiors.[46]

Figure 7. Seven Sources of Conflict in Project Environments

Sources of Conflict	Definitions
1. Conflict over Project Priorities	View of project participants differ over sequence of activities and tasks.
2. Conflict over Administration Procedures	Managerial and administrative oriented conflicts over how the project will be managed.
3. Conflict over Technical Opinions and Performance Trade-offs	Disagreements over technical issues, performance specifications, technical trade-offs.
4. Conflict over Manpower Resources	Conflicts concerning staffing of project team with personnel from other areas.
5. Conflict over Cost	Conflict over cost estimates from support areas regarding work breakdown structures.
6. Conflict over Schedules	Disagreements about the timing, sequencing, and scheduling of project-related tasks.
7. Personality Conflict	Disagreements on interpersonal issues.

While these three sources of conflict seem to cause over 50 percent of all conflict among the seven categories, considerable conflict seems to originate in other areas as well.[47]

Conflict over technical opinions is usually found in technically oriented projects. These "... disagreements may arise over technical issues, performance, specifications, technical trade-offs, and the means to achieve performance."[48] Conflict over administrative procedures primarily concerns how the project will be managed. In this area there are differences concerning "... the project manager's reporting relationships, definition of responsibilities, interface relationships, project scope, operational requirements, plan of execution, negotiated work agreements with other groups, and procedures for administrative support."[49] Conflict over cost objectives can have a great impact on the success of a project. Conflict from this source consists primarily of "... differences in views concerning fund allocation and cost estimates."[50] Frequently, this conflict develops over cost estimates from support areas concerning project work breakdown packages. Personality conflicts "... tend to center on interpersonal differences rather than on 'technical' issues,"[51] and "are some of the most difficult to deal with effectively."[52] All of these conflict sources are important; however, they vary in intensity among the various participants in the project, according to Thamhain and Wilemon. Their data show that a high degree of conflict exists with the functional departments. Project man-

Conflict Management for Project Managers

agers cannot control these departments, and conflict often develops over the "… timing of project activities which in turn impact the allocation of manpower resources, project priorities, etc."[53] Conflict with assigned project personnel ranked second to that with the functional department in most cases. Project personnel tend to have a narrow view of the project and look forward to returning to their functional environment. Conflict with subordinates ranked the lowest in most cases because "… project managers tend to have more control over their immediate team members, and team members are often more likely to share common project objectives with the project manager than with the functional departments."[54] Thamhain and Wilemon also found it interesting to note the intensity of conflict with superiors over schedules and administrative procedures. First, the superior did not recognize the complexities involved in the project. Second, they are held directly accountable for the accomplishment of the project. Third, project scheduling problems can impact many other areas; and if these areas are affected, it may require the intervention of the project manager's superior and thus involve him or her in conflict situations.[55] Some of the sources are more intense than others in relation to the participants of the project environment. The overall intensity of conflict also varies over the project life cycle.

The project life cycle phases often have undefinable boundaries and constantly overlap. While a variety of terms are used, a frequently used four-stage model includes the conceptual, the planning, the implementation, and the phase-out stages of the project (see Figure 8).

The predominant sources of conflict vary by life cycle phase, as does the overall intensity of conflict (see Figure 9). In the conceptual stage, project priorities, administrative procedures, and schedules were ranked as the predominant three sources of conflict.[56] In this stage, the project manager must launch his or her project within the larger organization. "Frequently, conflict develops between the priorities established for the project and the priorities which other line and staff groups believe important."[57] The second source, administrative procedures, is concerned with several important management issues, such as the design of the project organization, reporting procedures, authority of the project manager, control over resources, and the establishment of schedules and performance specifications.[58] Schedules is an area where some flexibility is needed from the established groups in the organization. Scheduling "… may involve a reorientation of present operating patterns and 'local' priorities in support departments."[59] Overall, effective planning is needed in this stage to avoid the destructive conflict emanating from these potential conflict sources.

In the planning stage, the work of the project is mapped and major planning decisions are made. The three sources ranked highest as to intensity in the project are project priorities, schedules, and administrative procedures. These also ranked highest in the conceptual stage. Some of these sources of

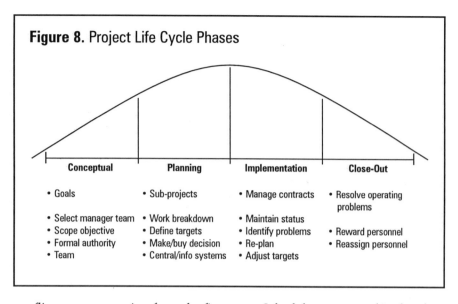

Figure 8. Project Life Cycle Phases

Conceptual	Planning	Implementation	Close-Out
• Goals	• Sub-projects	• Manage contracts	• Resolve operating problems
• Select manager team	• Work breakdown	• Maintain status	
• Scope objective	• Define targets	• Identify problems	• Reward personnel
• Formal authority	• Make/buy decision	• Re-plan	• Reassign personnel
• Team	• Central/info systems	• Adjust targets	

conflict are an extension from the first stage. Schedules are second in the planning stage and third in the conceptual stage. In the conceptual stage, conflicts develop over the establishment of schedules, whereas in the planning stage conflicts arise over the enforcement of schedules.[60] Conflict over administrative procedures becomes less intense in the planning stage, indicating that administrative problems are diminishing. Conflict over technical issues becomes more evident in the planning stage, primarily due to disagreements with a support group not being able to meet technical requirements, which can alter the project manager's cost and schedule objectives. Conflict over cost is still low in the planning phase, primarily because

> ... conflict over the establishment of cost targets does not appear to create intense conflicts for most project managers. Second, some projects are not yet mature enough in the build-up phase (planning) to cause disagreements over cost between the project manager and those who support him or her.[61]

In the implementation phase, the three highest ranked sources of conflict are schedules, technical issues, and manpower. In this phase, the adherence to the schedule becomes critical to project performance. The "management and maintenance"[62] of schedules is critical here. Technical problems appear because of the integration of subsystems and pitfalls in the design of a component. In this stage, disagreements may also arise over "... reliability and quality control standards, various design problems, and testing procedures."[63] The need for manpower reaches the highest levels in the implementation phase. Conflicts arise due to strains over manpower availability and project require-

Conflict Management for Project Managers

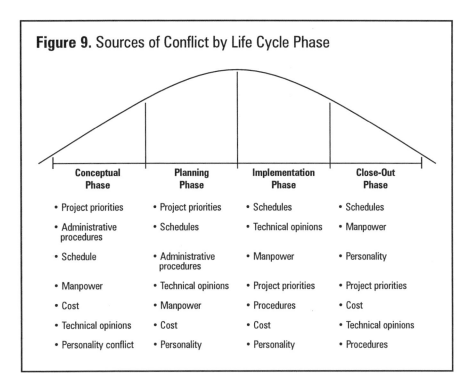

Figure 9. Sources of Conflict by Life Cycle Phase

Conceptual Phase	Planning Phase	Implementation Phase	Close-Out Phase
• Project priorities	• Project priorities	• Schedules	• Schedules
• Administrative procedures	• Schedules	• Technical opinions	• Manpower
• Schedule	• Administrative procedures	• Manpower	• Personality
• Manpower	• Technical opinions	• Project priorities	• Project priorities
• Cost	• Manpower	• Procedures	• Cost
• Technical opinions	• Cost	• Cost	• Technical opinions
• Personality conflict	• Personality	• Personality	• Procedures

ments. Conflict over priorities is declining in this stage and the other three sources were still ranked low.

In the phase-out stage, there is a shift in the sources of conflict. The top three ranked sources are schedules, personality, and manpower. Schedule slippages that were evident in the implementation stage carried over into the phase-out stage. Personality conflict, previously lower ranked, is second in this phase. Project participants are tense and uncertain about future assignments, and the pressure on project participants to meet stringent schedules, budgets, and performance objectives is intense at the end.[64] "Disagreements over manpower resources may develop due to new projects phasing in, hence creating competition for personnel during the critical phase-out stage."[65] Conflict over priorities is directly related to project start-up activities. Cost, technical, and administrative procedures are again ranked lowest.

Conflict Management and the Project Manager

As seen earlier, the project manager is a vital part of the organization's structure. Once personnel have been identified to work on the project, it is the project manager's job to assign and supervise tasks. In order that these

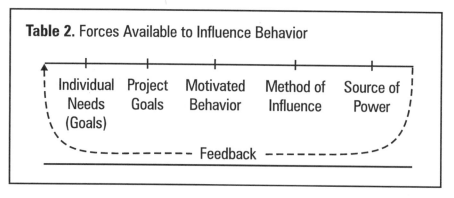

Table 2. Forces Available to Influence Behavior

Individual Needs (Goals)	Project Goals	Motivated Behavior	Method of Influence	Source of Power

Feedback

tasks will be successfully completed, the project manager must somehow influence or motivate these personnel. "The success of a project is very much dependent on the behavior of people internal and external to the project team."[66] An individual's behavior is directly related to goal and need fulfillment. Therefore, a project manager must effectively select tasks for the individual so that the goals of the individual can be met, along with the project goals. In order to influence and motivate the individual to this desired and optimal behavior, the project manager must use all of the five forces of power to the extent they are available in the specific situation. The project manager is also responsible for handling conflict situations as they occur either within or associated with the project. In this section the five sources of power are defined and explained in terms of how they can be applied by the project manager in managing the conflict situations of the project. Other methods exist which the project manager can use to influence project participants toward less destructive conflict. These are also reviewed in this section.

The forces of power available to the project manager determine the methods he or she can use to influence the behavior of project-oriented personnel. This entire complex phenomenon of motivating desired project-oriented behavior is represented in a highly simplified form in Table 2.[67]

The five bases of power identified by French and Raven describe the way in which people can be influenced.[68] Of the five basic sources legitimate, coercive and reward power are based primarily on organizational form. "The remaining two sources, expert and referent power, are based on individual factors and can be expected to vary among individual managers according to personal characteristics and such attributes as experience, management style, personality, and even physical stature."[69] The five sources of power are listed in Table 3.

Legitimate power is derived from the individual's position in the organization. Because of this person's formal authority or high position in the organization it is believed by the subordinate that this person has a right to direct certain aspects of behavior. Coercive power is predicated on fear. If the subordinate fails to comply with the superior's wishes, the subordinate feels like-

Table 3. Five Sources of Power
Legitimate Power
Coercive Power
Reward Power
Expert Power
Referent Power

ly to be deprived of something valued. Reward power is more positive. It "... involves positive reinforcement for desired behavior."[70] The person who obeys the person with reward powers does so in order to be granted desired rewards. Expert power is exercised when one person attempts to behave in a manner that is perceived to be desired by another person who is held in special esteem because of that other person's special knowledge or skill. Referent power "... is based on a less powerful person's identification with a more powerful person."[71] Some factors leading to this identification include the more powerful person's traits, past accomplishments, status. A project manager can adopt all of these bases of power as methods of influencing specific, desired behavior. According to Adams et al., there are three methods of personal influence in formal organizations: authority, persuasion, and control. Authority requires the use of legitimate power. Persuasion requires the use of expert or referent power. Control is based on reward or coercive power. "The power ... available to a project manager is determined by his or her degree of control, his or her position in the organizational hierarchy, his or her reputation, his or her knowledge and experience, and the organizational climate surrounding the project."[72] The relationship between these characteristics and power can be seen in the following table:

Project managers should generally avoid the use of coercive power. It does not positively influence desired goals and behavior, and may leave a residue of antagonism toward the project manager and the project. The forms of power which are most successful in creating a favorable climate while influencing behavior are reward and expert power. "Influence based on the ability to provide rewards intrinsic to the project itself by creating challenging tasks, shaping future work assignments, assigning responsibility, praising good performance and allowing individuals to correct poor performance themselves is a low-cost, powerful and available technique for project managers in a great many project situations."[73] Rewards extrinsic to the project itself, such as good performance evaluations and salary increases, are also important where available to the project manager, and can be powerful forces toward creating a satisfactory project climate. The project manager's influence can also be exerted through persuasion based on expert and referent power. Use of legitimate power should be exercised in conjunction with expert and reward power whenever possible. "That is, authority is most fully accepted when the desired behavior is in response to perceived desires of a high-status person and when positive rewards result from that behavior."[74] These bases of power, especially referent, expert and legitimate, are inherent in the project managers position. Legitimate power derives from the position and title, and provides a basis for demanding behavior to further project goals. Knowledge of all aspects of the project provides the necessary expert power. The continuing and extensive personal contacts that are part of the job provide the project manager every opportunity to develop referent power. These three sources thus become the principal basis from which the project manager can influence the behavior of project participants.

The five modes of conflict resolution were briefly defined and explained earlier in Part II as part of conflict management theory. As a review, the five modes are withdrawal, smoothing, compromising, forcing, and problem solving. The most effective of these is generally accepted to be problem solving, although each mode is appropriate depending on the particular circumstances and the desired result. Withdrawal and smoothing are temporary methods useful only in delaying the results of conflict, whereas compromising, forcing and problem solving deal directly with the issues involved.

Research has recently greatly increased our knowledge of the effect that the use of various conflict modes have on the project. Thamhain and Wilemon found that "... Forcing and withdrawal are significantly and positively correlated to increased conflict between project managers and their assigned personnel. This suggests that the more a project manager uses forcing or withdrawal as a mode of conflict resolution the more conflict he or she experiences."[76] Confrontation (problem-solving), compromise, and smoothing are negatively correlated with increased conflict, which means that project managers who rely on these modes experience less conflict in the long run than those who don't. Thamhain and Wilemon ranked the modes from most effective to least effective in resolving conflict as: (1) problem-solving, (2) compromise, (3) smoothing, (4) forcing, and (5) withdrawal. The most effective technique for minimizing conflict between project managers and superiors was found to be compromise, a mode that promotes both a free exchange of ideas and improved communication. The project manager can also effectively use this method in formal contract negotiations and in informal negotiations with project participants. Three modes are particularly important when considering conflict between project managers and functional departments. Forcing was found by Thamhain and Wilemon to be detrimental to this relationship because it increases the negative results of conflict. Withdrawal tends to minimize conflict, but as stated earlier also fails to resolve the issue. Problem-solving (confrontation) may increase the incidence of conflict, but it also tends to reduce its intensity. Thamhain and Wilemon also found in a study of the techniques actually used by project man-

Table 4. Characteristics of Power

Characteristics	Base of Power
Degree of control	Reward, coercive, legitimate
Position in organizational hierarchy	Reward, legitimate, referent
Reputation	Expert
Knowledge and experience	Expert
Organizational climate	Modifies strength of legitimate and others

agers that "while confrontation was the most favored mode for dealing with superiors, compromise was more favored in handling disagreements with functional support departments."[77] Table 5 provides a summary of these issues.

From this research, it appears that no single "best" method of dealing with conflict exists. Depending on the situation, the project manager needs to have the ability to use all of the conflict management methods as necessary. Smoothing will delay action and can be useful in situations where a "cooling off" period is required. Withdrawing cannot be used as a long-term strategy since others can exert pressure to have the conflict resolved. Compromise can be effectively used in contract and in informal negotiations, in situations where the project manager can afford to give something up. Forcing is generally a win-lose mode, i.e., a situation where one side wins only when the other loses. It can be used within the project indirectly through top management when necessary or when the project manager's power is high. Forcing can be used when time is of the essence, the stakes are high, and when no other alternatives may exist. Problem-solving actually can combine all modes to some extent, and should be used as the preferred approach where the necessary time is available and where sufficient trust exists among the conflicting parties. The project manager could not effectively employ these methods without possessing and exercising some power and authority.

Of course, the project manager may not have to worry about conflict resolution if project participants can be successfully influenced toward less destructive channels for pursuing conflict. To accomplish this task, a reevaluation of commitment, directions, goals, trust, and communication must be achieved, both for the project itself and for those who participate in it. Because of the incongruence of the background of the project team, the project manager needs to be more active in directing, coordinating, and controlling the efforts of those working on the project than is usually required of a manager of a typical functional organization. The project manager is responsible for accomplishing the project objectives and is thus responsible for providing direction and developing commitment to the project. However, the project team members also have

Table 5. Effects of Conflict Management Modes

	Dealings with project personnel	Dealings with superior	Dealings with support departments
Mode will minimize conflict	Compromise Smoothing	Compromise	Withdrawal
Mode will increase conflict	Withdrawal Forcing	Confrontation	Forcing Confrontation

a personal responsibility, apart from the project itself, to work together on a cooperative basis. How well these team members work together is largely a function of their commitment to the project. "Commitment is the key to overcoming many of the natural barriers to teamwork that exist in many projects, e.g., diverse specialties, infrequent contact, transient or part-time personnel, and lack of precedent."[78] The chances of successful project completion depend on the degree to which the project manager can secure and hold commitment to the project from superiors and other external individuals. This commitment is largely a function of directions, goals, trust, and communication.

In order to gain this commitment, the project manager must have a clear sense of direction. The project manager must keep track of himself or herself and the project. This direction does not include specific objectives that never change, but should involve some general long-range, written objectives that carefully define what the parent organization plans to achieve from the project. These long-range objectives lead us back to a consideration of goals. Congruence of goals between the project manager and both top management and the functional managers, as well as among the managers and the project participants, clearly leads to improved motivation and reduced destructive conflict among all those involved in the project.

Two other factors that reduce the destructive effects of conflict and increase the project manager's ability to influence project participants are high levels of trust and open, effective communications. Trust is actually a prerequisite to good open communications, and must be carefully developed by the project manager from the moment the project is initiated. Trust has a major impact on worker satisfaction and motivation. The presence of trust may prevent potentially conflictive situations from arising, while its absence is almost guaranteed to create conflict where actual conditions do not seem to warrant it.[79] If proper communication exists, conflict that does arise can also be challenged into less destructive avenues. In a project, communication channels are often not prescribed; rather, they are spontaneous and informal, arising out of the needs of the moment.[80] Project communication must therefore be flexible and very effective. Strong commitment, clear directions, well documented, congruent goals, and high levels of trust all lead to effective communications.

In summary, the power of the project manager provides the means for influencing the behavior of project participants. The five sources of power were defined and analyzed in this section relative to the project manager's ability to use them for the advancement of the project. Legitimate power is authoritative in nature and can be successfully used in a project, along with expert and referent power, to channel conflict into areas that can provide useful and productive results. Since conflict cannot be avoided, and since the project manager can appropriately use all five of the methods of dealing with conflict in different situations, care must be taken to understand the likely results of applying the various forms of power through the conflict handling modes to effectively avoid destructive conflict. Other factors that affect the management of conflict include the level of personnel commitment, the clarity of directions available, the specificity of the level of trust, and the clarity and openness of project communications. All of these factors have interactive effects on each other and, if used in a carefully coordinated manner, can help to avoid the destructive forms of conflict.

Two-Party Conflict Management

The previous four sections in this monograph have examined the theory and practice of conflict management from the individual's perspective—in this case, from the viewpoint of the project manager. Conflict management, however, is at least a two-party situation, and may involve several parties. While the multiple-party conflict situation can become very complex to analyze, a great deal of insight into the usefulness of the various conflict handling modes and the potential outcomes of completing conflict management styles can be obtained from a careful analysis of the two-party conflict situation.

Organizations typically use three separate strategies for dealing with two-party conflict. These strategies are labeled according to the results achieved from the confrontation by the competing parties. Thus there exist the "win-lose," the "lose-lose," and the "win-win" strategies. Perhaps the term "strategy" is inappropriately used here, for it implies that objectives have been set and a plan carefully evolved for dealing with the conflict situation. This may be true in a few isolated instances, and the individual participants in the conflict frequently have some objective they would like to achieve. By and large, however, the organization seldom has any specific plan for dealing with conflict. The "strategies" referred to here are actually simply classifications into which typical two-party conflicts can be neatly grouped. The term "strategy" is typically used in the literature, however, and will therefore continue to be used in this discussion.

Two-Party Conflict Strategies

Simply from its name it is clear that the "win-win" strategy has relative advantages over the other strategies. Both parties win—that is, both parties achieve what they need and desire from the conflict situation. The project manager can frequently structure the conflict situation to allow this set of results, and the more this approach is used the more likely it is that the project will be successfully managed. This approach is relatively new and, as will be pointed out shortly, cannot be used in all situations. In particular, it is dependent on achieving the active cooperation of all parties to the conflict, a task that may be very difficult in itself. Both the "win-lose" and the "lose-lose" strategies are widely practiced in projects and in business in general, due in part to (1) our tendency to compete with one another, (2) our tendency to continue using behavior learned in the past and to resist changing our approach, and (3) a failure to understand that in many cases it is possible to settle conflicts without one side losing. Perhaps another reason that the "win-lose" and the "lose-lose" strategies are used so frequently is that they encompass many of the commonplace actions we all use every day in doing our work, and these actions are seldom reviewed from the standpoint of their effect on conflict management in the organization.

Win-Lose

The win-lose strategy typically makes use of the power available to each party and treats the conflict as an open competition. For example, the project manager may in essence tell a subordinate to "do as I say because I'm boss," using his or her legitimate power to reward or punish organization members within the project's area of control, depending on whether or not they comply.[81] Alternatively, the project manager may threaten another person with dismissal, either overtly or covertly, thus using either mental or physical power to obtain compliance. Using still another approach, the project manager may choose to ignore a suggestion or comment from a subordinate concerning a controversial issue. This failure to respond places the subordinate in the losing position and is clearly an exercise of the project manager's power.[82]

Two other examples of the win-lose strategy deserving special note are majority and minority rule situations. The majority rule approach involves the time-honored formal or informal vote to determine a course of action. In this situation the project manager either declares that "the majority apparently agree that" one particular course of action is most appropriate, or may actually ask for a show of hands or even a secret ballot. This approach is frequently used in open meetings where a clear majority can be obtained in favor of the project manager's solution, or where there is really little reason from the project manager's viewpoint to choose one alternative over another. In many instances a vote may be a useful way to deal with conflict. If one group continuously loses the vote on a series of issues, however, the group members tend to become more personally involved and consider the vote to be a defeat or "loss."

The minority rule approach abounds with situations not usually recognized as examples of the win-lose strategy. A project manager may announce, for example, that "I think we'll need a special skull session on this issue, and it's urgent. What about 7:30 this evening?" Few would be terribly enthusiastic, but to object openly could publicly indicate a lack of commitment to the project. If no one objects, the meeting is held, and the project manager has "won." Another example involves a proposal described and enthusiastically supported by one individual in open meeting. A second cohort immediately picks up the issue, expressing the advantages from his or her viewpoint, and immediately calls for a vote. In this manner a two or three person minority can frequently "railroad through" a proposal before opposition has had time to organize.

In each of the cases described above, one or more of the sources of power have been exercised to create winners and losers over a particular issue. The project manager must frequently use these and other examples of the win-lose strategy to influence project participants toward project accomplishment. The participants will respond to accomplish the immediate task, but a heavy reliance on these techniques is unlikely to generate cooperation, a team effort, or a favorable climate in the long run. Excessive use of the win-lose approach can be expected to result in much destructive conflict throughout the project organization.

Lose-Lose

At first glance, it doesn't make much sense for two parties to deal with conflict in such a way that neither side accomplishes its goals. Nevertheless, the lose-lose strategy is frequently encountered in projects as well as in all other organization structures. The basic assumption of parties involved in a lose-lose conflict strategy is that getting something is better than getting nothing, even if that something does not accomplish the party's goal.[83] In many cases one or both parties are trying to avoid the conflict by smoothing or withdrawing from the issue, rather than dealing with the conflict with an open confrontation.

Compromise is one example of the lose-lose strategy. Compromises usually result in both parties accepting a second-best solution, with neither side accomplishing their real goals. Compromises are often necessary when managing a project, but the results of compromises on major issues are seldom either totally satisfactory or popular. Another common example of the lose-lose strategy involves side payments or bribes to get people to fake a losing position.[84] Extra pay is provided to get people to work overtime or an undesirable shift, or perform dirty, undesirable jobs. The organization loses the extra money, while the employee loses in that he or she performs a task he or she really would rather not do. Still another example involves resorting to rules, such as flipping a coin or referring to "the book."[85] Such approaches to dealing with conflict seldom take into account the unique aspects of the special situation which frequently invalidate the rule.

Perhaps the best example of a lose-lose strategy, however, is arbitration. The issue is submitted to a supposedly neutral third party for resolution, with everyone agreeing (formally or informally) to abide by the decision.[88] Typically two competing parties submit an issue to their common superior for a decision. Each party hopes to benefit from the decision while avoiding a confrontation. If the decision is made totally in favor of one party, then a win-lose strategy was used. In most cases, however, the resulting decision is some form of a compromise with neither party totally attaining their goal—a lose-lose strategy. Most labor disputes provide additional examples of this approach.

Project managers are frequently involved with the lose-lose strategy, particularly in their negotiations with functional department managers. Compromises must frequently be arranged, and in many cases issues must be carried to top management for final solutions. In fact, one frequently cited advantage of the project organization is that disputes can be quickly and easily brought to the attention of top management. The assumption, of course, is that top management will usually reinforce the project's position. While the specific issue may be resolved in this manner, the next result may well be a legacy of ill feelings and mistrust which can lead to much future destructive conflict.

At this point it is appropriate to review the attitudes surrounding both the win-lose and the lose-lose strategies, since they have several items in common. In both cases disagreements usually involve the means. The parties argue about how to do the job, rather than carefully defining the objective and searching for the best way to resolve the problem. The issue becomes "your way or my way." Thus, both the win-lose and the lose-lose strategies involve:

1. A clear we-they distinction, rather than a "we vs. the problem" orientation

2. Energies aimed at the other party, so both sides strive for total victory or a total defeat of the other party

3. Each party viewing the issue only from their own viewpoint, rather than defining the problem in terms of mutual needs

4. An emphasis on obtaining a solution, rather than on defining goals, values, or motives to be obtained with the solution

5. A personalization of the conflict, rather than an objective focus on facts and issues

6. Parties oriented toward conflict and emphasizing the immediate disagreement, rather than concentrating on the long-term effect of these differences and how they can be resolved.[87]

Win-Win

The win-win strategy involves a completely different atmosphere and view of the conflict situation. In this case, the focus is first on the ends or goals to be achieved, rather than on the obvious and frequently unnecessary alternative solutions that immediately present themselves. The key objective in using the win-win strategy is to *reach a solution which is not unacceptable to anyone*.

This last point is an important one. As shown in Figure 10, there are actually three groups involved in developing any solution in a two-party conflict situation; those who support the particular solution, those who oppose it, and those who just don't care. The win-lose and lose-lose strategies concentrate on the supporters and the opposers, pitting one group against the other. The win-win strategy directly recognizes the third group, the "don't care" group, and attempts to develop a solution that will cause the "opposers" to at least join the "don't care" group if they cannot become active supporters. The two approaches for achieving a solution which is "not unacceptable to anyone" are consensus and integrative decision-making.

Consensus demands a continuing discussion and analysis of the problem, carefully controlled to avoid polarized conflict and arguments over the means of achieving the objective. The discussion centers around ensuring that all parties have a clear and detailed understanding of the objectives desired by all participants. Rules have been developed for conducting a discussion aimed at arriving at a consensus, and these rules in themselves clearly describe the attitude that must be maintained. They are listed in Table 6.

Integrative decision-making methods are "concerned with sequencing the decision process through a series of steps,"[98] with the emphasis on pooling the goals of the parties after they have been polarized. To develop a positive gain for both parties from this process, the attention of both parties must be shifted from solutions to goals and then back to solutions.[89] One representative series of steps to accomplish this shifting of attention is presented in Figure 11. Each party comes to the meeting, as with most meetings, with preconceived solutions to the issue. The first major effort lies in clearly defining the problem and the goal to be achieved by the solution finally selected. Information is exchanged and/or collected concerning the problem and all of the group's needs and positions, and a series of potential alternative solutions are developed. These alternatives, which may or may not include all of the preconceived solutions brought to the meeting (the development of additional information may have eliminated several), are evaluated for their potential effects on all concerned. The most appropriate alternative is then selected and implemented. Note that implementing any alternative may lead to additional issues depending on the results achieved, and these new issues can be dealt with using the same decision-making process.

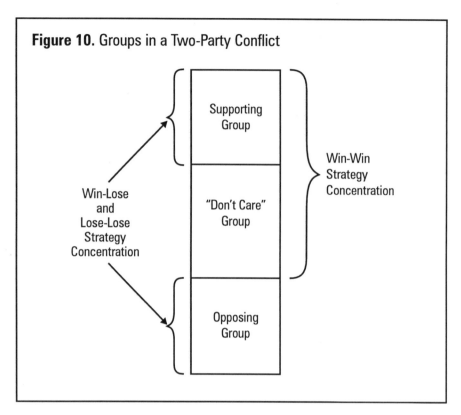

Figure 10. Groups in a Two-Party Conflict

Supporting
Group

"Don't Care"
Group

Opposing
Group

Win-Lose
and
Lose-Lose
Strategy
Concentration

Win-Win
Strategy
Concentration

Summary of the Strategies

Three key attitudes must be maintained in any effort to use a win-win strategy: (1) all parties must want a solution which achieves the objectives of all and is unacceptable to none; (2) all parties have the responsibility to be open and honest about facts, opinions, and feelings; and (3) all parties must agree to control the *process* for arriving at agreement, but not to dictate the content of that agreement.

A word of caution is in order. Not all two-party conflicts can be resolved, and the win-win strategy cannot be used to deal with all conflicts. A great deal of trust is required among all parties of the conflict anytime a win-win approach is to be attempted. If one party tries to develop a consensus through a problem-solving mode while another party uses power to force the issue, the situation will immediately revert to a win-lose strategy. All parties must work toward consensus or integrative decision-making if the win-win strategy is to prevail.

Further, the win-win strategy takes a great deal of time, time which may not be available to the project manager. When time is a paramount consideration, one of the other strategies becomes essential. In fact, all of the strate-

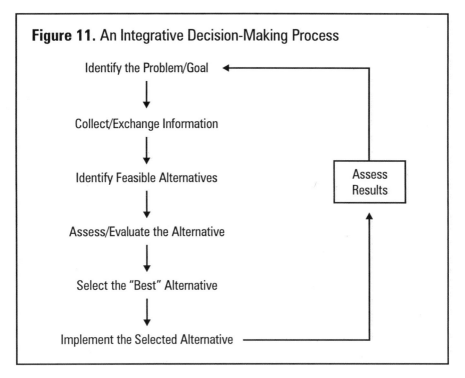

Figure 11. An Integrative Decision-Making Process

Identify the Problem/Goal

Collect/Exchange Information

Identify Feasible Alternatives

Assess/Evaluate the Alternative

Select the "Best" Alternative

Implement the Selected Alternative

Assess Results

gies should be used to deal with conflict depending on the situation involved. It should also be noted that all five of the personal modes for handling conflict discussed earlier are inherent in the three two-party conflict strategies. Problem-solving is the predominant mode used in the win-win strategy, while forcing is the major mode used by the winner in the win-lose strategy. Withdrawal is frequently seen used by the losers in the win-lose and the lose-lose strategy, while smoothing is frequently evident in the win-win and lose-lose strategies. Compromise is frequently used in the lose-lose strategy, but is a mode sometimes attempted by the loser in the win-lose strategy as well. The inference here is that certain individual modes of handling conflict can be associated with winning or losing in a two-party conflict. This inference holds true in general, but only when the conflict-handling modes of both parties are compared. The most recent findings of the relative power of various conflict-handling modes have been developed in research on formal negotiations, and these findings are summarized briefly in the next paragraphs.

Conflict Handling Modes in Two-Party Conflicts

It has been stated several times in this monograph that the project manager's job includes managing all aspects of the conflict that is inherent in the project

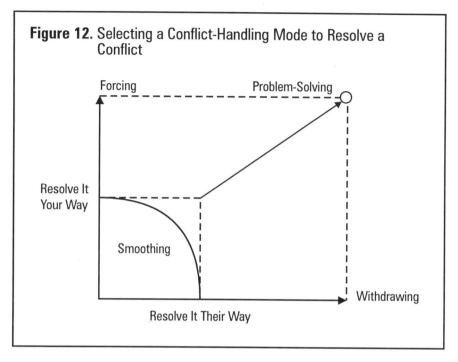

Figure 12. Selecting a Conflict-Handling Mode to Resolve a Conflict

management position and that is unique to the particular organization and project. In essence, this means that the project manager must be able to select from among all five of the conflict-handling modes that particular approach which will be most useful for the project at any particular point in time. Conflict situations, like any other management situation, are best handled for the benefit of the project if the situation is foreseen and analyzed well in advance, and if the project manager then takes the approach most likely to achieve the desired result. As diagrammed in Figure 12, there are only two ways for a two-party conflict to be resolved, your way or their way. The diagram demonstrates the likely results from using the various conflict-handling modes from the individual project manager's viewpoint. As noted earlier, smoothing does not resolve a conflict. In essence, nothing happens when this mode is attempted except that the conflict remains. Forcing denotes an attempt to get your way, if necessary at the expense of the other party. Withdrawing essentially leaves the field to the other party, who is free to resolve the conflict to his or her own advantage. Compromising is an approach that essentially "splits the difference" between the desires of the two parties, with neither party achieving their goals or desires. All four of these modes are associated with the win-lose and the lose-lose strategies. Problem-solving is uniquely associated with the win-win strategy and provides a means for both parties to achieve their goals and desires. Note, however, that both parties must be will-

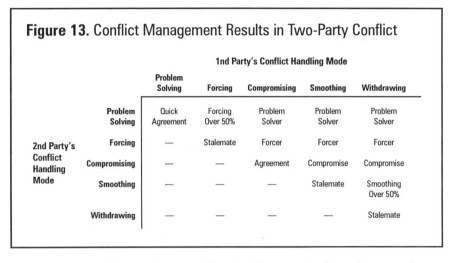

Figure 13. Conflict Management Results in Two-Party Conflict

| | | 1nd Party's Conflict Handling Mode | | | | |
		Problem Solving	Forcing	Compromising	Smoothing	Withdrawing
2nd Party's Conflict Handling Mode	Problem Solving	Quick Agreement	Forcing Over 50%	Problem Solver	Problem Solver	Problem Solver
	Forcing	—	Stalemate	Forcer	Forcer	Forcer
	Compromising	—	—	Agreement	Compromise	Compromise
	Smoothing	—	—	—	Stalemate	Smoothing Over 50%
	Withdrawing	—	—	—	—	Stalemate

ing to use the problem-solving conflict-handling mode if a realistic resolution to the conflict is to be developed which fully satisfies both parties.

In fact, the results of a two-party conflict do not depend only on the conflict-handling mode selected by one party, in our view the project manager. Rather, the results are dependent on the interplay of conflict-handling modes chosen and used by the two parties. In examining and preparing for a conflict situation, the project manager should specifically try to determine in advance the conflict-handling mode the other party will use. He or she can then select the mode which is most likely to lead to the desired results.

Figure 13 presents the findings of extensive research into the formal bargaining process, applied to the interplay of conflict-handling modes in two-party conflict situation, and is largely self-explanatory. The figure assumes that the two parties have approximately equal power at the beginning of the conflict. Note that if both parties use the problem-solving approach, a quick agreement is to be expected and both sets of goals are likely to be satisfied and a win-win strategy will have been used. If one party resorts to a forcing mode, however, the forcer is likely to win in over 50 percent of the cases, and the situation will have regressed to a win-lose strategy. Overall, the problem-solver is likely to win, that is, achieve the desired goals, in all cases except when the other party chooses forcing mode. The forcer, on the other hand, is engaged only in a win-lose strategy and will win at the expense of the "opponent" except when the other party chooses the forcing mode as well. In this case, a stalemate is to be expected. It is interesting to note that when both parties withdraw, a stalemate occurs. In essence, neither party is willing to recognize and address the issue, so the conflict is simply not dealt with and continues to exist. This figure deserves careful review by the project manager in preparation for a conflict confrontation. The prerequisite to using this approach to

---

Table 6. Rules for Developing a Consensus

- Focus on defeating the problem, not each other.
- Avoid voting, trading, or averaging.
- Seek facts to avoid dilemmas.
- Accept conflict as helpful, and don't allow it to elicit threats or defensive actions.
- Avoid self-oriented behavior which excludes the needs, views or positions of others.

---

managing conflict, of course, is that the project manager must have carefully observed and studied the behavior of all other parties associated with the project so as to accurately predict each potential "opponent's" likely response to the conflict situation.

An Example of Conflict Management

It is possible to influence the intensity of conflict to be expected in any group with some fairly simple, straightforward managerial actions. As an example of this, consider the allocation of office space among four projects and four functional departments responsible for supporting the projects. The first situation, diagrammed in Figure 14, illustrates high levels of conflict within the functional departments. The project and functional managers each have their own offices, and in all cases conflict over the allocation of personnel, financial, and physical resources can be expected among them. All personnel associated with a project, whether assigned to the project or functional manager, are assigned work locations in the project office areas. This creates strong positions for the project managers, since all of their work direction and coordination can be accomplished in one location with relative ease of communications among all project participants. The functional managers, however, must move from office to office to find and work with their assigned personnel. Communications within the functional departments are likely to be difficult, disagreements and misunderstandings are likely to be frequent, conflict will be the rule, and the intensity of that conflict is likely to be quite high. The reverse situation, with high levels of conflict expected within the projects and between program and functional personnel, is presented in Figure 15. With the project participants distributed among the four functional department offices, an already difficult and critical project communication problem is intensified. Not only must the project manager effectively establish communications among a wide diversity of technical specialties and skills with critical

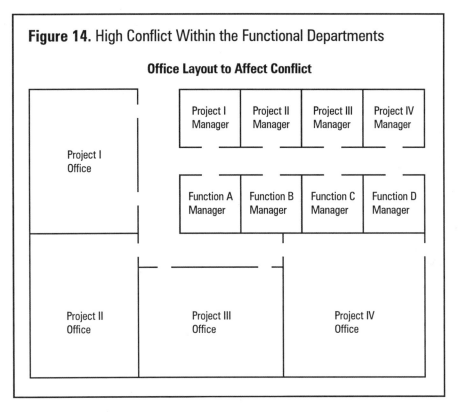

Figure 14. High Conflict Within the Functional Departments

Office Layout to Affect Conflict

Project I Office

| Project I Manager | Project II Manager | Project III Manager | Project IV Manager |

| Function A Manager | Function B Manager | Function C Manager | Function D Manager |

Project II Office

Project III Office

Project IV Office

milestones and goals to be enforced, this activity must be accomplished with the project participants physically scattered in different locations among personnel who are likely to be unsympathetic to the project. While the functional manager was in a difficult situation in the first scenario, the project manager is in a much more difficult situation here. Conflict and conflict intensity within the project and between the project and functional personnel can be expected to be extremely high.

The third situation, depicted in Figure 16, represents the potential for an extremely high level of conflict within Projects III and IV and functions C and D. Apparently, Projects I and II are high-priority efforts and have been assigned their own offices. The same is true of Functions A and B. For these projects and functions the situation is similar to those depicted in the first and second situations respectively, except that the projects will find it more difficult to obtain support from functions A and B. The Project III and IV personnel as well as the Function C and D personnel, however, are distributed among the offices apparently as space permits. This entire situation can only lead to extremely high levels and intensities of conflict. In addition to the communication and coordination difficulties described in the previous two situations,

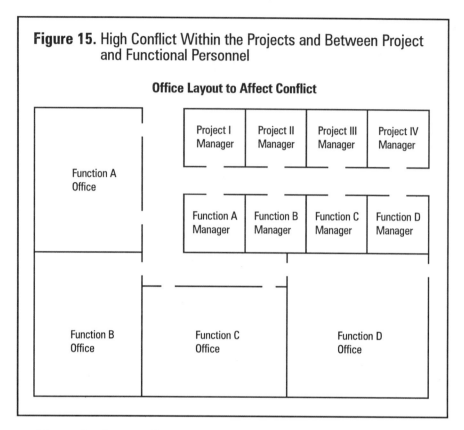

Figure 15. High Conflict Within the Projects and Between Project and Functional Personnel

Office Layout to Affect Conflict

problems of jealousy and envy are likely to exist as well. Few project participants or project managers are likely to wholeheartedly agree with the organization's assessment of the relative priorities among projects and functions, and there is also likely to be an unhealthy and time-consuming competition for positions within the high-priority projects and functions.

It is clear from the basic organizational structure of project situations that conflict will inevitably exist between the project managers and the functional managers. It is equally clear that the level and intensity of conflict within and among the project and functional personnel can be significantly influenced by as simple a managerial decision as the allocation of office space. The point is that the likely location of conflict, as well as its likely level of intensity, can frequently be predicted and planned for, channeled into specific areas where the project manager can prepare to deal with it. Projects tend to run much more smoothly when managerial planning of this type is carefully integrated into the technical planning efforts for the project.

In summary, although much of the theory of conflict management is based on an individual's viewpoint of the conflict situation, conflict is actually an in-

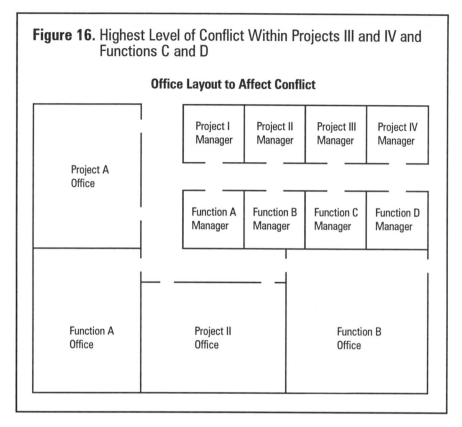

Figure 16. Highest Level of Conflict Within Projects III and IV and Functions C and D

Office Layout to Affect Conflict

| Project I Manager | Project II Manager | Project III Manager | Project IV Manager |

Project A Office

| Function A Manager | Function B Manager | Function C Manager | Function D Manager |

Function A Office

Project II Office

Function B Office

teraction between two or more parties. Few generalizations can be made with today's state of knowledge about the multi-party conflict situation. Much insight into that situation can be obtained by extension, however, from a careful analysis of the two-party conflict situation.

As two parties interact in conflict, three classes of results can be seen to exist within organizations. Loosely called "strategies," these classes of results are named after the results achieved by the two parties involved. Thus, the "win-lose," "lose-lose," and the "win-win" strategies are defined and discussed in some detail. The anticipated results of two-party conflicts when the parties involved use different conflict-handling modes are tabulated and discussed as well. Finally, an extended example is provided to demonstrate how the project manager can anticipate, channel, and plan for two-party conflict situations as the project progresses.

This section on managing two-party conflict situations in projects is necessarily incomplete. The theory itself is incomplete, and few useful generalizations based upon documented research are available to assist the project manager. The intent in this section is to identify and review that useful information that does exist, and to emphasize the importance of early planning by the project manager for control of the conflict environment, which can so significantly affect the results.

Summary

Conflict is inevitable in all organizations, primarily due to the ever-increasing complexity of our modern society, the innate nature of human beings, and the interaction of the two. As the complexity of society increases, the classical, traditional organization has declined in importance. The newer projectized and matrix organization styles are becoming more relevant to today's business and government environments. Inherent in these newer organization styles are the high incidences of rapid change and incongruent human goals that lead to high levels of conflict. Even more important, these conditions are made extremely clear and obvious to project participants by the nature of project work. The project manager, the person with the key responsibility to make the project successful, has no choice but to deal with this high level of conflict. Project management is in fact managing in a highly conflictive situation, and in many ways can be considered almost synonymous with conflict management.

The project manager is a manager of conflict. Much of his or her time and effort is consumed in dealing with one form of conflict or another as the project progresses through the inevitably problem-filled life cycle. In a few cases the project manager may actually be able to resolve the conflict by personally making some decision. Much more frequently, however, the project manager must choose to delay a decision or to bring the conflicting parties together in a carefully controlled situation, or lend his or her support to one side or the other, or provide additional information, or otherwise use his or her knowledge and managerial skill to influence the result toward the needs of the project. This is the rare managerial skill needed for the project manager, and those possessing it find themselves in great demand. It is a skill of personal behavior, one that is very difficult to teach. By understanding the sources of conflict, the power available to deal with it, the methods through which that power can be applied, and the likely results when two methods meet each other, the project manager is armed with the tools necessary to deal with this uniquely conflict-prone situation called project management.

Conflict Management for Project Managers

Endnotes

1. George Ritzer, *Working: Conflict and Change*, Englewood Cliffs, N.J.: Prentice-Hall, Inc., 1977, p. 8.

2. Ibid., p. 40.

3. Harold Kerzner, *Project Management: A Systems Approach to Planning, Scheduling and Controlling*, New York: Van Nostrand Reinhold, 1979, p. 42.

4. Ibid., p. 42.

5. Ibid., p. 48.

6. Arthur G. Butler Jr., "Project Management: A Study in Organizational Conflict," *Academy of Management Journal*, March 1973, p. 89.

7. Ibid., p. 86.

8. David B. Guralink, editor, *Webster's New World Dictionary*, Cleveland, Ohio: William Collins and World Publishing Co., Inc., 1947, p. 298.

9. Alan C. Filley, *Interpersonal Conflict Resolution*, Glenview, Ill.: Scott, Foresman and Company, 1975, p. 4.

10. Ibid.

11. Ibid.

12. Ibid., p. 5.

13. Ibid.

14. Ibid.

15. Ibid., p. 6.

16. Ibid., p. 7.

17. Ibid.

18. Ibid.

19. See R.R. Blake and J.S. Mouton, *The Managerial Grid*, Houston, Texas: Gulf Publishing Company, 1964, and application by Hans J. Thamhain and David L. Wilemon, "Conflict Management in Project Life Cycles," *Sloan Management Review*, Vol. 16, No. 3, Spring 1973, pp. 31–50.

20. Hans J. Thamhain and David L. Wilemon, "Conflict Management in Project-Oriented Work Environments," *Proceedings of the Sixth Annual Seminar/Symposium*, Drexel Hill, Penn.: Project Management Institute, 1974, p. 3.

21. Ibid., p. 87.

22. Ibid.

23. Ibid.

24. Filley, p. 51.

25. Ibid.

26. Ibid.

27. Ibid., p. 52.

28. Ibid.

29. John R. Adams, Stephen C. Barndt and Martin D. Martin, *Managing by Project Management*, Dayton, Ohio: Universal Technology Corp., 1979, p. 45.

30. Kerzner, p. 54.

31. Filley, p. 10.

32. Kerzner, p. 55.

33. Filley, p. 10.

34. Ibid., p. 11.

35. Adams, Barndt and Martin, p. 23.

36. Ibid.

37. Ibid., p. 32.

38. John R. Adams and Nicki S. Kirchof, "The Practice of Matrix Management," in *Matrix Management Systems Handbook*, ed. David Cleland, New York: Van Nostrand Reinhold, 1982.

39. Adams, Barndt and Martin, p. 38.

40. Hans J. Thamhain and David L. Wilemon, "Conflict Management in Project Life Cycles," as quoted in Kerzner, *Project Management: A Systems Approach to Planning, Scheduling and Controlling*, New York: Van Nostrand Reinhold, 1979, pp. 253–254.

41. Eschman and Lee, "Conflict in Civilian and Air Force Program/Project Organizations: A Comparative Study," September 1977, LSSR 3-77B, A047230, 168 pps.

42. Peter A. Stoycheff, "Conflict in the Management of Education, Business and Military Projects: A Comparative Study," unpublished Ph.D. dissertation, Ohio State University, 1980, p. 1.

43. Thamhain and Wilemon, "Conflict Management in Project Oriented Work Environments," p. 88.

44. Thamhain and Wilemon, "Conflict Management in Project Life Cycles," p. 253.

45. Ibid.

46. Ibid., p. 254.

47. Thamhain and Wilemon, "Conflict Management in Project Oriented Work Environments," p. 4.

48. Thamhain and Wilemon, "Conflict in Project Life Cycles," p. 254.

49. Ibid.

50. Adams, Barndt and Martin, p. 144.

51. Thamhain and Wilemon, "Conflict Management in Life Cycles," p. 254.

52. Ibid., p. 257.

53. Thamhain and Wilemon, "Conflict Management in Project Oriented Work Environments, p. 89.

54. Ibid.

55. Ibid.

56. Thamhain and Wilemon, "Conflict Management in Project Life Cycles," p. 258.

57. Ibid., pp. 258–258.

58. Ibid., p. 259.

59. Ibid.

60. Ibid., p. 260.

61. Ibid.

62. Ibid., p. 261.

63. Ibid.

64. Ibid., p. 262.

65. Ibid.

66. Adams, Barndt and Martin, p. 137.

68. Ibid.

69. Ibid.

70. Ibid., p. 139.

71. Ibid.

72. Ibid., p. 141.

73. Ibid., p. 142.

74. Ibid.

75. Thamhain and Wilemon, "Conflict Management in Project Oriented Work Environments," p. 89.

76. Thamhain and Wilemon, "Conflict Management in Project Life Cycles," p. 264.

77. Ibid., p. 265.

78. Adams, Barndt and Martin, p. 135.

79. Filley, p. 15.
80. Adams, Barndt and Martin, p. 136.
81. Filley, p. 22.
82. Ibid., p. 23.
83. Ibid.
84. Ibid., p. 24.
85. Ibid.
86. Ibid.
87. Ibid. p. 25.
88. Ibid., p. 26.
89. Ibid.

References

Adams, John R., Stephen E. Barndt, and Martin D. Martin. *Managing by Project Management*. Dayton, Ohio: Universal Technology Corp., 1979.

Adams, John R. and Nicki S. Kirchof. "The Practice of Matrix Management." In *Matrix Management Systems Handbook*, ed. David Cleland. New York: Van Nostrand Reinhold, 1982.

Butler, Arthur G. Jr. "Project Management: A Study in Organizational Conflict." *Academy of Management Journal*, March 1973, p. 89.

Eschman and Lee. "Conflict in Civilian and Air Force Program/Project Organizations: A Comparative Study." September 1977, LSSR 3-77B. A0A047230, 168 pp.

Filley, Alan C. *Interpersonal Conflict Resolution*. Glenview, Ill.: Scott, Foresman and Company, 1975.

Guralink, David B., ed. *Webster's New World Dictionary*. Cleveland, Ohio: William Collins and World Publishing Co., Inc., 1974.

Kerzner, Harold. *Project Management: A Systems Approach to Planning, Scheduling and Controlling*. New York: Van Nostrand Reinhold, 1979.

Ritzer, George. *Working: Conflict and Change*. Englewood Cliffs, N.J.: Prentice-Hall, 1977.

Stoycheff, Peter A. "Conflict in the Management of Education, Business and Military Projects: A Comparative Study." Unpublished Ph.D. dissertation, Ohio State University, 1980, p. 1.

Thamhain, Hans J., and David L. Wilemon, "Conflict Management in Project Life Cycles." In Kerzner, *Project Management: A Systems Approach to Planning, Scheduling and Controlling*. New York: Van Nostrand Reinhold, 1979.

Thamhain, Hans J., and David L. Wilemon. "Conflict Management in Project-Oriented Work Environments." *Proceedings of the Sixth Annual Seminar/Symposium*. Drexel Hill, Penn.: Project Management Institute, 1974, p. 87.

Negotiating & Contracting for Project Management

Penny Cavendish
and
Martin D. Martin

Introduction

A key concern of the project manager is the identification and acquisition of the goods and services that will be required for the implementing and completing of project plans. The goods and services usually span a wide range of items, such as architectural and engineering services, materials, equipment, and supplies. Quite often a large percentage of the dollars provided for the project will be expended in this manner. Therefore, the successful project manager needs to have a knowledge of contracting and negotiation to enhance his or her skills and to ensure success. Contracting is referred to by various names, such as procurement, purchasing, acquisition, and buying. Certainly an argument can be made for the use of each of these terms. In a specific context each is probably relevant; however, in this monograph the term *contracting* will be used to refer to the process whereby a project manager, working within the organizational structure and policies of the company, takes action to acquire goods and services in support of his or her project. Contracting is the process of acquiring the required goods and services so that they will be available when needed, in the proper quantity and at the right price.

Contracting is a boundary spanning function that usually involves individuals from both the project office and the contracting function of the parent organization. These individuals will interact in the marketplace with specific sellers to acquire needed goods and services. This relationship is illustrated in Figure 1. If Project A involves the construction of a plant addition which will provide the firm with additional production capacity, then materials, supplies, and equipment must generally be obtained from other firms to complete the project. Once the additional plant capacity is in existence, then it will produce more goods to better serve the firm's markets.

Having established the role of contracting, the relationship can be better understood as outlined in Figure 2. The detailed contracting process will be considered later, but for now assume that the project manager has a requirement for an item of equipment. He or she will initiate a request to his or her contracting function and specify his or her need. The contracting people will contact one or more firms that manufacture and sell the equipment. The process of structuring and completing the transaction is negotiation. Not all contracting actions result in negotiation, as will be discussed later. The purpose of this monograph, however, is to examine the contracting and negotiation processes as they relate to the project manager and his or her position in the organization. It is necessary first to examine some pertinent project organizational issues.

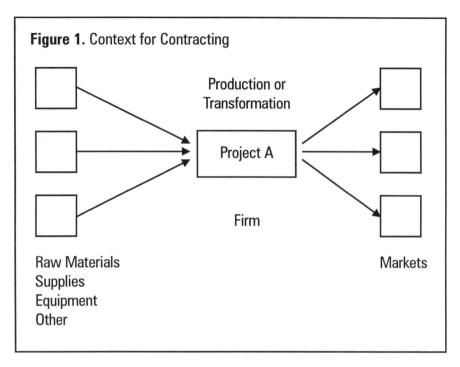

Figure 1. Context for Contracting

Production or Transformation

Project A

Firm

Raw Materials
Supplies
Equipment
Other

Markets

Organizational Issues

No one best way exists to structure an organization. Rather, the decision must be made in the context of the firm's objectives, its products, the demands of the environment, and other factors. Typically, organizations are structured on a functional basis. Such a structure is displayed in Figure 3. In this case the key organizational elements involve production, engineering, personnel, and marketing as line components, and accounting and legal as staff elements. Functional organizations tend to be characterized by tall structures with managerial layering, long lines of communication, rigid information flows, and sequential product flows. As the environment for the organization becomes more complex and more characterized by uncertainty in terms of markets and other economic, political, social, technological, and ecological factors, the organization becomes increasingly complex, and it becomes ever more difficult for managers to successfully accomplish organizational objectives. A solution to these problems has been found in the use of organic or systems structures, best represented by project organizations, which are tailored to environmental demands and permit specific managers to be assigned to key projects. The project management approach permits visibility, flexibility, and accountability for organizational activity. The resulting organization structure depends on the conditions that the company encounters in the environment. Each project is

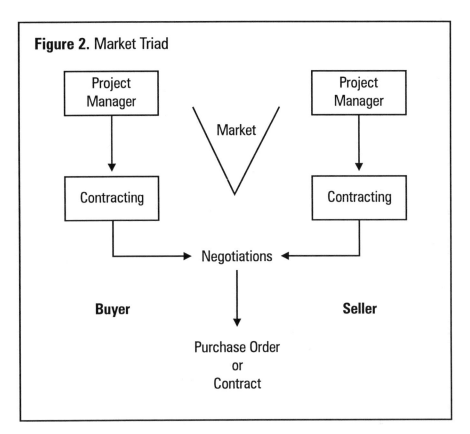

Figure 2. Market Triad

managed as an entity within the goals, policies, procedures, and other organizational constraints. In other words, this approach is basically contingent in nature and relies on the contingency theory of organization. It is not possible to examine all of the possible organizational structures that could include a project management subsystem. Rather, three structures are briefly reviewed and then the last part of this section examines how the contracting function may be organized within the firm and the internal organization of contracting.

The Project Management System

Initial moves toward project management usually involve the use of committees, task forces, steering groups, project expeditors, and coordinators. However, the management actions taken are still governed by the functional organization. Thus, work is performed within the functional department on a specialized basis. This situation can benefit the project; but since personnel are still working for the functional manager, flexibility can and is often sacrificed by subordinating the project goals to the good of the functional department.

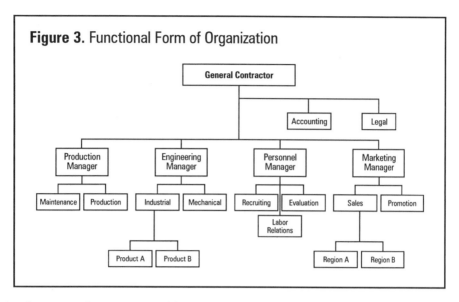

Figure 3. Functional Form of Organization

It becomes almost impossible to maintain cost, schedule, and performance goals as a consequence of the existing functional controls and the inevitable conflict that results. Contracting support for the project coordinator or expeditor must be obtained through the functional structure and may not be available when needed. The projectized structure is one solution.

Projectized Form of Organization

In the projectized form, the project manager has people from the various functional departments assigned directly to his or her project. For example, a person in the marketing department may be temporarily assigned to a project manager for the purpose of working on a certain project. This situation is outlined in Figure 4. The project manager is given a considerable amount of authority over the project and the personnel. This has a number of advantages for the project. Activities tend to be directed toward the same goal, creating an environment of unity of purpose and resulting in more open communication channels. In this organization structure, contracting support is provided by assigning contracting personnel directly to the project manager. This organizational form is not without disadvantages, the major one being a possible increase in the cost of maintaining the organization. There is a probability that equipment and facilities will be duplicated among several projects and resources will not be used efficiently, causing costs to be higher than necessary. Another problem is what to do with the personnel once the project is complete. As a project comes to a close, people begin to get uneasy as they worry about where to obtain the next job. Personnel may be retained on the project long after they are needed. In an attempt to combine the advantages of the

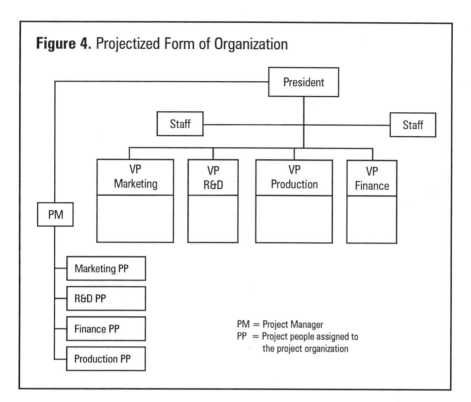

Figure 4. Projectized Form of Organization

PM = Project Manager
PP = Project people assigned to
the project organization

functional and projectized structures, a matrix organizational structure is often used.

Matrix Form of Organization

In the matrix structure, individuals from the various functional areas are not assigned to the project on a full-time basis. Rather, the project manager must task the functional department for their services. This condition is portrayed in Figure 5. Although highly complex, there are a number of advantages to using this type of organization:

• The project manager controls the resources necessary for project work. There is more flexibility in resource allocation.

• Functional departments support the project, allowing people to be shared, thus decreasing cost. Contracting support is provided by providing "shared" people from the functional contracting department. As a result of this type of delineation, people maintain a job after project completion.

• Since projects have different demands, policies and procedures can be developed for each project as needed; but they cannot counteract company policies and procedures.

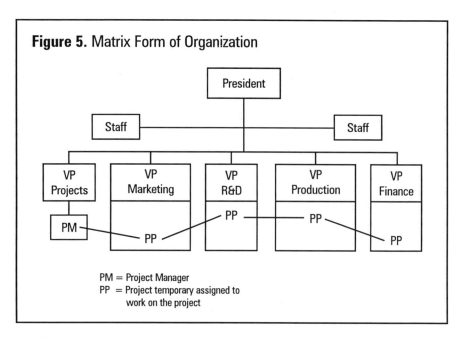

Figure 5. Matrix Form of Organization

PM = Project Manager
PP = Project temporary assigned to
work on the project

- The structure enhances rapid response to change, conflict, and project needs.

This structure is not without its disadvantages. A major disadvantage is that more administrative personnel are needed, thus increasing costs. Since the project managers work independently, there is the possibility for duplication of effort. The project manager does have access to project people within the functional departments. Access is not automatic, however, and this increases the possibility of conflict. For this complex organizational form to function, there must be a high degree of understanding between the project manager and functional managers, for they must constantly work together. Open channels of communication must be maintained, not only between the project manager and functional units, but also within the functional department itself.

Organic or Systems Organization Structure

For best results, the organizational structure adopted by the company should meet the competing demand of factors such as organizational objectives, management needs, product types, and environmental conditions. In Figure 6, an organic structure is displayed. It involves functional, matrix, and projectized elements and represents the approach that one company has chosen to deal with the organizational issue. In this case there is a separate, centralized contracting function. Project managers in the matrix must obtain their contracting support by negotiating with the director of contracting. On the other hand, the projectized project has its own contracting people assigned. The use

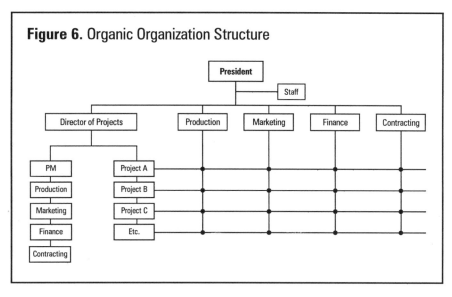

Figure 6. Organic Organization Structure

of project management thus raises the issue of whether contracting should be centralized or decentralized and how its internal structure should be impacted in an environment where either the matrix, projectized, or some combination structure is used.

Organization for Contracting

Within every project management organizational structure there is some type of internal organization for contracting, be it centralized, decentralized, or some combination of the two. When discussing centralization versus decentralization, the distinguishing factor depends upon where contracting authority lies; that is, who actually has the authority to sign contracts. For efficient contracting operations, the contracting organization should be appropriate for the job at hand. No consensus exists as to the best or ideal organizational contracting system. Therefore the structures are varied and change often as companies attempt to find a suitable structure. Probably the main factors used to determine the contracting form should be the basic structure and strategy of the project at hand.

Centralized Contracting

Centralized contracting exists when a single function is responsible for the entire contracting process. The director of this function is held accountable to management for the proper performance of contracting activities. Contracting procedures are typically stringent and standard across projects when the contracting function is centralized. When operating properly, centralized contracting has a number of benefits.

- It is more economical in terms of efficiency and effectiveness.
- Management control is facilitated when a single department is responsible for the contracting function.
- Fewer orders are processed, thus reducing duplication of effort. By decreasing duplication in contracting, receiving and inspection costs are also reduced.
- Centralization develops a higher degree of contracting specialization. Contracting specialists are more accustomed to the market and consequently buy more efficiently.
- Contracting coordination is achieved through face-to-face communication between the contracting specialist, project personnel, and the seller.
- The contracting manager is better able to deal with sellers because sellers have fewer people to call on.

Along with the advantages of a centralized contracting function, there are disadvantages. One disadvantage is that requisitions may be received sporadically, creating a bottleneck effect. For example, at the beginning of a fiscal year when funds are more readily available, the contracting department may have an excessive amount of orders without enough personnel to place them, thus creating a backlog. Another disadvantage is that requisitions may be processed without considering of the special needs of the project manager. The volume of actions may be too great to permit individual treatment.

Decentralized Contracting

At the other extreme is a decentralized contracting department. The contracting function can be considered decentralized when each project manager has control over the contracting process for his or her project. In most cases there is one person responsible for contracting activities under each project manager. Like centralized contracting, decentralized contracting has its advantages and disadvantages. Some of the strengths of decentralized contracting include:

- The project manager controls contract award. Contracting people are familiar with project needs and are under the supervision of the project manager.
- Contracting is tailored to a single project. The project manager is more knowledgeable about the project and contracting needs.
- The contracting person appointed to the project is available and under the project manager's direct control.
- When the contracting function is confined to one project, the contracting person is more responsive to the project.
- Since in most cases the centralized contracting department is geographically removed from the project, the location of contracting people with the project manager minimizes geographical distance and thus communication problems.

One of the disadvantages associated with decentralized contracting is that there tends to be duplication of effort involved in contracting, receiving, inspection, and accounts payable. As a result of this duplication, costs are higher. Another disadvantage is that contracting procedures tend to vary from one project manager to another. Thus there are no standard contracting policies.

In some situations, centralized contracting may be appropriate. For example, in an organization where projects are using the same types of materials, centralized contracting may be satisfactory. When projects are diversified in their contracting needs, decentralized contracting may be more appropriate. In most cases, neither rigid centralization nor loose decentralization of contracting meets the overall organizational need. In an attempt to maximize the advantages and minimize the disadvantages, usually some compromise between a centralized and decentralized contracting structure is needed to meet the needs of the project manager.

Organizing the Contracting Effort

In most cases the structure of the project management system, projectized or matrix, will impact the contracting organizational form. In a projectized organizational structure, contracting activities are basically decentralized, with contracting personnel usually assigned to a particular project. This makes the contracting organizational structure in a projectized project management environment more responsive and flexible, adaptable to the needs of the project.

In the matrix form of organization, the internal organization of contracting is basically centralized. A separate contracting department exists. The project manager has access to personnel in the contracting department, but he or she must gain contracting support by negotiating with the director of contracting.

With the more practical and complex organic form of organization structure, the organization for contracting can be some combination of centralized and decentralized. The organic structure in Figure 6 is made up of projectized, matrix, and functional structures. In the projectized portion, where personnel are assigned directly to a project manager, the contracting activities are carried out in a decentralized fashion. In the matrix and functional portions of the structure, contracting personnel remain under the control of the contracting department. In this figure, there is a decentralized and a centralized contracting organization, but the contracting structure is primarily centralized. Within this structure, contracting operations can vary from centralized to decentralized depending upon the demands of the project. For instance, if one project is structured so that continued operation of the firm is dependent upon the successful completion of the project, top management may be well advised to decentralize contracting operations to this project while maintaining centralized contracting for other projects.

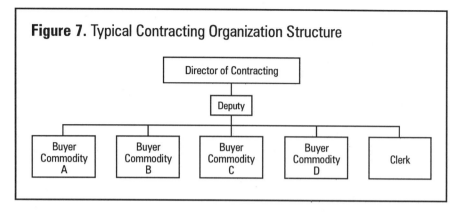

Figure 7. Typical Contracting Organization Structure

The organization for contracting can appear in various forms, but some type of specialized organization is essential for efficient operations. Figure 7 is just one example of a typical structure internal to a contracting department. This type of structure would most likely be appropriate in a matrix project management system. Responsible to top management, the director of contracting is mainly involved with management duties. Some of the project managers' duties include directing overall contracting policies, coordinating the contracting program and procedures, handling major aspects of contracting relations with suppliers, and a host of other duties. He or she is usually not involved in contract negotiations except on major contracts. The deputy is in charge of the buying staff and general office operations. In this representative structure, the buyers are organized on a commodity basis so that each has the sole responsibility for buying certain products. This allows the buyers to become more specialized in their field and acquire better knowledge of the product and sources of supply. In this case the project manager would need to negotiate with the director of contracting to gain support for his or her particular project. For example, the buyer of Commodity A may do some work with a number of different project managers, yet the director maintains control over all buyers. This arrangement makes the contracting operation basically centralized.

It should be stressed that the organization for contracting can take various forms within the project management system. The above example is just one possibility. In most cases the form of the internal contracting structure is dependent upon the project management system. The type of structure for the organization as a whole and the contracting organizational structure is a decision which is made by top management. When determining the structural type, management should consider the economics of the structure and what is best for the company. It is possible for adjustments to be made as necessary, depending upon the contracting system used.

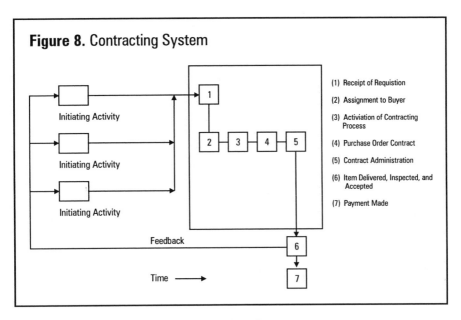

Figure 8. Contracting System

(1) Receipt of Requistion

(2) Assignment to Buyer

(3) Activiation of Contracting Process

(4) Purchase Order Contract

(5) Contract Administration

(6) Item Delivered, Inspected, and Accepted

(7) Payment Made

Contracting System

The contracting system as an organization entity involves the contracting function and a specific initiating or using activity for each transaction involving goods and services. This relationship is illustrated in Figure 8. The contracting function is basically reactive in nature. The using activity has a requirement for some goods or services. In most organizations the using activity will prepare a requisition and send the document to contracting for action. Contracting is usually not involved in the preparation of the requisition; however, for large complex purchases, an argument can be made for early contracting involvement. The specifications, drawings, and other attachments to the requisition are very crucial because they will structure and impact all actions taken by contracting, including the design of the resultant contract or purchase order. As portrayed in Figure 8, the first contracting action is triggered by the receipt of the requisition. The document is normally checked for accuracy and completeness. The next step is the assignment of an individual to be responsible for the transaction. The contracting process is activated by contacting one or more suppliers, depending on the nature of the goods or services to be acquired. The result of this contracting activity is either a purchase order or a contract. For a low-cost item, contract administration may be as simple as a follow-up action if the item is not delivered on a timely basis; whereas, for a contract involving the construction of a building, the contract administration may be extensive and of long duration, involving an entire project to manage the contract. At some point in time, the item will be

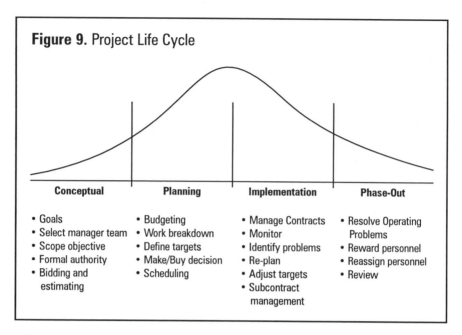

Figure 9. Project Life Cycle

Conceptual	Planning	Implementation	Phase-Out
• Goals	• Budgeting	• Manage Contracts	• Resolve Operating
• Select manager team	• Work breakdown	• Monitor	Problems
• Scope objective	• Define targets	• Identify problems	• Reward personnel
• Formal authority	• Make/Buy decision	• Re-plan	• Reassign personnel
• Bidding and	• Scheduling	• Adjust targets	• Review
estimating		• Subcontract	
		management	

delivered; and assuming it is of the proper quality based on inspection, it will be accepted and payment will be made to the supplier.

Project Life Cycle

The relationship of contracting to the project life cycle is demonstrated in Figure 9. In many cases the project starts with contract award. In other cases contract award coincides with the implementation phase. The implementation phase may also involve subcontract management. The exact relationship will depend on the overall project strategy. For example, if a general contractor is used to manage the construction of a building, then subcontract management and the integration of work efforts will be the general contractor's responsibility. On the other hand, if the project manager is pursuing a component breakout strategy and has retained the integration function, then subcontract management may well be a project management responsibility. Figure 10 illustrates the many opportunities for contract management involvement during all phases of the project.

The contracting process is represented overall in Block 3 of Figure 8. This process may be activated and completed in any one or all of the life cycle phases. For example, in the planning phase for a building, an architectural-engineering contract may be awarded for the design and layout of the building with a construction contract awarded for the implementation and phase-out phases. The contracting process is examined in more detail below.

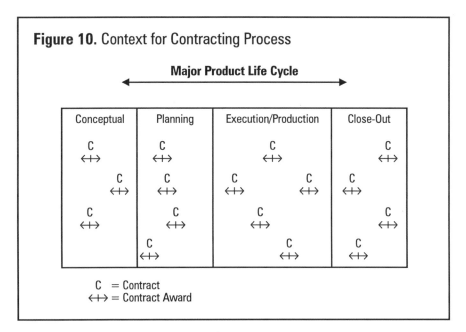

Figure 10. Context for Contracting Process

Major Product Life Cycle

Conceptual	Planning	Execution/Production	Close-Out
C ←+→	C ←+→	C ←+→	C ←+→
C ←+→	C ←+→	C ←+→ C ←+→	C ←+→
C ←+→	C ←+→	C ←+→	C ←+→
	C ←+→	C ←+→	C ←+→

C = Contract
←+→ = Contract Award

Contracting Process

The contracting process is detailed in Figure 11. It basically consists of three phases and five cycles. The phases are keyed to contract award. Thus, there is a pre-award phase which begins with project approval and ends during the solicitation cycle with the beginning of negotiations. The award phase follows and ends with the completion of negotiations. The post-award phase covers the writing and execution of the contract and ends when the contract is retired from the active contract list.

Requirement Cycle

The requirement cycle is basically the responsibility of the project manager. This individual controls the project budget, which is a product of the overall corporate planning process. He or she knows when and where the goods and services in support of his or her project will be needed. These requirements are generally portrayed by means of a network involving the Critical Path Method (CPM) or by means of the Program Evaluation and Review Technique (PERT). Thus, the project manager is responsible for describing his or her need by means of specifications and drawings, for specifying the schedule parameters in the form of delivery dates, and for estimating the cost of the goods or services in the context of its life cycle. Another major responsibility of the project manager and his or her staff is to deal with the "make or buy" aspects

Figure 11. The Contracting Process

The Contracting Process				
Pre-Award Phase		Award Phase	Post-Award Phase	
Requirement Cycle	Requistion Cycle	Solicitation Cycle	Award Cycle	Contractual Cycle
Cost Estimating		Cost Uncertainty Analysis Cost Analysis Risk Analysis		Milestones Info/Comm Performance Quality Control Payment Document Schedule Control Cost Control
		Invitation for Bid		
Project Approved	Requistion Initiated	Request for Proposal Request for Quote Released Contractor Cost Estimate	Completion of Negotiation	Contract Distribution — Contract Retired Phase Up/ Phase Down Reallocate/ Dispose of Resources Reassign People

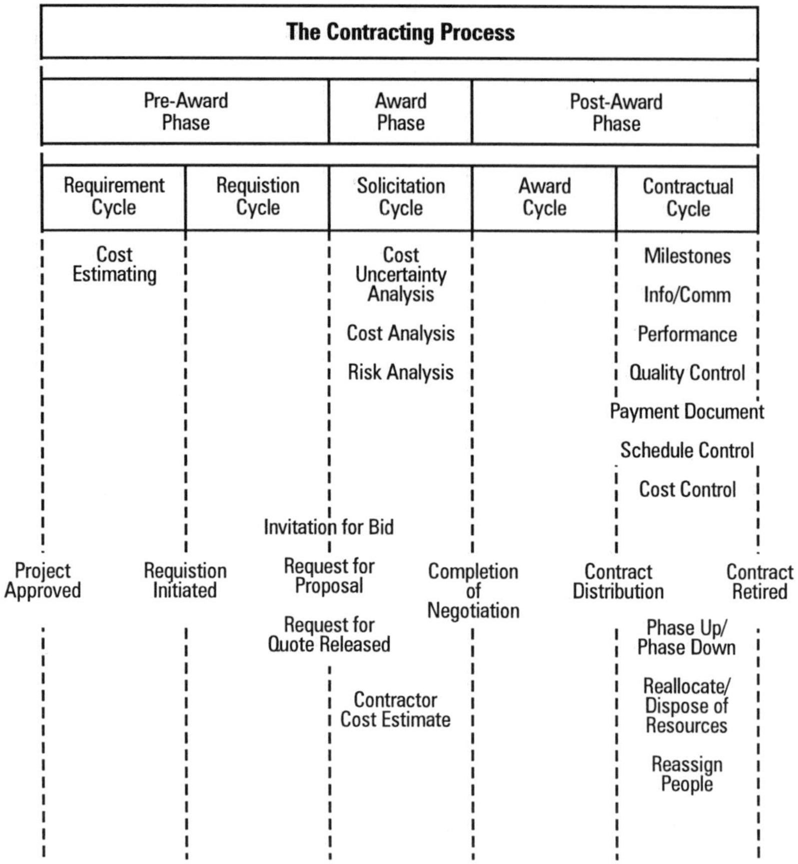

of the project. If the firm has idle capacity suitable for producing needed goods and services, the most economical method for acquiring them may be to use in-house resources. On the other hand, economics and other factors may dictate that the items be procured from external sources. In many firms the project management staff has the responsibility to maintain and forward to contracting a list of firms who are qualified to provide the needed goods and services. Although not covered in detail in this monograph, the most critical responsibility of the project management staff is to develop the specifications and drawings that must accompany the requisition to the contracting function. It is at this point that the contracting staff may be invited to attend meetings where the specifications are developed for the acquisition of complex items. This is the reason that the requirements cycle is included as a part of the contracting process. The specifications will drive the process. If they are exact and detailed and if contracting understands the requirement, the probability for a good purchase is increased. Once the requisition and accompanying documents have been developed and any needed management approvals obtained, the requisition is then forwarded to contracting. This description assumes a centralized contracting function. The initiation and forwarding of the requisition to contracting thus starts the requisition cycle.

Requisition Cycle

The requisition cycle for contracting essentially starts with the receipt of the requisition. This document and its attachments will be reviewed to ensure accuracy and completeness. While the responsibility for developing the specifications belongs to the project manager, the contracting staff has a responsibility to review and possibly challenge the specifications. The contracting staff, for example, may believe the specifications to be overly restrictive, thereby limiting the number of firms who can provide the goods or services. The project manager may have specified a sole source, whereas contracting may believe the transaction amenable to a multi-source solicitation. If this be the case, then these issues must be resolved in this cycle. Once the requisition has been reviewed and accepted, then contracting will initiate planning, which will culminate in issuing some type of solicitation to industry for the goods and services. The nature of the goods or services being procured, its urgency, the dollar value involved, and the available firms are among the factors that will determine if the solicitation will be verbal or written, if it will be an invitation for bid, request for proposal, or a request for quotation. The technical differences between these types is beyond the scope of this monograph, but basically for most low dollar value, standard items, the firm will solicit quotations. As the item becomes more unique, of higher dollar value, and more technology-oriented, the firm will pursue the bid or proposal route. A key consideration for this planning is the amount of uncertainty that may be associated with the technical nature of the goods or services. This uncertainty may well impact cost and schedule. For this reason, the type of contract that will be used to procure the goods or services becomes a critical concern for the project manager.

Strategy of Contract Type

The type of contract used is dependent on the degree of uncertainty facing the project manager. When entering into a contract, the objective of the buyer is to place on the seller the maximum performance risk while maintaining a degree of incentive for efficient and economical performance. The objective of the seller should be to minimize his or her degree of risk while increasing profit potential. There are basically two principal types of contracts—fixed price contracts and cost contracts. In a fixed contract, the seller agrees to perform a service or furnish supplies at the established contract price. In a cost contract, the seller agrees to use his or her best effort to fulfill the contract within the estimated contract amount; but if the amount is exceeded, the seller is no longer obligated for further performance unless the buyer increases funds. Given these two basic types of contracts, there are variations of contract types, with each bearing different degrees of risk. Thus, these variations can be placed on a continuum, with the buyer absorbing the risk at one extreme and the seller absorbing the risk on the other, as can be seen in Figure 12. Generally speaking, buyers prefer the fixed price contract, which places more risk on the seller, and sellers prefer cost contracts, which place more risk on the buyer. Five contract types are examined, beginning with one extreme of the continuum where the buyer absorbs the risk, moving through an intermediate range where risk is shared, and ending at the other extreme where the seller bears the risk.

The cost-plus-percentage-of-cost contract provides for reimbursement to the contractor for allowable costs due to contract performance. Additionally, the contractor receives an agreed-upon percentage of the estimated cost as profit. From the buyer's standpoint, this is the most undesirable type of contract because the seller has no incentive to decrease costs. In fact, the seller may be motivated to increase costs since, by increasing costs, the profit potential will also increase. For example, if the estimated cost is $100,000 and the agreed-upon percentage is 10 percent, the estimated total price is $110,000. If the seller increases costs to $110,000, the total price would be $121,000. Thus, there would be an increase in profit of $1,000. In this situation the project manager will want to pay particular attention to the control of labor and material costs so that the seller will not be able to purposefully increase these costs. Although this type of contract is prohibited for federal government use, it is used in private industry, particularly in the construction industry. As can be seen from Figure 12, 100 percent of the risk is borne by the buyer.

The cost-plus-fixed-fee contract provides that the seller be reimbursed for allowable costs of performing the contract, and in addition the seller receives as profit a fixed fee payment usually based on a percentage of estimated costs. This fixed fee does not vary with actual costs unless the scope of work is changed. For example, if the estimated cost for performance is $100,000 and a 10 percent profit fee is agreed upon, the fee is $10,000. Even if costs rise to $110,000, the fee remains at $10,000. Under this type of contract, the project manager assumes a high degree of risk while the seller assumes minimum risk. This type of contract is also susceptible to abuse in that there is a ceiling placed on profit potential, but there is no motivation for the seller to decrease costs. Therefore, the project manager should keep tight control on labor and

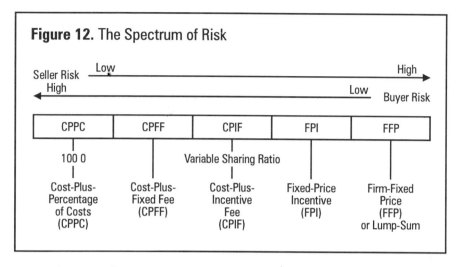

Figure 12. The Spectrum of Risk

CPPC	CPFF	CPIF	FPI	FFP

100 0   Variable Sharing Ratio

Cost-Plus-Percentage of Costs (CPPC)   Cost-Plus-Fixed Fee (CPFF)   Cost-Plus-Incentive Fee (CPIF)   Fixed-Price Incentive (FPI)   Firm-Fixed Price (FFP) or Lump-Sum

material costs. This type of contract is primarily used in research projects where the effort required to achieve success is uncertain until well after the contract is signed.

Another cost reimbursement type of contract, the cost-plus-incentive-fee, means the seller is paid for allowable performance costs along with a predetermined fee and an incentive bonus. If the final cost is less than the expected cost, both the buyer and seller benefit by the cost savings based upon a pre-negotiated sharing formula. This sharing formula is an agreed-upon percentage reflecting the degree of uncertainty each party will bear. For example, expected cost is $100,000, the fee to the seller is $10,000, and there is a sharing formula of 85/15 where the buyer absorbs 85 percent of the uncertainty and the seller absorbs 15 percent of the risk. If the final price is $80,000, resulting in a cost savings of $20,000, the seller is reimbursed for the final cost and the fee, plus an incentive of $3,000 (15 percent of $20,000), for a total reimbursement of $93,000. Both the buyer and the seller share the risk in this situation, but both can gain. The seller can increase his or her fee if costs are below the target cost, thus giving the seller an incentive to decrease costs so as to increase profit. The cost-plus-incentive-fee contract is primarily used when contracts involve a long performance period with a substantial amount of hardware development and test requirements.

The most complex type is the fixed price-plus-incentive-fee contract, which is composed of a target cost, target profit, target price, ceiling price, and share ratio. Based on a ceiling price of $120,000, target cost of $100,000, target profit of $10,000, target price of $110,000, and share ratio of 70/30, for every dollar the seller can reduce costs below $100,000 the savings will be shared by the buyer and seller based upon the negotiated sharing formula which reflects the degree of uncertainty faced by each party. Assuming the seller tries to maximize profits, he or she is provided an incentive to reduce his or her costs by producing more efficiently. If costs exceed the ceiling price of $120,000, the seller receives no profit and the maximum price to the buyer is $120,000, regardless of the costs incurred by the seller. Consequently, risk is shared by both the buyer and seller. This incentive type contract is usually used when contracts are for a substantial sum and involve a long production time. This enables the seller to develop production efficiency during the performance of the contract.

Used most often, the firm-fixed-price or lump-sum contract, is an agreement where the contractor agrees to furnish supplies or services at a specified price that is not subject to adjustment because of performance costs. The seller bears the greatest degree of risk while the potential for profit is at a maximum. In this situation the seller is motivated to decrease costs by producing efficiently because, regardless of what the costs are, the seller receives the agreed-upon amount. As a consequence, the seller should place emphasis upon controlling costs. This type of contract is best suited when reasonably definite production specifications are available and costs are relatively certain.

By now, many of the key decisions concerning aspects of the contract such as price, quantity, quality, and other specifications have been made. The type of contract desired has been established. Approval by top management to continue contracting procedures has been received. Planning for future contract negotiations has begun. These accomplishments trigger the start of the solicitation cycle.

Solicitation Cycle

During this cycle of the contracting system there is actual contact with the marketplace. The project manager has established his or her project needs. It is now the responsibility of the contracting department to fulfill these needs through the market. There are three major concerns of the contracting personnel during solicitation. The first concern is the method of contract origination. The second concern is source qualification. The third concern is the negotiation meeting.

Origination

There are basically two ways in which a contract can originate—unilaterally or bilaterally. When made unilaterally, the contract usually takes the form of a purchase order, which is a relatively simple type of legally binding document. The purchase order is usually a standardized form with approximately seven copies. Each of these copies has a different purpose for satisfying internal and external communication needs. For example, one copy may go to the receiving department to be used to check the incoming order, while another copy remains on file for purposes of follow-up. In most cases the contracting department sends out the purchase order, expecting the seller to accept it automatically. Usually, the purchase order is used when routine, standard cost items are needed. Because a purchase order is a legal document, care should be taken when preparing it. Such aspects as quantity, quality, price, delivery, and other factors affecting product acceptability should be clearly specified. Terms and conditions usually appear on the purchase order in written form. In most cases these terms and conditions are standardized, but in some cases special conditions may be included. Very rarely is the negotiation process involved when consummating a purchase order. Therefore, the wording of the purchase order should be prepared such that there is little room for misinterpretation. Once the authorized signature is on the purchase order, it is sent to the supplier. Many companies want a written acceptance of the order and usually the seller returns the acknowledgment copy of the purchase order for confirmation. Relying on customers to adhere to ethical business practices, most sellers do not worry about the terms and conditions on the purchase order. Generally, the items ordered are stock items which will be automatically delivered to the customer. In some cases the supplier may want to negotiate on some of the terms and conditions written on the purchase order, but this is not done very often.

When originated bilaterally, there are three ways in which a contract may be developed. The first way is when the buyer requests a quotation for the contract from different suppliers. The project manager will inform the contracting department as to the goods or services needed, and the contracting department will proceed to develop a request for quotation. This is usually done when the items are of relatively low dollar value, such as supplies and materials. A survey of potential sources of supply is completed. The quotation request informing suppliers of the services to be performed or the goods needed is sent out to a scaled-down number of possible suppliers. It is advantageous for the contracting department, with the aid of the project manager, to develop a form with complete information regarding what is required so that prospective suppliers will be working with the same information. This form will also be useful when reviewing and appraising the competitive quotes from suppliers. The record will aid in comparing factors such as set-up, freight, and tooling costs, which must be considered before making a selection. In some cases it will be necessary for some negotiation to take place. For instance, if there is a wide gap between quotes from two suppliers on the price of the item, it may be due to some misunderstanding; it would then be beneficial to hold a meeting to clear up misunderstandings and negotiate to an appropriate price.

The second manner in which a contract is developed bilaterally is by releasing a request for proposal. This type of request is usually made when there is a high dollar value involved and the item or service is not standardized. Examples of when a request for proposal may be sent out is for a construction project, a research and development project, and a made-to-order, highly complex piece of machinery. With the aid of the contracting department, the project manager should develop a specific description of his or her needs. Blueprints, drawings, specifications, and other appropriate data should be included. The contracting department should select possible suppliers and mail the request to them. Suppliers will return the desired information such as price, schedule, and performance. This information will be reviewed by the contracting department and the project manager. Each proposal should be reviewed thoroughly for omissions or exceptions. To a degree, this type of request involves more uncertainty than the previous solicitation types. Therefore, this is a key area for future negotiations. Based on the different suppliers' proposals and their own knowledge, the contracting department should be able to identify satisfactory proposals. Very often, some criteria is lacking and features offered by suppliers differ, such as on complex equipment, so that the buyer will resort to negotiations in order to obtain the best advantage for the company. Since there is some uncertainty involved, negotiation on price, quality, and schedule may take place, with some trade-offs being made.

The last method of bilateral contracting is conducted by releasing an invitation to bid. A prerequisite to this type of process is a clear and accurate description of the supplies, equipment, and services required. It is most appropriate for high dollar value, standard items. Prepared by the project manager and the contracting department, specifications are of written form, including drawings, industry standards, performance requirements, and other pertinent information. This must be done so as to ensure fair competition among all bidders. Provisions should be stated in such a manner to avoid misinterpretation. Implicit in this concept, an invitation for bids is open to all qualified potential bidders who may wish to participate. Most often, newspaper advertising is used along with advertising in trade papers. Since advertising for bids cannot be relied upon to reach all bidders, invitations to bid may also be sent directly to interested prospective bidders. For example, if the project manager has worked with a certain supplier before, he or she may request that an invitation to bid be sent directly to the company. A reasonable amount of time should be allowed the prospective bidders for the preparation and submission of bids. Formal bids are submitted to the contracting department in sealed envelopes. All bids are opened at a specific time. Bidders are allowed to attend the bid opening. Most of the time, bids are opened and read aloud for those that are present. In most cases the contract award goes to the lowest responsible bidder. This allows for consideration of other criteria besides price, such as quality and time. Professional judgment is critical. If the contract is not awarded to the lowest bidder, reasons as to why should be carefully documented. This type of contracting method is open to fraud, collusion, and other dishonest conduct. Therefore, project managers and contracting personnel must practice carefully defined ethical business procedures. Since the contract is usually awarded to the lowest bidder, negotiations do not usually take place between the buyer and seller.

Source Qualification

With input from the project manager, the contracting department is responsible for developing a list of qualified sources of supply. The contracting department should maintain information files on firms that have previously done work for the company. Information about the product, delivery history, desirability as a supplier, and other general information should be included in the file. Since many contracting operations are repetitive, it is advantageous for the contracting department to maintain these files so that the department need not spend time researching this information anew for each contract solicitation.

Assuming that the project is different from any other previously undertaken, thus requiring different goods and services, a source qualification list must be developed. Sources of information about suppliers are easily accessible. Through their associations with professional organizations, the project manager as well as other company personnel may be able to provide information about possible suppliers. Usually well informed about the capabilities of their products along with competitors' products, sales personnel are an excellent source of information concerning possible sources of supply. Contracting departments in other companies are another potential source of information. Other sources of information that may be used to further develop the source list include supplier catalogs, trade journals, trade exhibits, and trade registers.

Once the prospective supplier list is completed, the contracting department should collect information about each source to determine if the supplier will be able to fulfill the requirements. Since the collection of information can be time consuming, the contracting department should obtain only the data necessary to make the decision. How extensive this evaluation will be depends upon the nature, dollar value, and complexity of the contract. For example, if the contract is to involve an expensive, complex piece of machinery, the supplier evaluation will be more extensive than if the contract involves a low dollar value, common office supply item.

The project manager along with the contracting department should assess the management capability of the supplying firm. The ability to control a firm can influence successful performance. For instance, if the contract is for the construction of a bridge, activities must be integrated and coordinated, which obviously requires extensive management skills.

Technical and manufacturing capabilities need to be evaluated in some cases. When expertise is needed in a particular field, technical capability should be examined. For example, the project manager may desire to have the supplier knowledgeable in the area of design to aid in constructing a building.

The manufacturing capability should also be considered. Suppliers with suitable, more modern equipment will probably be more capable of meeting quality and time requirements. Equipment needed for the process should be available along with personnel possessing the right skills. The supplier should be able to control production by acquiring material of required quality within a realistic time period. The supplier should attempt to create a smooth flow of materials to the buyer.

An investigation of the financial strength of a potential supplier should be made. Financial strength can reveal if the firm is capable of performing without supply interruption. For example, if the financially troubled supplier is behind in production and will not be able to meet a delivery date, the supplier will probably not be willing to work overtime in order to meet the terms of the delivery schedule. The contracting department may also want to evaluate the capability of the supplier to finance a large dollar value contract in order to avoid progress payments.

The result of the evaluation should be a list of several acceptable sources of supply with whom the contracting department could confidently award a contract. There probably will not be one best source. Therefore, the contracting department is assured of alternative sources of supply along with maintaining competition, which can prove beneficial in the negotiation process. Several suppliers may be very close when at a decision point. In the process of appraising and narrowing the choice, however, a negotiation meeting may be held where terms and conditions are considered in order to determine which supplier will best satisfy the needs of the project in the best interests of the company.

Negotiation Meeting

Assuming all of the planning for negotiations is complete, the actual negotiation meeting occurs during the solicitation cycle of the contracting process. Negotiations can be conducted by one person or by a team of individuals. Usually in contract negotiations where there is a high dollar value project involved a team of individuals will do the negotiating. The team might be composed of representatives from engineering, accounting, marketing, legal, or other departments depending upon the nature of the project. Before entering the meeting, the team should understand the objective of the negotiation and be briefed on technical and economic matters. In order to avoid confusion, it is essential to designate a leader of the team. The authority of this person to commit the company and the limits of authority of other team members should be clearly established. Basically, the authority to commit company funds lies with the contracting department. Therefore the leader of the team is usually a contracting specialist. The project manager should also be included on the negotiating team in order to protect the project interests. Inclusion of the project manager also helps to ensure that specifications are accurately interpreted.

A negotiation meeting is a dynamic situation that brings a buyer and seller together, but each party has different objectives when they come to a meeting. The buyer wants something such as a piece of equipment or new building which increases the possibility of future profit, but he or she wants it at as low a price as possible. On the other hand, the seller wants to do the service for the buyer, but he or she desires to make as much profit as possible.

The period covered by the negotiation meeting can be divided into five stages—protocol, probing, scratch bargaining, closure, and agreement. These five negotiation stages can be considered as a sequential process. For ease of analysis, the negotiation meeting has been divided into stages, but there is no sharp dividing line between the stages in actual negotiations. By examining the activities of the negotiators, it should be possible to determine what stage the negotiations have reached in the process. The negotiators should be aware of what stage in the process they are working so they can focus on the problems inherent in the particular stage. Negotiators should not rush the process nor attempt to leave one stage incomplete and move to the next stage too quickly.

It is during the protocol stage that introductions are made and the negotiators get to know each other. During this stage, the atmosphere in which the rest of the negotiation meeting is conducted will be determined.

During the probing stage, the negotiators begin the search process. Each party will identify their issues of concern. Issues are not debated to any extent, only reviewed in an attempt to get a feel and understanding for where the other party stands. This is the time to identify strengths and weaknesses of the opponent and possible areas of interest. The negotiation plan may need to be modified at this time to take into account any information disclosed by the opponent during this stage which the negotiator did not anticipate.

Stage three, scratch bargaining, is the essence of the meeting. Here the actual bargaining occurs and concessions are made. The differences between the two parties' approach, basically concerned with time, cost, and performance criteria, are discussed with some outcome deemed appropriate by both negotiating parties. During this stage, points of concession are identified. The gap between the two parties narrows, marking the beginning of the next stage.

During the closure stage, the two positions are summed up and final concessions are reached. A summary of the agreements reached is documented. Arrangements for recording the results are initiated, leading into the last stage.

The main difficulty in the agreement stage of negotiation is making sure both parties have an identical understanding of the agreements that have been reached. Differences in language and terminology contribute to misunderstandings, and clarification may be necessary. It is possible that negotiations may be reopened concerning a point that was previously thought settled. This stage marks the end of the negotiation meeting, but plans for recording the agreements in a written contract should be established before the meeting is dismissed.

Included in the appendix to this monograph is a checklist designed to aid the project manager and contracting department when participating in a negotiation. Throughout the negotiation meeting, each party will attempt to obtain the best deal possible. There are a number of tactics negotiators can use in an attempt to gain an advantage.

Negotiation Tactics

Negotiation is not only a technical process. It also involves humans. Since negotiation is actually a bargaining process between individuals, the process involves personalities, attitudes, feelings, motives, and, to a large extent, psychology. When used by competent negotiators, these techniques can be a powerful working tool. There are many negotiation tactics that can be used, and it is impossible to cover them all in this monograph. Some of the more prominent tactics are cited below.

- By imposing a *deadline* for reaching an agreement, one party limits the time involved in negotiating. A deadline can be a powerful tactic because it implies a possible loss to both parties involved. The other party does not necessarily have to accept the deadline as their own, but in most cases they do.
- Using another type of timing technique, one party can take the other party by *surprise*. One party may have some information, such as a price change, and present it to the other party who was not aware that they possessed this information.
- Once an agreement is reached, one party may claim that it cannot be finalized because the negotiator has *limited authority* and cannot commit the company's resources. This is a stalling tactic. It would be advantageous to know the authority of the opponent early in the negotiation meeting.
- Along the same line as limited authority, the party may claim that the person with final authority is absent. This *missing-man* technique may also be used when the party does not have the information asked for by the other party.
- The negotiator may use the tactic of *fair and reasonable*. Comparisons to other like situations may be used. For example, he or she may claim the price for the computer is equitable because that is what another company is paying.
- In some cases, the tactical use of delays can be beneficial. The meeting can be delayed when a party leaves the room for some reason, or upon the strategic arrival of refreshments, or based on a request for recess. Delays may be desired because a team member is going astray, tempers are beginning to flare, to divert from the subject, or for some other reason.
- Although the objectives of the two parties differ, both parties need each other. Therefore, *reasoning together* by working problems out to the benefit of all involved may be a useful technique.

- In some cases, one party may use the tactic of *confusing the opponent*. In this situation the party may deliberately distort issues and figures, creating confusion. If this is done, someone should speak up before agreeing to anything.
- *Withdrawal* is another technique sometimes used. One party may make a false attack upon an issue, then retreat. This is usually done to divert attention from an area of possible weakness.
- Another method that may be used to the advantage of one party is to make the other party appear *unreasonable*. For instance, say the buyer concedes on a number of minor issues asked for by the seller, then a major issue comes up on which agreement cannot be reached the buyer points out all of the areas in which they made concessions, thus making the seller appear unreasonable.
- If an agreement cannot be reached, one party may suggest that the issue go to *arbitration* where a third party becomes involved. Since the third party may be biased, there is a possibility that one or the other party may be hurt. Therefore, the party using this technique usually hopes it will scare the other party into agreement.
- *Fait accompli* may be a tactic. One party may claim that what is being asked for has already been accomplished and cannot be changed. For example, a supplier may say he or she shipped the order because he or she knew that was what the buyer wanted, therefore it is not a necessary issue to be negotiated.

These are just a representative few of the tactics negotiators may use during the meeting. There are a number of others such as speed, confession, threats, and small bites which may be used, but this does not complete the possible list. The use of tactics is inevitable. We are not proposing that the project manager use or not use any one of these tactics. The project manager should be aware of them because there is a possibility that these tactics may be used on him or her. It is suggested that the project manager learn all he or she can about his or her opponent, including the tactics he or she may use during the negotiation meeting. Negotiation is difficult. Throughout the meeting, the project manager should keep in mind the objectives to be achieved.

Objectives of Negotiation

Throughout the negotiation meeting, negotiators should keep in mind the objectives of the negotiation meeting and key the tactics they may use in order to achieve these objectives. Working for the betterment of the company, the project manager wants to obtain a fair and reasonable price, while still getting the contract performed within the time and performance limitations. The buyer will want to put clauses in the contract so that he or she will be assured of some degree of control over how the contract is performed. While maintaining some control, the buyer should persuade the seller to give maximum cooperation to the buyer when carrying out the terms of the contract. The last objective of the buyer is to develop a good relationship with the supplier. This objective cannot be overemphasized for the buyer will have to carry on the relationship throughout the contract period. A cooperative attitude during negotiations makes it easier to work together on possible contested matters that may occur during the contract period. Also, if the buyer-seller relationship is good, the groundwork is laid for possible future projects for which the seller would be an appropriate selection.

After an agreement has been reached in the negotiation meeting, the contracting process enters the post-award phase. This phase, basically administrative in nature, is made up of the award cycle and the contract administration cycle. The award cycle involves the writing of the contract and contract acceptance. An examination of the negotiation process should also occur during this cycle. Activities in the contract administration cycle range from change control, quality control, inspection and acceptance, through to contract completion and payment.

Award Cycle

The completion of negotiations marks the beginning of the award cycle. The actual contract between the two parties must be written based upon the agreement reached during the negotiation meeting. Both parties must agree to the contract as it is written. A post-negotiation critique is conducted, including a critique of the planning done for the meeting as well as the conduct of the meeting itself.

A contract is comprised of a number of clauses expressing the agreement reached between the buyer and seller. Some representative clauses, which may be negotiated and included in the contract, are as follows:

- At the beginning of the contract, certain definitions may be clarified. The buyer and seller may be spelled out. Ambiguous terms may be defined.
- The scope of responsibilities of the buyer and seller may be included.
- How the price will be determined—such as fixed-fee contract or cost-plus-incentive contract—and how payments will be made—partial or lump-sum, within 30 days after delivery, or some other method—may be set forth.
- Both parties may want to determine how changes to the work effort are to be made and who must approve of them.
- The project manager may desire to have some written guarantee concerning the goods or services provided.
- Insurance concerns such as workmen's compensation, title change, and damage to equipment may be covered.
- Conditions under which requirements can be wavered may be defined.

- Inspections may be desired at set intervals or in some other manner by the project manager. Decisions may be made as to who will bear inspection costs.
- The buyer and seller may desire to set forth terms of termination. For example, the buyer may terminate the contract for convenience and the seller may ask for a penalty. The project manager may want to cover himself or herself if the seller defaults.
- Results of a delay in completion, excusable or unexcusable, may be determined. For instance, there may be a penalty to the seller if the equipment is not delivered in the specified time frame.

There are many more clauses that can be included in the contract; other examples include subcontracts, performance bonds, notices. In fact, a contract can include almost any legal provision, but the project manager should not go overboard with unnecessary clauses because everything has a cost. Clauses included should express the intent of the buyer's side while also satisfying the seller. Once the clauses are selected, the contract must be written.

A contract is a legal document of purchase or sale which is binding on both parties. Certain elements must be present in a contract situation. If any of these elements are absent, the contract is no longer enforceable. When entering into a contract, the people involved must have the legal capacity to do so. There are variations from state to state as to the definition of legal capacity. In the situation of the contracting department, the person who signs the contract must also have the authority of the firm. A contractual relationship is a relationship that is voluntary. The two parties must have a mutual meeting of the minds and an understanding as to what the contract means. Therefore the terms and conditions of the contract should not be ambiguous. If force, coercion, or duress are used to develop the contract, the contract is not legally binding. There must be a sufficient cause to contract; that is, consideration must be provided to both parties. The two parties enter into the contract to get something for something. For instance, the seller provides a service in return for money. The purpose of the contract must not be illegal or against public policy. Besides the above elements of a contract—legal capacity, mutual assent, consideration, and legality—the form of the contract must be appropriate. The form must follow applicable state laws and laws governing businesses. All of these elements must be evident in the written contract if it is to be legally enforceable. In many cases it is advisable to have the legal department or a lawyer oversee the process of writing the contract.

Once the contract is written, it is sent to the seller for signature. The seller can refuse to sign the contract, whereby the contracting process will start over again. On the other hand, the seller can accept the contract as written, making the next step the action taken by the seller to comply with the contract by providing the goods or services. It is possible for the seller to conditionally accept the contract. This implies that the seller will sign, but there are some changes in the contract he or she would like to see incorporated. In this situation, the buyer can turn down the change, accept the change, or do some more negotiations on the proposed change. To prevent this type of activity, it is advisable for the project manager to have representatives from both sides evaluate the contract as it is being negotiated and written. The status of the seller must also comply with the basic elements of the contract as stated above. Once the contract is signed, the seller is obligated to perform the services or deliver the goods, and the buyer is obligated to pay the price of the contract. Even after the contract is signed and the negotiations are complete, the negotiation process is not quite finished.

Once the contract is signed by both parties, a post-negotiation critique should be conducted. This critique provides feedback to the project manager as to how well the negotiation was planned and conducted. Since there is a possibility of future negotiations, neither party involved wants to feel as if they lost in the process. In other words, if there is a "winning party," the feeling of winning should not be communicated to the other party. So that both parties can maintain their self-esteem, both the buyer and the seller should be able to walk away from the meeting with the feeling that they actually won.

The project manager should critique the planning process that occurred when preparing for negotiations. By performing this evaluation, the project manager will be able to identify areas where improvements for future negotiations are desired. For example, the project manager may be able to identify areas in which information was lacking, such as cost data. When conducting the planning critique, the project manager should focus upon the primary considerations discussed previously under planning for negotiations. Reference to the checklist for the pre-negotiation phase, which is included in the appendix, is a good starting point when conducting this critique.

In addition to evaluating the planning process, the project manager should also critique the negotiation meeting. A good starting point would be to establish how well the negotiations were able to achieve the objectives of the negotiation. The project manager may want to consider the causes and resolution of conflict. Since the buyer will be working with the seller for a period of time, communication aspects, both verbal and nonverbal, should be considered. Areas in which communication between the parties could be improved should be evaluated. Other considerations may be found in the checklist for the negotiation phase, included in the appendix.

The project manager can answer the questions in the negotiation critique, included in the appendix, to help in evaluating the meeting. By conducting a critique of the meeting, the project manager should be able to define areas where improvements may be made so that future meetings can run more smoothly.

In addition, the project manager should analyze the strategy and tactics both parties used, thus maintaining his or her information base. He or she should identify what tactics were used to achieve the objectives and how each party handled the approach of the other party. Areas where emphasis was placed should be defined. For instance, if emphasis was placed on the scheduling portion for the conduct of services, the project manager should determine if the negotiators had adequate information on which to base their analyses.

In many cases, there is a tendency to leave this last step out of the negotiation process. This feedback process is important to the project manager. The outcome of the process identifies areas of strengths and weaknesses. This type of information will aid the project manager and the contracting department in future negotiations. It should also help the project manager when carrying out activities specified by the provisions of the contract. In the appendix of this monograph, a checklist for the post-negotiation phase is provided for the project manager to aid in his or her evaluation of the negotiation process. After both the contract is executed and the negotiation process is evaluated, the contracting process makes a transition into the contract administration cycle.

Contract Administration Cycle

Once the contract has been signed by the buyer and seller, performance marks the beginning of the contract administration cycle. This cycle consists of all actions involved with the delivery of goods or services, acceptance, payment, and close-out of the contract. The purpose of this cycle is to make sure the seller performs according to the contract and receives proper reimbursement. For example, in the construction of a building, the project manager will want to monitor the contractor to make sure the contractor constructs the building to the specifications and drawings provided, and that he or she does not make arbitrary changes. In most cases, many small problems will occur; but with close surveillance and appropriate action by the project manager these problems can be overcome. During this cycle, the project manager, along with other individuals, will interface with the contractor frequently. Contract provisions will be interpreted, with disputes and appeals being processed. All contract changes should be negotiated and properly executed. Finally, progress payments must be approved.

As a consequence of environmental factors, change is inevitable. The proposed change can add new work or delete some work from the existing contract, or it can be some combination of adding certain requirements while deleting others. Therefore, definite procedures to incorporate a contract change are usually outlined in the agreement. Clauses stating who can initiate changes and who can authorize changes should be included. Changes are not necessarily bad. However, it is important to control the changes. A thorough evaluation of the potential change should be made before actually making the change. Once a change is made, the change should be incorporated into the project plans or problems can occur. Then, the configuration should be managed based on the changes.

The major concerns in the change control process include funds, schedule, performance, and, in some cases, other special interest items. These concerns are particularly important in the project environment. When there is a change to be incorporated, the impact on costs should be analyzed. How the change is going to affect the project schedule should be considered. Along with funds and schedule, the project manager should determine how the change will impact the anticipated performance. For instance, he or she may want to determine if adding structural components will increase the life of a proposed building. When considering change, all of these concerns should be analyzed simultaneously. The project manager will want to look at the trade-offs among the concerns. For instance, he or she may want to increase the available funds in order to meet the established delivery schedule.

In order to control change, it is suggested that the project manager develop and use an information system. In controlling costs, the project manager should consider both direct and indirect costs. It would be beneficial if he or she acquires and retains appropriate information which enables him or her to calculate variances between proposed and actual costs. With the scheduling concern, an information system would aid the manager in determining the effect of the change in terms of the critical path, concurrency, and integration. The system should be able to establish specification conformance and completion points which the project manager can use to analyze the impact change will have on the performance of the goods or services resulting from the project.

Throughout the term of the contract, the project manager, with the aid of the contracting department, should attempt to ensure that the goods or services conform to specifications and performance standards by conducting periodic inspections. The quality desired for the goods or services will be defined in the contract clauses. It is especially true in the project environment that quality control does not occur at the end of the contract period. Surveillance should occur throughout the process. In some cases, the project manager may be interested in investigating the contractor's quality control program to see if it corresponds to contract standards.

During the negotiation meeting, the project manager should negotiate warranty clauses which are deemed applicable to the particular project. A warranty clause provides the buyer with additional time after delivery for correction of defects or some other type of adjustment. This clause will run for a specified amount of time with a definite beginning point. When setting up such a clause, a good beginning would be to define a defect or failure which, if there is an occurrence, the seller must correct at no extra cost. The clause may cover such aspects as defective material and poor workmanship. It is impossible to cover all items that may fail, but the project manager should attempt to cover major details. Provisions should be made for situations over which the seller cannot be held responsible, such as floods, earth-quakes, and acts of God. When covered by a warranty clause, problems that develop in performance are to be handled by the project manager and the contracting department. Once the buyer is aware of defects or failures in the product or service, the project manager and contracting department are contacted. It is their joint responsibility to determine if the contract covers the defect or failure and if it is within the warranty period. They must examine the types of remedies available, such as repair or replacement, then select the remedy that will best satisfy the needs. In some cases, this process may involve more negotiation between the buyer and seller.

Although the warranty clauses may cover the goods or services for an extended period of time, steps for contract completion may begin. At this point, excess resources can be disposed of or transferred. For instance, members of the project team may be placed back in their functional department in the case of a projectized organizational structure. With the aid of the members of the project team, a performance evaluation measuring how well the seller did in meeting the terms of the contract should be prepared. Such aspects as cost, delivery, and performance should be included in the evaluation. Also, a statement as to the status of the relationship between the buyer and seller may be included. This information will comprise a performance data file on the particular seller, which can be added to the source file that the contracting department maintains. Contract completion is the final step of the contract administration cycle within the post-award phase, thus marking closure for the contracting and negotiation processes.

References

Adams, John R., Stephen E. Barndt, and Martin D. Martin. *Managing by Project Management*. Dayton, Ohio: Universal Technology Corp., 1979.

Aljian, George W. *Purchasing Handbook,* Third edition. New York: McGraw-Hill, 1973.

Beckmann, Neal W. *Negotiations: Principles and Techniques*. Lexington, Mass.: D.C. Heath and Company, 1977.

Beckmann, Neal W., and Myron A. Carpenter. *Purchasing for Profit: An Approach to Measuring Purchasing Performance*. St. Louis, Mo.: Warren H. Green, Inc., 1979.

Evans, Stuart J., Harold J. Margulis, and Harry B. Yoshpe. *National Security Management Procurement*. Washington, D.C.: Industrial College of the Armed Forces, 1968.

Heinritz, Stuart F., and Paul V. Farrell. *Purchasing: Principles and Applications,* Fourth edition. Englewood Cliffs, N.J.: Prentice-Hall, 1965.

Karrass, Chester L. *The Negotiating Game*. Cleveland, Ohio: The World Publishing Company, 1970.

Kerzner, Harold. *Project Management: A Systems Approach to Planning, Scheduling, and Controlling*. New York: Van Nostrand Reinhold, 1979.

Lee, Lamar, Jr., and Donald W. Dobler. *Purchasing and Materials Management: Text and Cases*. Third edition. New York: McGraw-Hill, 1977.

Lewis, David V. *Power Negotiating Tactics and Techniques*. Englewood Cliffs, N.J.: Prentice-Hall, 1981.

Marsh, P.D.V. *Contract Negotiation Handbook*. Epping, Essex: Gower Press Limited, 1974.

Riemer, W.H. *Handbook of Government Contract Administration*. Englewood Cliffs, N.J.: Prentice-Hall, 1968.

Stuckenbruck, Linn C. (ed.). *The Implementation of Project Management: The Professional's Handbook*. Reading, Mass.: Addison-Wesley, 1981.

Warschaw, Tessa Albert. *Winning by Negotiation*. New York: McGraw-Hill, 1980.

Appendix

Checklist for Negotiation—Pre-Negotiation Phase

1. Know what you need to buy.
2. Determine urgency of requirement.
3. Develop strategies and tactics in detail.
4. Thoroughly research your opponent.
5. Develop a contingency plan.
6. Determine individual or team approach.
7. Designate the team leader.
8. Develop an independent negotiation objective with minimum/maximum limits.
9. Identify give and take points.
10. Ascertain the limits of your authority.
11. Know your strengths and weaknesses.
12. Ensure that team personnel are qualified as to traits and training.

Checklist for Negotiation—Negotiation Phase

1. Establish a common ground for negotiation.
2. Observe protocol.
3. Do not make the first major concession.
4. Use team members skillfully.
5. Don't be afraid to say no.
6. Establish the rules for negotiation, such as an appeal individual.
7. Always keep your main objective in sight.
8. Be willing to change strategies and tactics.
9. Be willing to compromise.
10. Be calm, poised, and patient.
11. Permit your opponent to save face.
12. Allow each party to claim a win.
13. Negotiate a deal fair to both parties.
14. Obtain written concurrence at the end of each session.
15. Use surprise as required.
16. Be confident.

Checklist for Negotiation—Post-Negotiation Phase

1. Reduce the total agreement to writing on a prompt basis.
2. Avoid disparaging remarks relative to your opponent's skill, etc.
3. Don't discuss negotiation results with opponent.

4. If required, make agreements public.

5. Conduct a self-critique for results.

6. Obtain and maintain feedback.

Negotiation Critique

1. Was an attempt made by either of the parties to take control of the meeting? If so, what tactic was used and was it successful?

2. What factors surfaced as significant bargaining points during the course of the negotiation?

3. Did it appear that both parties were prepared for the meeting? Were facts and figures used for support?

4. Were the participants willing to compromise? Who conceded the first point? What was conceded?

5. Were the negotiation results summarized by the parties and final agreement confirmed?

6. What were the final dollar amounts as negotiated? If negotiations were not completed, what was the last offer/counteroffer involved?

7. Additional comments or observations:

Contract Administration for the Project Manager

Martin D. Martin,
C. Claude Teagarden
and
Charles F. Lambreth

Introduction

A significant characteristic of the project management concept is that an individual is selected and given the responsibility of managing a major project for its duration. In this role he or she is singularly accountable for the control of project costs, schedule and performance or quality. Also he or she is highly visible to top management. There is high potential for advancement if he or she succeeds and of course the reverse is also true. Being a project manager requires a knowledge of many areas. One of the most critical areas is that of contract management, since the project manager is typically responsible either for fulfilling contract requirements which constitute the project, or for assuring that subcontractors accomplish their portions of the project.

It is unfortunate that, generally speaking, the project manager is frequently not selected until early in the execution phase of the project.[1] The perspective for this statement is the seller side of the market. Many clients or buying firms also assign a project manager for a major capital project. Quite often this individual has the luxury of being involved in the conceptual and planning phases of the project life cycle as well as in the latter phases. These relationships are outlined in Figure 1. For example, if a major plant addition is involved, the project manager in the client organization may contract with an engineering service firm to design the building. This work starts in the conceptual phase and will in most cases extend through the total project life cycle. For the project manager in the client organization the functions of contract management are exercised in his or her relationship with the engineering services organization. During the planning phase the negotiations begin for the follow-on construction contract. A construction contractor is selected and the construction work begins in the execution phase. This monograph is written to illustrate the situation that faces the project manager in the seller organization who is assigned, for example, to build the building. An earlier monograph was written from the perspective of the project manager in the client organization.[2]

It is enlightening to examine a funding profile for a project from a life cycle cost (LCC) concept and thus see the relationship to the project life cycle. This funding profile is illustrated in Figure 2. It is during the development phase that the project is designed and thus in this phase of the LCC model that the project life cycle conceptual and planning phases occur. Execution and closeout occur during the production phase of the LCC model. Once the project is completed the client firm must operate and maintain whatever product was created. Two concerns surface at this point. One deals with the possibility of trade-offs between the costs of production as opposed to the costs of operation and maintenance. The project that is designed with high quality may incur high production or acquisition costs, but in the long run dollars may be saved in operation and maintenance costs. A continuum of possible combinations can be envisioned. These decisions have to be made in

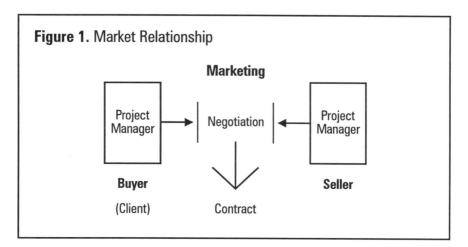

Figure 1. Market Relationship

Marketing

Project Manager → Negotiation ← Project Manager

Buyer

(Client)

Contract

Seller

the design part of the development phase of the LCC model. This leads to the second point. Once a design is selected and the project is started, the latitude for changes decreases over the project life cycle. Thus, the magnitude of the changes that can be made without significant cost increases decreases. This places a premium on the nature of the contract negotiated and written to govern the execution phase of the project life cycle.

For a contract to be enforceable it must possess certain characteristics for both parties. While this material was covered in the earlier handbook,[3] it is important to review these characteristics for clarity. From a format standpoint, a contract usually consists of a page or two that includes selected *administrative data* such as the names and addresses of the contracting parties and other administrative recitals. The next section is the *schedule*, which contains the statement of work, specifications, payment provisions, delivery instructions and other special clauses that have been agreed to by the parties. The last section includes *general provisions* that are somewhat standard and generally accepted in the specific industrial sector. However, a contract may be negotiated and written to meet the needs of the instant situation and the interest of the parties. This is sometimes termed "creative contracting" as opposed to those situations where the parties seek to validate their understandings by use of a standard contract. These issues are important because the contract will be one of the mechanisms that will constrain the project manager as he or she attempts to discharge his or her responsibilities. In some cases, for a very unique product, the contract may weigh several pounds and contain several thousand pages.

Obviously, a major contract is not required for all goods and services which are involved in supporting the development and production of a major project. Figure 3 contains the market structure spectrum. Standard homogeneous items that are to be acquired are usually obtained using a purchase order. Very

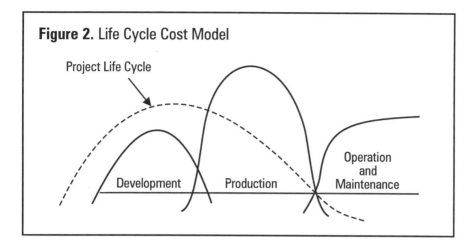

Figure 2. Life Cycle Cost Model

Project Life Cycle

Development

Production

Operation
and
Maintenance

little contract management is involved. The main control is a follow-up by the expediter. Delivery will normally be required 90–120 days after receipt of the order by the vendor or supplier. If the delivery is suspended, and if the item is not received as scheduled, follow-up action is taken. However, as one moves across the spectrum, the complexity, cost and magnitude of the project generally increases. In the ultimate project, such as a hydroelectric dam across a river, the specific design makes it the only one of its kind. A project such as described will be built under the specific provision of a major contract. This effort will probably take years. In this case contract management becomes more significant and crucial to success.

Not all theorists agree on the specific functions of contract management. The approach taken in this monograph is shown by the generalized model outlined in Figure 4. Each of these functions will be discussed in the following sections, and specific actions for the three primary functions are summarized in Appendix A. Section II includes a review of the model for the contracting process. In Section III the relationship between the project life cycle and the contracting process is explored. Section IV highlights the importance of planning and considers the impact of the contract on the planning process. In Section V the key contract management concerns which the project manager should highlight are discussed. In this section selected legal perspectives are included to highlight specific issues that the project manager may want to consider. However, these comments are general in nature. When the project manager is faced with a given situation he or she may find it advisable to seek specific legal counsel tailored to the instant situation.

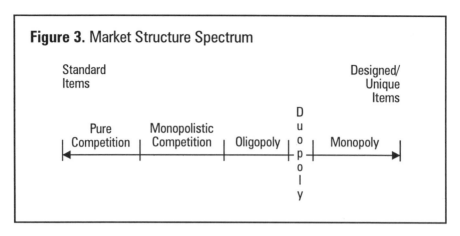

Figure 3. Market Structure Spectrum

The Contracting Process

There are three basic phases for the contracting process: pre-award, award and post-award.[4] For this monograph the frame of reference is the negotiation and legal execution of a contract. These phases are outlined in Figure 5.

The pre-award and award phases include the requirement, requisition and solicitation cycles. Included are all of the actions which must be accomplished to select a firm and to negotiate the specific terms and conditions of a major contract. The phases are sequential and are concluded when negotiations are complete. The post-award phase includes two cycles; award and contract management. Contract management is also known as the contract administration or contractual cycle. It is during these two cycles that the contract is written, signed by the two parties, and the work under the terms of the contract is completed. As pointed out in the introductions the focus of this monograph is two fold. First, the primary perspective is from that of the project manager. Seldom will he or she have the total responsibility for negotiating and signing the contract. Generally, this activity will be accomplished by the firm's contracting department. Depending on company policy, however, he or she will probably be involved and he or she certainly needs to have an overview of the process. Thus, the pre-award and award phases will be reviewed with an eye to project manager involvement. Second, the focus of this section is of the contract management cycle, so it will be overviewed here, while specific and major concerns will be discussed in Section IV. The contracting process will be examined at the cycle level of detail.

Requirement Cycle

The actions in this cycle relate to the identification and delineation of the need by the client's project manager. It includes the development of the statement of work,

Figure 4. Contract Management Functions

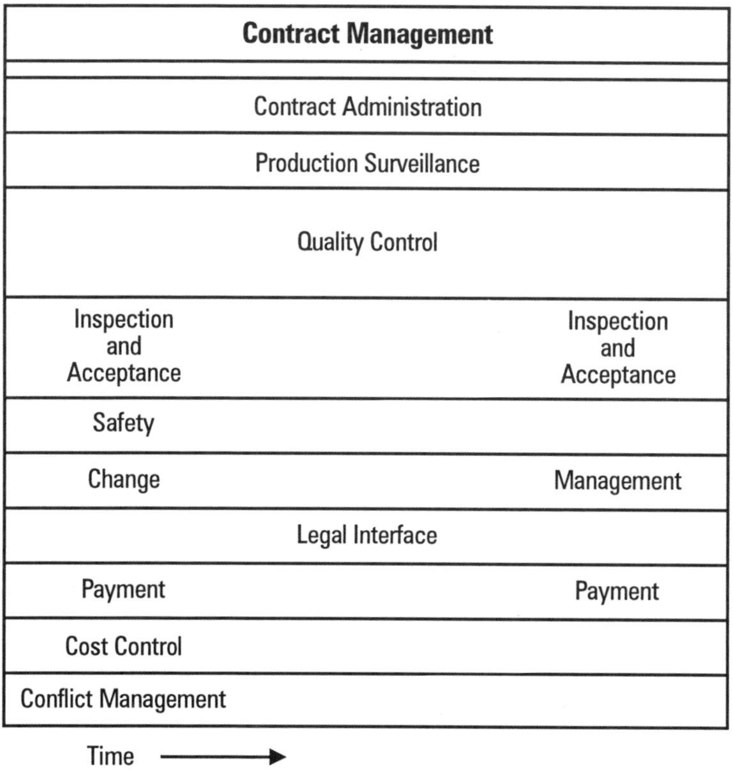

Contract Management
Contract Administration
Production Surveillance
Quality Control

Inspection and Acceptance		Inspection and Acceptance
Safety		
Change		Management
Legal Interface		
Payment		Payment
Cost Control		
Conflict Management		

Time ———⟶

specifications, and other details of the contemplated project. The make-or-buy decision becomes a consideration. Will the project be designed and constructed with in-house personnel, will it be totally contracted out, or some combination of the two? Assuming a combination approach with the overall integration process being retained by the client, the project must be totally defined. A work breakdown structure needs to be developed and specific work packages identified. Major milestones and time schedules are usually developed through the use of networks, critical path method (CPM), or by use of the Program Evaluation and Review Technique (PERT) or some other technique. Cost estimates must be completed using the above information. The emphasis in this cycle is on planning, programming, and budgeting from the client firm's perspective. After the project is totally delineated and pertinent approvals are obtained, a requisition will be prepared and the paperwork forwarded to contracting.

Figure 5. The Process

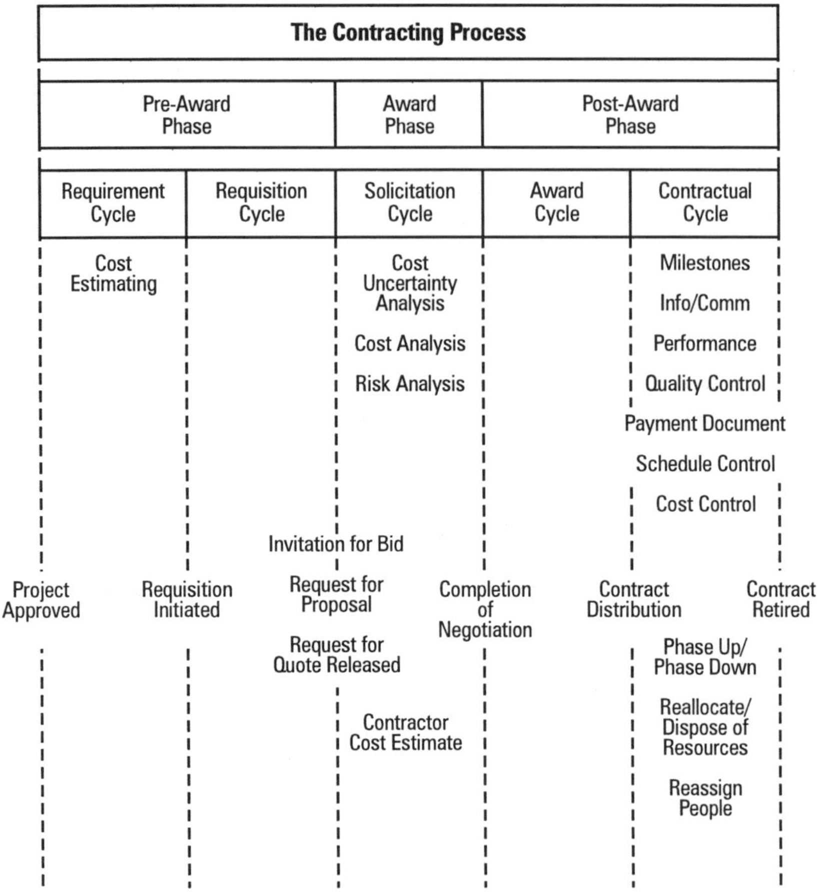

The Contracting Process				
Pre-Award Phase		Award Phase	Post-Award Phase	
Requirement Cycle	Requisition Cycle	Solicitation Cycle	Award Cycle	Contractual Cycle
Cost Estimating		Cost Uncertainty Analysis Cost Analysis Risk Analysis		Milestones Info/Comm Performance Quality Control Payment Document Schedule Control Cost Control
		Invitation for Bid		
Project Approved	Requisition Initiated	Request for Proposal Request for Quote Released Contractor Cost Estimate	Completion of Negotiation	Contract Distribution — Contract Retired Phase Up/ Phase Down Reallocate/ Dispose of Resources Reassign People

Requisition Cycle

Receipt of the requisition will activate the contracting process by the contracting department. It is during this cycle that action is initiated to verify the details of the anticipated contract. The specifications are reviewed for scope and completeness. Source files are reviewed to identify firms that possess the technical, managerial and financial resources to do the work. Performance on past contracts becomes important in qualifying potential bidders. The bid package or solicitation request is developed. The next cycle involves solicitation of bids from industry.

Solicitation Cycle

The critical issue in the solicitation cycle is the identification and selection of a firm or contractor to accomplish the project work. At the end of the requisition cycle firms were mailed the request for proposal, the invitation for bid, or some other solicitation device. These documents normally stipulate a date for the response to be submitted. Assuming a request for proposal (RFP), after the proposals are received they must be evaluated to ensure that they conform to the terms and conditions of the RFP. Thus, technical and cost considerations will be involved in the evaluation. If the lowest bidder is qualified technically, formal contract negotiations will be initiated. This subject is covered in an earlier monograph and will not be reviewed at this point.[5] Many practicing project managers consider the negotiation aspects of developing a contract to take place during the award cycle. In fact, in terms of contracting theory, these negotiations are part of the solicitation cycle, and this cycle ends with the completion of negotiations. Figure 5 illustrates this issue by showing the "completion of negotiations" as a boundary-spanning process separating the solicitation cycle from the award cycle.

Award Cycle

During this cycle contract award is completed. This involves the actual writing of the formal contract to reduce the agreements of the parties to the written word. The contract may be written by either party. Assuming that the client organization has this responsibility, the contracting and legal personnel will write and select clauses as mentioned in the Introduction to clearly delineate the intention of the parties. The contract will be mailed to the seller for review and signature. The signing of the document by both parties results in the formal contract that will form the basis for the subsequent project work.

Contractual Cycle

The primary responsibility for contract performance rests with the seller under the terms of the prime contract as negotiated. The seller at this point will generally assign a project manager to fulfill these obligations. The context now shifts from the client's project manager to that of the seller. Usually the contract spells out how the relationship between the two individuals will be structured. Both will have contract management responsibilities. Since these vary from situation to situation, a generalized approach to the subject will be taken. Unless otherwise stipulated, the term "project manager" from this point on will relate to the seller and his or her project team.

The project manager must exercise the typical management functions of planning, organizing, staffing, directing, control, and communication in order

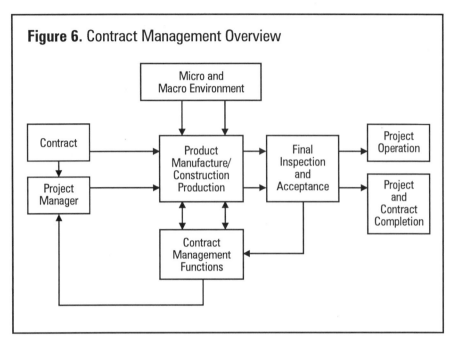

Figure 6. Contract Management Overview

Micro and Macro Environment

Contract

Project Manager

Product Manufacture/ Construction Production

Final Inspection and Acceptance

Project Operation

Project and Contract Completion

Contract Management Functions

to produce the contracted product. These functions will be interrelated with the contract management functions delineated in Figure 4 of the Introduction. The overall contract management process is outlined in Figure 6. The contract terms and provisions will structure and impact the contract management processes of the project manager as his or her or she and his or her team produce the product. In turn the macro and micro environment of the project will interface with the management and production processes. As progress is made, the project manager will need to periodically assess the state of affairs, comparing planned activity to actual.[6] This assessment will be based on information flows as illustrated in Figure 7. These specific information flows place a premium on the ability of the project manager to use the tools at his or her disposal to meet the problems that are created daily by changes in top management guidance and the uncertainties of a changing environment. Each information flow will be examined in the sections that follow.[7] However, as reflected in Figure 8, the project manager does have various tools at his or her disposal that can facilitate the contract management job. These tools make use of the information that the system provides and gives the project manager a systematic approach to contract management.[8] The use of milestone charts, schedule tracks, work breakdown structures, and statements of work not only help the project manager maintain a close watch on the time schedules, but also point out to whom the responsibility for each task is assigned.[9] This helps the project manager manage his or her project through the management of indi-

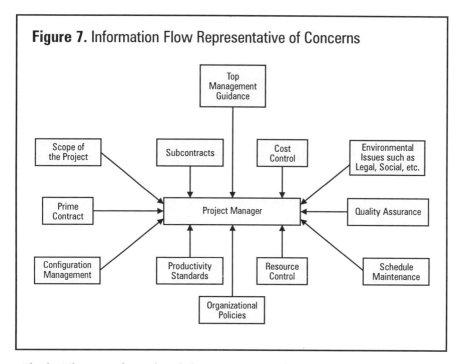

Figure 7. Information Flow Representative of Concerns

viduals. The use of cost breakdown reports and project specification break-downs allow the project manager to keep a close watch on the financial aspects of the project. Prior to examining the constraints that impact the project manager's planning ability and some special contract management issues, there is a need to focus on the relationship between the project life cycle and the contracting process.

Relationship Between the Project and Contract Life Cycles

As suggested earlier, the contracting process and the project life cycle are intimately related. The project life cycle is represented in Figure 9.

In the conceptual phase the project parameters are delineated. The need is identified. Alternative project configurations are evaluated. Basic schedules and budgets are developed. If feasibility is established, activities after approval move into the planning phase. The overall schedule is prepared. Studies and analyses are initiated to examine various design alternatives for affordability and essentiality, and the system parameters are clarified. In some cases proto-types or models are fabricated and tested. The make-or-buy decision becomes an important concern.[10] The parallel nature of the contracting process, where

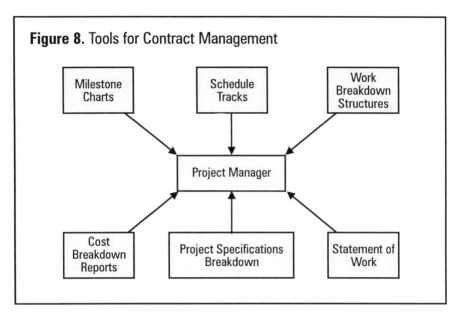

Figure 8. Tools for Contract Management

| Milestone Charts | Schedule Tracks | Work Breakdown Structures |

Project Manager

| Cost Breakdown Reports | Project Specifications Breakdown | Statement of Work |

a major contract is the planned support vehicle, is obvious. These project life cycle activities take place during the pre-award and award phases of the contracting process. This relationship is illustrated in Figure 10. The execution (the term "execution" as used here is not to be confused with the signing of the contract by both parties) and termination phases coincide with the post-award phase of the contracting process. It should be noted, as illustrated, that the contract can be managed as a project. This condition is shown in the lower right-hand part of Figure 10.

Assignment of Project Manager

Unfortunately, the project manager is frequently not assigned to the project until the execution phase. A high premium for good project managers exists in the marketplace today. It is due to this apparent shortage of top-notch project managers that the project manager is not assigned to a project during the conceptual phase. This late assignment places a great deal of responsibility on the project manager to step into a project and digest a great deal of planning material in a short period of time. If the seller's project manager was brought in during the conceptual phase then he or she could help plan and negotiate the contract that is to be administered. This earlier introduction to the project would not only increase the quality of work, but also be cost beneficial. With a more thorough understanding of the project specifications and requirements, the project manager could identify key problems earlier and thus prevent financial waste. Many problems occur when the project manager is

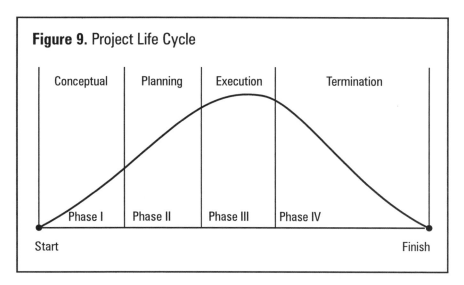

Figure 9. Project Life Cycle

not assigned to the project during the conceptual phase. The problems cause increased costs to the project, misinterpretation of specifications of a project and difficulty in working with pre-established contracts. The authors of this monograph suggest an earlier orientation to the project than is traditionally practiced. The project life cycle and the contracting process are detailed in Figure 11. This figure shows the traditional as well as the proposed involvement of the project manager in the project life cycle. Some might argue that this early assignment would increase contract and project cost. However, it is also argued that overall savings would exceed such cost increases. Regardless of when the project manager is assigned, the critical function to be accomplished is project planning—which is typically constrained.

Contractual and Related Impacts on Project Planning

The discussion in this section assumes that the project manager is assigned to the project at the beginning of the execution phase of the project life cycle. While this is obviously not always true, and the authors have argued for earlier assignment, from a practical basis it is the premise for the generalized approach considered in this monograph. Project managers are highly trained and valuable individuals and companies try to maximize the return on the use of such persons. However, assignment at the beginning of the execution phase places a premium on the project manager's ability to get oriented to the project parameters as soon as possible. Such a practice also may tend to hamper the individual's ability to plan effectively.

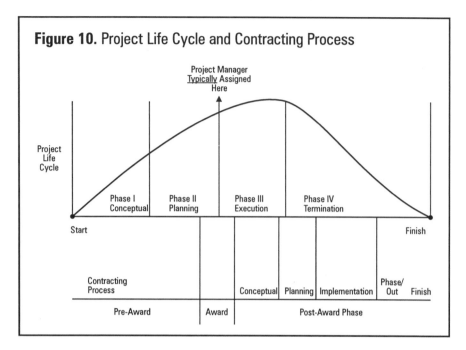

Figure 10. Project Life Cycle and Contracting Process

Project Manager
Typically Assigned
Here

Project
Life
Cycle

Phase I	Phase II	Phase III	Phase IV
Conceptual	Planning	Execution	Termination

Start   Finish

Contracting
Process   Conceptual | Planning | Implementation   Phase/ Out   Finish

Pre-Award   Award   Post-Award Phase

Project planning is the primary function of the project manager.[11] It provides a basis and framework for the exercise of the other management functions of organizing, staffing, direction, control, and communication. In the main, the individual's latitude in the area of organization is limited. It is accepted as a given in the project environment. Generally, the project manager is responsible for structuring his or her project team in order to govern the relationships between the members of the project team. He or she must adapt his or her approach to the project within the context of the project management system of the specific firm.[12] The emphasis here is on planning concerns, as it is assumed that the reader is knowledgeable of the planning process.

Project Management System Context

The project management system and its implementation is directly impacted by the firm's make-or-buy policy. One option available is for the client firm to staff sufficient manpower resources to perform all the tasks necessary to complete a project. This approach has drawbacks in that full-time people must be paid at all times and with full benefits. The nature of most productive enterprise is that there may be periods of inactivity when resources are idle and thus the firm must support a burden of excess capacity. On the other hand, the firm may contract for its project management system. In the first case the integration effort is totally on the company. In the fully contracted effort, the

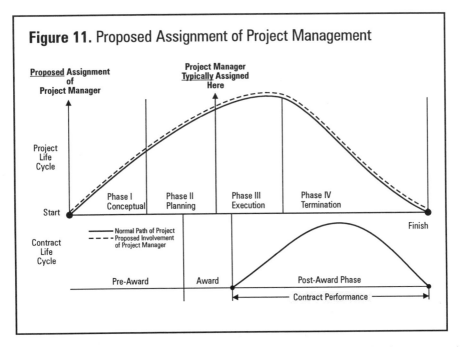

Figure 11. Proposed Assignment of Project Management

Proposed Assignment of Project Manager

Project Manager Typically Assigned Here

Project Life Cycle

Start

Phase I Conceptual | Phase II Planning | Phase III Execution | Phase IV Termination

Finish

——— Normal Path of Project
– – – Proposed Involvement of Project Manager

Contract Life Cycle

Pre-Award | Award | Post-Award Phase

◄——— Contract Performance ———►

contract places this responsibility on a contractor. A third method is a combination of the two, as outlined in Figure 12.[13] In this case both in-house and contracted tasks are involved. The project manager is responsible for supervising the overall effort and for structuring and maintaining the interface between the in-house and the contracted portions of the project. The key is management of the two efforts as specified in an overall plan. The important aspect of the project management system design is that the project manager needs to have a high-degree of knowledge relative to contract management, organizational relationships, and top management philosophy and policy, as these variables place constraints on the capacity to plan.

Planning Constraints

The most obvious constraints that the project manager must cope with are the contract provisions. The work statement, specifications, drawings, blueprints and other quality and performance parameters must be interpreted. Schedule provisions must be scoped and integrated with orders for materials so that as construction proceeds concrete, steel, and other items will be available as needed. Other provisions dealing with site accessibility, inspection, scrap removal, and other issues must be identified and included in activity plans. These provisions will be considered in more detail later. However, these constraints will relate in some form or fashion to the concepts of performance,

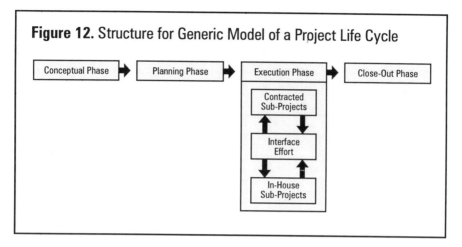

Figure 12. Structure for Generic Model of a Project Life Cycle

Conceptual Phase → Planning Phase → Execution Phase → Close-Out Phase

Contracted Sub-Projects

Interface Effort

In-House Sub-Projects

schedule and cost, which must be dealt with early in the planning process. Since, in most cases, the project manager will not have been involved in the negotiation of the contract, he will need to read and understand the details of the contract provisions.

Although not used widely, the project charter, when available, will bound and scope the planning efforts of the project manager. Whether or not a formal written charter is used, the guidance from top management will still be germane and must be clarified and considered during the planning phase.[14] In general, a project charter covers:
• Project justification and background
• Scope and objectives of the project
• Available resources
• Organizational relationships and responsibilities
• Delegation of authority to the project manager
• Authority and responsibilities of other organizational elements
• Project schedule
• Estimates of project cost
• Schedules of equipment, material, and supplies which must be acquired, and
• Management approval and any limitations that top management wants to highlight.

As is obvious, the project charter can be quite comprehensive and can either restrict the project manager or provide him or her with operating flexibility.

The final direct constraint on the project manager is a consequence of the firm's organizational structure. If the project manager is operating in a matrix, a premium will be placed on coordination and communication with other organizational elements such as contracting or engineering. However, if the project manager is operating in a totally projectized environment he will proba-

Contract Administration for the Project Manager

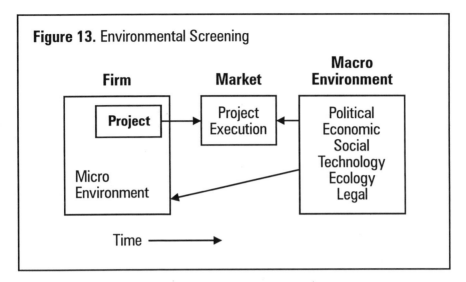

Figure 13. Environmental Screening

bly have contracting and engineering personnel, for example, assigned to the project team.[15] There will still be a need for coordination and communication but with lesser emphasis placed on these issues during planning. An example will illustrate this constraint. If contracting is centralized, the project manager will have to work closely with contracting to ensure that materials and supplies are purchased and made available at the work site in conformance with the work schedule. If the materials or supplies are received too early there is a possibility of damage. Long-term storage may be needed. On the other hand, if the materials or supplies are received late, work may be halted and there may be the invocation of a contractual penalty such as liquidated damages, which will reduce profitability as costs are escalated unnecessarily.

Environmental Screening

A concern for the project manager is the multiple environments which impinge on the project and the contract.[16] This situation is illustrated in Figure 13. The micro environment for the project consists of those organizational relationships identified earlier as a planning constraint. This environment needs to be screened to deal with competing projects and possible organizational changes. However, a significant aspect of environmental screening deals with the macro environment. Project management in the context of this monograph is a marketing aspect of the organization. The project manager as a representative of his or her firm and his or her team are producing a product for a client or customer. His or her actions thus assume a boundary-spanning nature. The project manager must deal with the customer on a daily basis and with the environmental variables of a political, economic, social, technological, and ecological nature. The political and legal dimensions involve laws that limit and bound the operational area for project management. For example, on a construction project involving the federal government, there is a requirement for an environmental analysis (E.A.), which could result in an environmental impact statement (E.I.S.). In this case the political and ecological variables combine to cause additional planning activity, with its associated cost. The economic variable relates, among other things, to the overall condition of the economy. An inflationary situation requires certain allowances when dealing with cost budgets and the prices of equipment, materials and supplies that have to be acquired. The social variable deals with culture, subculture values, as well as with social legislation requirements that must be dealt with by the project manager. For example, the work ethic is alive and well in some parts of the United States, whereas in others, workers demonstrate low productivity for a comparable time period. The concern with ecology requires that action be taken to preclude situations where the project effort might result in air and water pollution. Many manifestations of these variables exist. The project manager will need to assess his or her specific contract and environment to identify specific concerns that must be considered. This environmental screening can become crucial, especially if the project manager encounters conditions in project execution which were not anticipated when the contract was negotiated. This possibility illustrates the nature of the uncertainty that may be present in the project manager's many environments.

The Role of Uncertainty

The project manager will inherit the cost estimates, time schedule, and performance parameters which were developed for the project prior to contract negotiation. The estimates were developed in the planning phase of the project life cycle and are just that—estimates.[17] These numbers contain varying provisions for the uncertainty that was assessed for the project. As he develops his or her project plan and the derivative activity plans, using such tools as PERT, CPM, and other technique, he or she will want to verify the known unknowns and determine how valid the estimates are.[18] This process will help validate the size of the management reserve or contingency provision and will assist in identifying the controls which need to be incorporated in the plans. High levels of uncertainty will dictate strict controls and periodic reviews to ensure that cost, time, and performance targets are being met as the project progresses. Uncertainty dictates that planning and control be related activities. Variances from plan must be detected promptly. As shown in Figure 14, actual and budgeted costs can deviate markedly. Reports such as these help the project manager detect changes so that corrective action can be taken. One certain factor is that changes will be necessary during contract and project execution.[19] Change management and associated topics including subcontract management, contract specifications, work delays and special clauses, are the concerns of the next section.

Contract Administration for the Project Manager

Special Considerations for Contract Execution

The contract and project life cycle execution stages normally overlap if the project manager is assigned at the beginning of the execution phase of the project. Interpretation of contract clauses becomes critical to the project's success. While each contract clause must be evaluated and applied on its own merits and in the context of the project charter, the macro environment and the organizational climate or culture, there are certain clauses which need to be highlighted by the project manager. Several such clauses are discussed in this section.

Changes

Changes to the project scope have been documented as one of the major causes of cost growth.[20] For major projects which take several years to complete, changes in technology and the other environmental factors have a high probability of creating the need for changes in the project itself. Admittedly, some contracts are negotiated with the tacit understanding that scope and dollar value will be expanded as the work progresses. This tactic is a convenient way to tap the management reserve and to keep the project going for an extended period of time. This practice, in the opinion of the authors, is an ethical issue. The work should be clearly defined in the planning phase of the project life cycle and funds should be added to the contract under the changes clause to fund only those situations where an actual change is justified by the occurrence of unanticipated events. As stated previously, change is inevitable, and the key to cost control becomes a sound system to manage change as it occurs.

The control of change is a critical responsibility of the project manager. The system should be defined and included in the changes clause of the contract. If it is not, then the project manager should develop one. The system should cover who initiates a change request, how it is processed and funded, and who has the final approval authority. For a major project, such as the construction of a building, power plant or other structure, a configuration control committee needs to be established. It becomes the responsibility of this committee to establish the need for a change based on a change request. A request for a change may be initiated by either the project team or the client. The first question to be answered deals with the essentiality of the change. Is it really necessary? Assuming that the answer is positive, then the impact of the change should be ascertained. What will the effect of the change be on the overall project? How will it affect cost, schedule, and performance? To the extent it is practical, the change should be priced in its entirety at this point. The types of pricing or contractual arrangements have been covered in an earlier monograph and need not be restated here.[21] The practice in many industries is to price changes on a cost-plus basis. This practice should be avoided if at all possible. The change

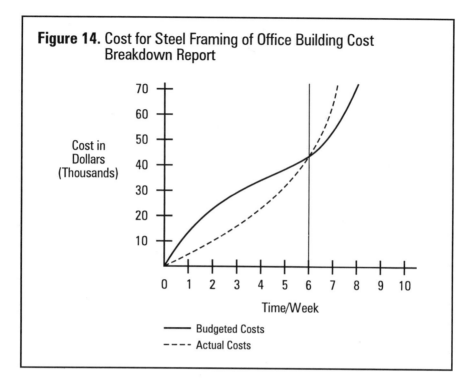

Figure 14. Cost for Steel Framing of Office Building Cost Breakdown Report

Cost in Dollars (Thousands)

70
60
50
40
30
20
10

0 1 2 3 4 5 6 7 8 9 10

Time/Week

——— Budgeted Costs
- - - - Actual Costs

proposal should be priced on a lump-sum basis. If time appears to be of the essence, the change may be priced initially on a cost-plus basis with the provision that it be converted to a lump-sum basis as soon as possible, but not later than 30 days after initial approval. This time period permits the collection of information and cost data which should permit a more exact determination of what the total cost of the change will be.

This condition highlights the need for a good information system to assist in project control. The system needs to be tailored to the project and of a simple design so as to provide timely and accurate information as to project status. It must be flexible and adaptable so that team members can use the system on a daily basis and at the project site.

The change proposal needs to be explicit in terms of the impact of the change on the contract work statement, specifications, and drawings. Several alternatives need to be examined and may be used as a basis for negotiation. Trade-offs among cost, schedule, and performance may be required. In a specific case familiar to the authors, cost was a datum and could not be increased. The negotiations for the change proposal focused primarily on performance. Substitute materials were identified and blueprints and drawings were modified to provide a design which was affordable so that cost and schedule targets were maintained. The identification of such trade-offs requires that the project team be thoroughly knowledgeable of the contract specifications.

Legal Perspective: Changes

Simply stated, a change is a modification of the contract done to alter the specifications, delivery time, price, quality, or any other provision of the contract. A change may be accomplished by mutual agreement of the parties to the contract[22] or by unilateral action if pursuant to the exercise of options contained in the terms of the original contract.[23]

Except in a contract for the sale of goods[24] or the "changes" clause in a government contract, there must be mutual agreement to modify a contract and that agreement must be supported by consideration.[25] Therefore, it behooves the project manager to ensure that a changes clause is contained in the original contract giving him or her the authority to direct change and providing an orderly procedure for determining added cost/extra work.

Modification of a contract, as discussed above, should not be confused with reformation which is a judicial remedy in equity by which a court construes the contract so as to express the real intention of the parties.[26] Nor should it be confused with "constructive change." The latter can take place when the project manager's conduct is such as to have the effect of requiring performance differing from that prescribed by the contract. The project manager's conduct in effecting constructive change may either be affirmative or a failure to act.[27]

Contract Specifications

Specifications are basically of two types. They are either standard in nature, where a specific design has been accepted throughout an industry, or they are tailored and unique to the situation at hand. Most project managers will have to deal with tailored specifications. Few projects can be built to standard specifications, especially those that must be constructed to meet the requirements of a specific terrain or where the design is dictated by a new technology. Since in most cases the project manager will not have participated in the development of the specifications and the subsequent contract negotiations, he or she must study the specifications in detail. Often this examination will reveal the potential for change and for subsequent cost savings. A fact that is often overlooked but which should be recognized is that the development of specifications includes a behavioral component. Based on extensive experience with designers, one of the authors has defined several classes of design propensities:
- Drive for competency
- Safety margin coefficient
- Indifference methodology

- "Monument" syndrome
- Budget expansion
- Sole-source shelter.

The drive for competency approach typifies the individual who cannot come to closure. The person is driven to keep changing the design and often this approach results in increasing complexity and accompanying cost escalation. The project manager must be able to deal with the changes that will be suggested by this class of designer. The safety margin coefficient type deals with design parameters in terms of how much is enough. Minimal weighting factors for a building could be unsafe but the question becomes one of how much safety margin is really required. At some point costs increase exponentially but safety gains do not. Again there is a closure problem and the project manager must maintain control of this type of designer. Indifference methodology relates to an attitude that tends to promote a contingency approach to specifications even when such an approach is not warranted. The design becomes too flexible. The engineer or architect is indifferent to the structure of the final product. The goal is to please everyone and consequently no one is pleased. The "monument" syndrome is based on the desire to build a product that will last forever, regardless of cost. The designers of the pyramids certainly took this approach. Again the question is, "how much is enough?" The design should be safe and functional but "gold plating" should be avoided. The budget expansion designer develops the specifications with an eye to available funds. The more money available, the more complex and costly the design. The sole-source shelter encompasses the situation where specifications are developed so that equipment, materials, and supplies are tailored to require the products of a specific manufacturer or supplier. This approach has the tendency to eliminate competition and to increase the cost of the project.

This area has been identified as a significant cause of cost growth.[28] It must, therefore, be a major concern of the project manager. The authors recognize that the daily management activities of the project manager often are so hectic that he or she is precluded from adequately dealing with the interpretation and maintenance of the specifications. However, it is a significant task that must be addressed. Some companies make a living handling this task for the project manager on a sub contracted basis. This approach is certainly acceptable. The job must be done if the project is to be completed and if cost, schedule, and quality parameters are to be maintained.

Legal Perspective: Specifications

Problems discovered after the contract has been signed rarely may be corrected without costly and time-consuming negotiation or litigation.[29] Frequently, these problems could have been avoided by a careful review during the draft-

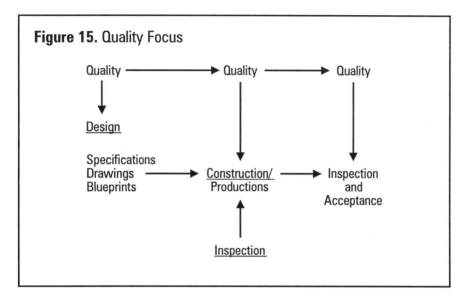

Figure 15. Quality Focus

ing stage of the contract.[30] This particularly concerns the specifications and the item descriptions contained therein. These descriptions must be stated with sufficient specificity to clearly establish the minimum acceptable requirements. Often this description may of necessity include more than one performance standard, (for instance, if, in addition to the worded specification, reference is made to drawings; physical or functional interchangeability with another item; chemical, electronic, dimensional, or mechanical requirements; and/or manufacturing detail). When this occurs, the contract must specify which standard is to control in case of conflict. Should the contract fail to do this and the delivered item, for example, conform to the drawings but be electronically incompatible with interfacing equipment, then the contract may be deemed to be fulfilled.

Quality Control

All is for naught if the project doesn't perform to specifications once it has been produced or completed. Quality is a frame of mind that must pervade the project environment from design through production to completion. It cannot be inspected into the product. It must be built into the product. This is illustrated in Figure 15. The attitude of quality must be present when the project is designed. It must be examined in the context of cost affordability and schedule maintenance. These ideas must find expression in the specifications, drawings, blueprints and statements of work, and must be transmitted to the project team. As discussed under the changes section, changes should be approved only after their impact on project quality is ascertained. During construction, controls must he or she established to ensure that quality is kept in mind as the work progresses. Periodic checks for specification conformance are a must. Nonconforming work should be evaluated by the configuration control committee to ensure quality maintenance. Nonconforming work that will degrade overall quality should not be accepted but should be reworked. The cost of rework can be prohibitive; therefore, the emphasis should be on doing things right the first time. Correction of deficiencies should be thorough and timely. Some issues that come into play are warranties and latent defects. From a legal perspective these issues can be costly and result in damage to the company reputation and to the reputation of the project manager and his or her team. This concern for quality applies equally to subcontracts.

Legal Perspective: Warranties

The project manager should be aware of two types of warranties: express and implied. The concept of warranty is based upon one party's assurance to the other that the goods will meet certain standards of quality; including condition, reliability, description, function, or performance.

This assurance may be express or implied. Recognizing the principal function of a warranty is to establish a level of quality (and title—not discussed herein); it thus gives a source of remedy for loss due to a defect in the quality of the goods. The contract may and should establish a level of quality, and if it does, it is an express warranty recognized under Section 2–313 (1) (a) of the Uniform Commercial Code.

Warranty clauses in a contract must be carefully drafted to meet the circumstances of the particular desired end, and so as not to limit any rights afforded the project manager by any other provisions in either the contract or law.[31] A warranty clause can give the client project manager a contractual right to assert claims for deficient supplies or services. It may be drafted in such a way as to allow additional time following acceptance and even payment in which to assert rights to correct deficiencies or defects without additional costs to the client or for the client project manager to effect the correction or replacement at the faulted party's (sellers) expense.

Implied warranties are measured by "merchantability" or "fitness for a particular purpose." Goods are not considered to be merchantable if they are not reasonably fit for the ordinary purposes for which such goods are used. The implied warranty of merchantability arises in every sale of goods made by a merchant who deals in goods of the kind sold.[32] Unless the party to the contract is making an isolated sale of goods, he or she will be considered a merchant with respect to the goods and the implied warranty will exist.[33]

Merchants and non-merchants alike are subject to the implied warranty of fitness for a particular purpose.[34] The warranty is implied where, at the time of contracting, the seller knows a particular purpose for which the item is be-

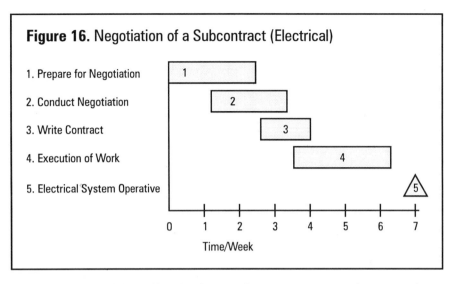

Figure 16. Negotiation of a Subcontract (Electrical)

1. Prepare for Negotiation

2. Conduct Negotiation

3. Write Contract

4. Execution of Work

5. Electrical System Operative

0   1   2   3   4   5   6   7

Time/Week

ing purchased and the seller also knows the project manager/buyer is relying on the seller's skill or judgment in selecting or furnishing suitable goods.[35] If, however, the client project manager is knowledgeable of the product, inspected it, and made his own independent judgment without relying on the seller's skill, the warranty will not be created.[36] Likewise, if the product delivered is in accordance with the specifications and plans furnished by the client project manager, the fact that the product is unfit will not excuse the client project manager from the defect in the plans and specifications and the warranty will not provide a remedy against the seller.[37]

Subcontract Management

In this era of industrial specialization, many companies find it convenient to subcontract various work tasks. For example, a construction contractor may subcontract for plumbing, electrical and other work packages. This requires that the project manager be involved in the basic make-or-buy decision. Generally, it is better to subcontract when:

- The subcontractor possesses special technical and engineering skills
- The contracting firm possesses limited capacity in an area
- The subcontractor can augment the contractor's labor force at a lower cost than an in house capability can be maintained, and
- The work represents a small part of the overall work effort.

Subcontracting one or more work packages places the project manager in the role of an integrator, contract negotiator, and contract administrator. The schedule for the negotiation of a subcontract is included in Figure 16 and reflects how a milestone chart can assist in planning the subcontract effort. He or she should at least be knowledgeable of the contracting area even if contracting is centralized in his or her company. Assuming a projectized structure, the project manager will be responsible for negotiating the subcontract. It will be necessary to cost out the work to arrive at a negotiation-cost position. Generally speaking, it is best to subcontract on a lump-sun basis with a clearly defined work statement and specifications. Clauses will need to be selected for the subcontract to ensure that the prime contractor's interests are protected. The subcontract clauses should conform and augment the clauses which are governing the project manager under the terms of the prime contract. For example, the subcontract should include a work statement, specifications, changes, quality, payment terms, inspection bonding, and other clauses as specified in the earlier contracting monograph.[38] Under this assumption of a projectized structure, the project manager will also be responsible for administering the subcontract.[39] It will be necessary for the project team to interpret and administer the provisions of the subcontract. This activity will involve production surveillance and quality assurance functions. The project manager will be in charge of negotiating and executing any changes to the subcontract as a consequence of design and environmental changes. He or she will have to process and deal with any disputes or appeals with the subcontractor. In general, the project manager and team will have to maintain control without hampering the work of the subcontractor. The exact management actions required will depend on the terms and conditions of the subcontract.

The integrator role also is of paramount importance. This is outlined in Figure 17. As can be observed, the project manager must schedule the overall work effort as the work progresses. He or she must ensure that the subcontractor work is either completed early or on time. Late delivery or completion of subcontractor work could bring the overall project to a stop. This condition could possibly result in costly delays that impact both cost and schedule under the prime contract. Thus, a premium is placed on planning and control by the project manager under the terms of the client contract. Production surveillance ensures that activities are checked on a periodic basis.

Production Surveillance

This contract management area is concerned with on-site visits to determine progress on the project. As with the other contract management functions, it contains a planning component. The contract work statement and delivery schedule are the basis for the production plan. The production plan includes a complete delineation of significant progress checkpoints, partial deliveries, and other critical production, construction or manufacturing data. This data is usually portrayed on milestone charts or some other visual tracking technique.[40] For this area to be adequately covered during manufacturing, on-site visits are a must. The project manager and his or her team members are usually on-site

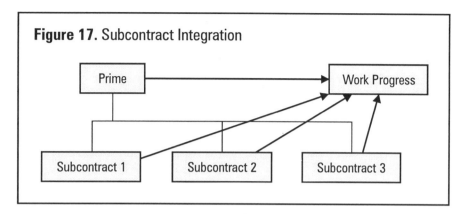

Figure 17. Subcontract Integration

as necessary. However, production surveillance is also a concern of the client personnel who have access to the work area. The project manager must assure that these visits do not interfere with the work effort; however, client visits should not be resisted. Such resistance could increase the natural adversarial relationship and should be avoided. This is an area that needs frequent attention and should be monitored daily to preclude client personnel from initiating unnecessary changes. As discussed earlier, all changes should be handled by the project manager and the configuration management committee.

Production progress should be documented and reports generated to keep all interested parties apprised as to schedule slippage problems. As problems are detected, corrective action should be initiated to bring production back on schedule, so that inaction is not construed as a waiving of performance requirements. Production surveillance activity often will identify the need for a change proposal. Production surveillance often identifies problems that lead to conflict between the project team and the client.

Legal Perspective: Waiver

A pitfall of which the client project manager must be continually aware is "waiver." Under the doctrine of waiver it is possible for a party to relinquish rights he or she otherwise has under the contract.[41] If, for example, a selling party to the contract tenders incomplete, defective, or late performance and the client project manager knowingly accepts that performance without objection or does not demand the defects be remedied, the project manager has waived his or her right to strict performance.[42] In some circumstances the party at fault may remain liable for provable damages caused by the incomplete performance; however, the waiver will prevent the project manager from calling the breech a material breech and thus from calling the contract to an end (discharge).

Conflict Management

Cost, schedule and quality concerns are frequently the root of conflict between the project team and the client, as well as between federal and state regulatory personnel. The nature of the product will be instrumental in identifying the players in the conflict drama. These conflicts emerge primarily as a result of differing objectives, values, backgrounds, personalities, and status considerations. For example, the interpretation of a specification or the need for a change to the project design may well trigger a conflict. These conflicts may occur between project team members, between the project team and top management, between the project team and the client or between the project team and other individuals and groups. The identification of conflict and its resolution by the project manager are crucial to project success. This subject is covered in excellent detail in an earlier monograph and will not be addressed to that specific level in this section.[43]

Other Applicable Contract Clauses

The nature of contracts and lack of space preclude coverage in this monograph of every possible clause that could be included in a contract. Contracts reflect the negotiation process that lead to their creation and clauses that cover special situations and conditions can be agreed to by the parties and subsequently be reduced to writing. Several other more common concerns will be presented later in this section. Where there is doubt relative to a special clause, legal advice should be sought.

Delays

Most contracts contain clauses dealing with work delays. The key issue becomes that of who caused the delay and the nature of the interruption. For example, a flood that ravaged a construction site would hardly be the responsibility of the prime or any subcontractor, whereas the late delivery of materials to the work site which caused a lengthy delay might well be construed as a fault of the prime contractor or project manager. This latter situation would probably result in the client imposing some type of penalty on the project manager's company under the terms of the contract. This condition places a premium on the management effort of the project manager and his or her team. Attention to the other topics covered in this section should, hopefully, assist in avoiding lengthy delays where the prime contractor could be adjudged at fault. Each delay will require the development of a cost and schedule impact statement. Rescheduling of events will be necessary to get the project back on track.

Legal Perspective: Bonds

When drafting the contract, the project manager should consider provisions for certain types of bonds which contain penal amounts sufficient to assure performance and payment. Under certain circumstances fidelity and patent infringement bonds may also be required.

A performance bond, as the name implies, secures to the project manager the performance and fulfillment of all the undertakings, terms and conditions of the contract. Certainly, in the case of construction contracts, such a clause should be required and, in no event, should the penal amount of the bond be less than 100 percent of the contract price.

Payment bonds secure the payment of subcontractors, laborers, and material persons by the prime contractor. Additionally, the project manager should consider including a contract clause requiring the prime contractor to secure payment bonds from any subcontractor on the project in an amount sufficient to insure payment of the latter's suppliers of labor and material.[44]

It should be noted that the Miller Act,[45] covering bonds on federal projects, requires both performance and payment bonds on all but minor construction contracts in which the United States government is a party to the contract.[46]

Payment

Payments may be based on a percentage of progress or on the delivery of an item at some intermediate point or at the end of the contract. To preclude conflict, the manner of determining the progress percentage should be clearly defined and included in the contract. If not, then the project manager should seek to set up a system to govern this area. The system should be discussed with the client. After agreement the details should be reduced to writing and signed by both parties. It is necessary to have the product inspected and accepted before the payment will be made, so the need for quality control throughout the contractual cycle of the contracting process cannot be overemphasized. Disputes over payment should be avoided as the contractor usually depends on these payments to generate cash flow to meet salary, material, and other cost commitments. The payment dates should be included in the master production and other schedules so that personnel understand their importance.

Termination

Most contracts contain a clause as to the circumstances that may lead a client to terminate a contract. In most cases the reasons center on the concept of nonperformance. Where the project manager and his or her team fail to do their job and the lack of progress can be clearly traced to their negligence, most terminations occur as performance defaults. However, as a consequence of the lead time to negotiate a new contract with another contractor, most clients are reluctant to terminate if there is a high probability of recovery by the prime contractor. Again, this type of clause reinforces the need for appropriate and timely management actions by the project manager and his or her team.

Legal Perspective: Breech

Failure to perform a contractual obligation constitutes a breech of contract.[47] Stated another way, a party to a contract is obligated to perform as promised.

The measure of damages for a breech of a contract is the amount of loss that the injured party has sustained thereby. Should the breech be occasioned by the project manager preventing the performance of the contract, without fault on the part of the other party, who is willing to perform, the loss to the latter may consist of two distinct grounds for damage: first, what he or she has already expended toward performance; second, the profits he or she would have realized had he or she been allowed to perform.

More likely the breech would occur when a party fails to comply with the terms and conditions of the contract. In this case, damage might consist of excess cost in repurchasing or the diminished value of the defective work or the delay.

It is important that the project manager recognize the distinction between a breech of contract and a *material* breech of contract. Both are grounds for damages. In the case of a *material* breech, however, the non-faulted party is discharged from any further obligations under the contract. What is material in some situations may not be in others. As stated above, a breech of contract is the failure to perform a duty imposed by the contract. A material breech, however is so serious as to deprive the non-breaching party of the benefit of the bargain—the benefit expected to be received from the breeching party's performance.[48]

The time in which a party to the contract is to complete performance may or may not be critical to the project manager. Should no time for performance be stated or implied in the contract, performance must be completed within a reasonable time.[49] If, however, the project manager deems time of completion to be critical, the contract should expressly stipulate "time is of the essence."

When the contract stipulates time is of the essence, failure to perform within the allotted time will constitute a material breech of the contract and the project manager will not be required to accept late performance.[50]

The foregoing discussion supports the need for a complete understanding of the contract by the project manager. Its provision, must be understood and must support the planning efforts of the project manager and his or her team. It also reinforces the need to hold periodic progress review, to ascertain cost, schedule, and quality status for the project and the contract. Thus, contract

Contract Administration for the Project Manager

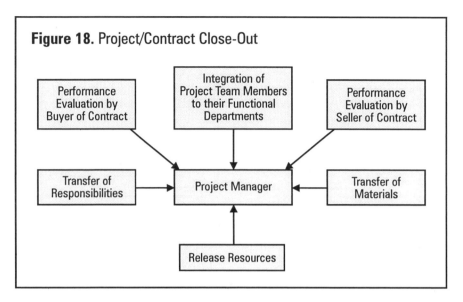

Figure 18. Project/Contract Close-Out

Performance Evaluation by Buyer of Contract

Integration of Project Team Members to their Functional Departments

Performance Evaluation by Seller of Contract

Transfer of Responsibilities

Project Manager

Transfer of Materials

Release Resources

management is critical to project success. Assuming successful project and contract completion, the question arises as to how clients evaluate performance under a contract and what should be accomplished for project and contract close-out.

Project/Contract Close-Out

The close-out in the final step of the project life cycle and the contracting process. A performance review is conducted to determine the degree to which the provisions of the prime contract and subcontract were met. Personnel are evaluated and rewarded accordingly. Where applicable, an important part of the close-out is the transfer of the functional personnel back to their departments once the contract is complete. The project manager must also release to inventory or dispose of any excess resources not used in the contract. The final job of the project manager becomes the transfer of the completed project to the client. Some of the major concerns of the close-out step are demonstrated in Figure 18, "Project Close-Out."

Performance Data File

Throughout the contracting process, a record of performance should he or she maintained. There are three major concerns which should be included in this file: cost, delivery, and quality. The project manager in both the buying and selling organization should keep a file on each of the contractors and subcontractors. The use of a Performance Data File will not only help the project manager monitor contracts and subcontracts, but it will also allow the project manager some input for his or her final performance evaluation. It is important that both the buyer and seller of the contract fill out a performance evaluation in order to provide quality of input into the Performance Data File. This information can be valuable in future source qualifying decisions and in personnel assignments.

An important step in the performance evaluation process is the rewarding of behavior based on results. There are a variety of methods to stimulate positive behaviors in the area of contracting. Some of these methods may include increased salaries, assignment of additional responsibilities, bonuses, awards, and even letters of commendation.

A self-evaluation of the project manager's contract performance becomes information that is quite valuable to both the individual and to the company in the future management of contracts and subcontracts.

Conclusions

The need for the project manager and his or her team to control costs, to meet schedules and to produce a quality product places a premium on the proper execution of the contract management functions. The relationship between the project life cycle and the contracting process must be clearly understood in order to facilitate the accomplishment of these goals. The assignment of the seller's project manager to the project at the beginning of the post-award phase of the contracting process dictates that project planning be emphasized and that the constraint on planning and the environmental influences be identified and controlled. Contract clause interpretation becomes a critical task. Special emphasis should be directed to selected clauses, such as changes, production surveillance, subcontract management. The issue is not whether the project manager should understand contract management. Rather the issue is whether he or she can afford not to!

Endnotes

1. John R. Adams, Stephen E. Barndt, and Martin D. Martin, *The Management of Project Management,* Dayton, Ohio: Universal Technology Corp., 1978, p. 18.

2. Penny Cavendish and Martin D. Martin, *Negotiating and Contracting for Project Management,* Drexel Hill, Penn.: Project Management Institute, 1982.

3. Ibid.

4. Ibid.

5. Ibid.

6. Jack Gido, *An Introduction to Project Planning*, Schenectady, N.Y.: General Electric Company, 1974, p. 132.

7. Wilbur B. England, *Modern Procurement Management,* Homewood, Ill.: Richard D. Irwin, Inc., 1970, pp. 201–203.

8. Linn C. Stuckenbruck, ed., *The Implementation of Project Management: The Professional's Handbook*, Reading, Mass.: Addison-Wesley, 1981, p. 150.

9. John R. Adams and Brian W. Campbell, *Roles and Responsibilities of the Project Manager,* Drexel Hill, Penn.: Project Management Institute, 1982.

10. Melvin Silverman, *Project Management: A Short Course for Professionals,* New York: John Wiley & Sons, 1976, Vol. 4, p. 13.

11. Martin D. Martin and Kathleen Miller, "Project Planning as the Primary Management Function," *Project Management Quarterly*, March 1982, p. 31.

12. Dwayne Cable and John R. Adams, *Organizing for Project Management*, Drexel Hill, Penn.: Project Management Institute, 1982, pp. 13–29.

13. John R. Adams, Stephen E. Barndt, & Martin D. Martin, *Managing By Project Management*, Dayton, Ohio: Universal Technology Corp., 1979, p. 26.

14. S.R. Mixon, *Monograph of Data Processing Administration, Operations, and Procedures*, New York: Amacom, 1976, p. 60.

15. Adams, Barndt, and Martin. 1976, p. 41.

16. Philip Kotler, *Marketing Management: Analysis, Planning, and Control,* Englewood Cliffs, N.J.: Prentice-Hall, 1960, p. 43.

17. John R. Adams and Martin D. Martin, "A Practical Approach to the Assessment of Project Uncertainty," *Proceedings of the Fourteenth Annual Seminar/Symposium*, Drexel Hill, Penn.: Project Management Institute, 1962, pp. IV-F.1—F.11.

18. Harold Kerzner, *A Systems Approach to Planning Scheduling, and Controlling,* New York: Van Nostrand Reinhold, 1979, p. 293.

19. David E. Ewing, *The Human Side of Planning: Tool of Tyrant*, New York: MacMillan, 1969, p. 201.

20. Eugene L. Scott, "The Cost Growth Phenomenon," *National Contract Management Journal*, Vol. 16, No. 2, Winter 1983, p. 39.

21. Cavendish and Martin.

22. Whitney v. Wyman, 101 US 392. Craig vs. Kessing, 297 NC 32, 233 SE2d 264.

23. See generally Section 3:35, *The Law of Modem Commercial Practices*, Revised Edition. Squillant and Fonseca. Lawyers Co-Op (1980).

24. Section 2–209 (1) V.C.C. But see New York General Obligations Law, Section 5–1103 (1163) and Hoffman v. Block, 20 Md. App. 284, 315 A2d551.

25. Utley v. Donaldson, 94 US 29.

26. American Sales Corp. vs. US 32 F2d 141 (5th Cir.) Cent. denied, 28 US 574. Rubinson vs. North American Accident Ins. Co. 246 NW 349. 36A Words and Phrases 188.

27. Anthony Tile and Marble Co. Inc. vs. H.L. Coble Const. Co. 16 NC App. 740, 193 SE2d 338. Also see generally 13 Am. Jur. 2d, Sections 17 and 19.

28. Scott, p. 38.

29. Henderson Bridge Co. vs. McGrath, 134 US 260.

30. Bentley vs. State, 73 Wis. 416, 41 NW 338.

31. Section 2–317. U.C.C.

32. Section 2–314. U.C.C.

33. Section 2–104 (1), U.C.C. See 67 Am. Jur. 2d, Sales, Sections 63–67, 728–738.

34. Section 2–315, U.C.C.

35. Addis v. Bernardin, Inc., 597 P.2d 250 (Sup. Ct. Kan.)

36. Koppar Glo Fuel, Inc. vs. Island Lake Co. 436 F Supp. 91 (E.D. Tenn.)

37. See 1 Anderson, Uniform Commercial Code 666. Lewis and Sims, Inc. vs. Key Industries, Inc., 16 Wash. App. 619, 557 P2d 1318.

38. Cavendish and Martin.

39. Adams, Barndt, and Martin.

40. Robert D. Guyton, Martin D. Martin, and Thomas R. Schaefer, *Prerequisites for Winning Government R&D Contracts*, Dayton, Ohio: Universal Technology Corp., 1982, p. 112.

41. See Sections 84, 246 and 247, Restatement, Second, Contracts and generally 66ALR 2d 570 et. Seg.

42. Harrison vs. Puga. 4 Wash. App. 52, 480P2d 247 Wheeler vs. Wheeler, 299 NC 633, 263 SE2d 763 Seismic & Digital Concepts Inc. vs. Digital Resources Corp., 590 SW2d718 (Tx. Civ. App.).

43. Nicki S. Kirchof and John R. Adams, *Conflict Management for Project Managers*, Drexel Hill, Penn.: Project Management Institute, 1982.

44. McGrath v. American Surety Co., 307 NY552, 122 NE2d906.

45. 40 US Code 270a—270e.

46. See Stickalls, Bond of Contractors on Federal Public Works—the Miller Act. 36 Boston vs. Law Review 499.

47. Section 235 (2) Restatement, Second, Contracts.

48. See Arthur L. Corbin, *Corbin on Contracts*, West Pub. Co., and John E. Murray, Murray on *Contracts*, Bobbs-Merrill Co.

49. U.S. vs. Smith, 94 US 214. Minneapolis Gaslight Co. vs. Kerr Murray Mfg. Co., 122 US 300.

50. Cheney vs. Libby, 134 US 68.

References

Adams, John R., Stephen E. Barndt, and Martin D. Martin. *Managing by Project Management*. Dayton, Ohio: Universal Technology Corp., 1979.

Adams, John R., Stephen E. Barndt, and Martin D. Martin. *The Management of Project Management*. Dayton, Ohio: Universal Technology Corp., 1978.

Adams, John R., and Bryan W. Campbell. *Roles and Responsibilities of the Project Manager*. Drexel Hill, Penn.: Project Management Institute, 1982.

Adams, John R., and Martin D. Martin. "A Practical Approach to the Assessment of Project Uncertainty." *Proceedings of the Fourteenth Annual Seminar/Symposium*. Drexel Hill, Penn.: Project Management Institute, 1982.

Cable, Dwayne, and John R. Adams. *Organizing for Project Management*. Drexel Hill, Penn.: Project Management Institute, 1982.

Cavendish, Penny C., and Martin D. Martin. *Negotiating and Contracting for Project Management*. Drexel Hill, Penn.: Project Management Institute, 1982.

Cleland, David I., and William R. King. *Systems Analysis and Project Management*. New York: McGraw-Hill, 1993.

England, Wilbur B. *Modern Procurement Management: Principles and Cases*. Homewood, Ill.: Richard D. Irwin, 1970.

Ewing, David W. *The Human Side of Planning: Tool or Tyrant?* New York: MacMillan, 1969.

Gido, Jack. *An Introduction to Project Planning*. Schenectady, N.Y.: General Electric Company, 1974.

Guyton, Robert D., Martin D. Martin, and Thomas R. Schefer. *Prerequisites for Winning Government R&D Contracts*. Dayton, Ohio: Universal Technology Corp., 1982.

Kerzner, Harold. *Project Management: A Systems Approach to Planning, Scheduling, and Controlling*. New York: Van Nostrand Reinhold, 1979.

Kerzner, Harold. *Project Management for Executives*. New York: Van Nostrand Reinhold, 1982.

Kirchof, Nicki S., and John R. Adams. *Conflict Management for Project Managers*. Drexel Hill, Penn.: Project Management Institute, 1982.

Kotler, Philip. *Marketing Management: Analysis, Planning and Control*. Englewood Cliffs, N.J.: Prentice-Hall, 1980.

Martin, Martin D., and Kathleen Miller. "Project Planning as the Primary Management Function." *Project Management Quarterly*, March 1982, pp. 31–38.

Mixon, S.R. *Handbook of Data Processing Administration, Operations. and Procedures*. New York: Amacom, 1976.

Scott, Eugene L. "The Cost Growth Phenomenon." *National Contract Management Journal*, Winter 1983, pp. 37–45.

Silverman, Melvin. *Project Management: A Short Course for Professionals*. New York: John Wiley & Sons, 1976.

Stuckenbruck, Linn C., (ed.), *The Implementation of Project Management: The Professional's Handbook*. Reading, Mass.: Addison-Wesley, 1981.

Warshaw, Tessa Albert. *Winning by Negotiation*. New York: McGraw-Hill, 1980.

Appendix

Included in this Appendix are representative contract management functions. In a centralized organization structure most of these functions will be the responsibility of the contracting department; in the decentralized projectized structure they will be shared. However, in most organizations the contracting staff is underpaid, understaffed, and lacks adequate training; it is therefore necessary that the project manager be knowledgeable of contract management functions. Also, placement of the functions under each area will vary from company to company.

Checklist for Contract Administration

1. Interpret and execute the terms and provisions of the prime contract.
2. Integrate all contract activities which involve production management, quality control and other contract management functions.
3. Act as the focal point with the other contracting party.
4. Exercise the functions of subcontract management.
5. Price and negotiate subcontracts and contract changes.
6. Act as the focal point for conflicts arising under the contract.
7. Develop and maintain contract file documentation.
8. Ensure adequate logistics support for project operations.
9. Certify invoices for payment.
10. Support and monitor configuration management committee.

Checklist for Production, Manufacturing, and Construction Surveillance

1. Track and maintain visibility and status of cost expenditures.
2. Maintain control of schedules.
3. Reschedule work as required.
4. Maintain periodic site inspections to ascertain work progress.
5. Interface with other contracting parties.
6. Generate status reports for distribution to management.
7. Operate value analysis program.
8. Maintain overall tracking system to evaluate progress against plan.
9. Assess work completion to certify progress payments.
10. Evaluate change proposals.

Checklist for Quality Control

1. Ensure that quality requirements are met.
2. Interpret specifications, drawings, and blueprints.

3. Perform inspections as required for work in progress and completed products.

4. Develop and maintain quality control documentation.

5. Develop and distribute quality status reports.

6. Ensure that health and safety requirements are adhered to at work site.